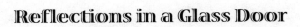

Reflections in a Glass Door

Reflections in a Glass Door

Memory and Melancholy in the Personal Writings of Natsume Sōseki

Marvin Marcus

University of Hawai'i Press
Honolulu

14 13 12 11 10 09   6 5 4 3 2 1

Library of Congress Cataloging-in-Publication Data
Natsume, Soseki, 1867–1916.
  [Essays. Selections]
  Reflections in a glass door : memory and melancholy in the
personal writings of Natsume Soseki / Marvin Marcus.
     p.   cm.
  Includes bibliographical references and index.
  ISBN 978-0-8248-3306-0 (hardcover : alk. paper)
  I. Marcus, Marvin.   II. Title.
  PL812.A8A6 2010
  895.6'442—dc22
                        2009010035

Publication of this book was assisted by a grant from the
Japan Studies Endowment Fund, Center for Japanese Studies,
University of Hawai'i, Mānoa.

University of Hawai'i Press books are printed on acid-free
paper and meet the guidelines for permanence and
durability of the Council on Library Resources.

Designed by Paul Herr

Printed by The Maple-Vail Book Manufacturing Group

For Ginger, Danny, and Steve,
  with much love,
and in memory of my parents,
  Michael and Fruma Marcus

Contents

Acknowledgments

Even for those like myself who work alone in small book-lined rooms, the study of literature is inevitably a collaborative effort. As a community of readers and scholars, we are beholden to those who hear us out, share their thoughts and ideas, and help expand our horizons and enrich the way we read and understand the world.

I owe debts large and small to those who have taught me, encouraged me, and provided intellectual and emotional sustenance over the years spent on this project. First, to my mentors at the University of Michigan—Robert Hopkins Brower and Robert Lyons Danly—who early on instilled in me an appreciation of literary art and a commitment to high academic standards. Their passing, many years ago, is still deeply felt, and their example has long remained an inspiration.

Among the many inhabitants of the Sōseki scholarly community, I owe a great deal to those whose work has been exemplary. Edwin McClellan and Jay Rubin, among a handful of others, have written about Natsume Sōseki and modern Japanese literature in ways that neither exclude nor intimidate the nonspecialist and that delight and instruct in equal measure. I have greatly benefitted from the sheer intelligence and integrity of their work. Moreover, their beautifully crafted renderings of Sōseki's novels have stood as models of the translator's art.

I've benefitted as well from discussions and correspondence with many colleagues and friends on various aspects of this project. Here I wish to acknowledge Puck Brecher, Rebecca Copeland, Mike Finke, Bob Hegel, Matthew Königsberg, Joel Marcus, Sharalyn Orbaugh, Elizabeth Oyler, Henry Smith, and Jonathan Zwicker.

I owe so much to those at Washington University with whom I've worked for nearly a quarter of a century. First and foremost, a collective word of thanks to my students—undergraduate and graduate—who have studied Sōseki as a captive audience in many courses taught over the years and on whom I tested my ideas and assorted manuscript drafts. To my colleagues in Japanese literature, past and present, my gratitude for sharing their expertise, and for their friendship and support. I am indebted as well to the larger community of colleagues in the Department of Asian and Near Eastern Languages and Literatures, for their literary insights, encouragement, and good fellowship. I am especially grateful to the two anonymous readers of my manuscript, whose comments and corrections benefitted me immeasurably.

Here I wish to acknowledge a departed colleague and dear friend, Bill Matheson—a peerless teacher, a good and wise man with a beautiful and generous spirit—with whom I experienced the classroom as a magical place, and literature as a gift to be savored and shared.

My heartfelt thanks go to our departmental office staff—to Debra Jones, who for decades has devoted herself to administering a large and diverse faculty, and to JoAnn Achelpohl and her predecessor, Shaaron Benjamin, for all they've done on my behalf and for my colleagues and students. I am also indebted to Asako Shiba of our East Asia Library, for her Japanese bibliographic expertise and for being instrumental in locating the images used in this book. The Iwanami shoten images are taken from a booklet, published by Iwanami shoten, entitled *Natsume Sōseki shashinchō*—a collection of photographs used as frontispieces in the individual volumes of *Sōseki zenshū*.

A word of thanks to Yōko McClain, professor emerita of Japanese at the University of Oregon, for sharing her thoughts (and her published reminiscence) on her famous grandfather. Thanks as well to Sammy Tsunematsu, director of the Sōseki Museum in London (and translator of many of Sōseki's works), for his insights on the author's experiences in London, and to Damian Flanagan, award-winning author of books on Sōseki—in English *and* Japanese—for his help and encouragement.

I owe a special debt to the International Exchange Center at Kokugakuin University in Tokyo, under the directorship of Nobukatsu Shimoyama, for making the center's facilities—and the university library—available to me during summer research visits. And thanks as well to the International Center at Kyoto University, with which I was affiliated in 2008, for inviting me to speak on my Sōseki project to the Kyōdai community. This was a most rewarding experience.

I wish to acknowledge dear friends of long standing, Tetsuya and Chizuko Takei—our Tokyo family—for everything they have done for me and my family over nearly thirty years. Their unstinting kindness has been a blessing. Thanks as well to Mitsuo Iijima, a retired Japanese diplomat and gifted literary essayist, for his gracious hospitality during visits to Japan.

My thanks to the Graduate School of Arts and Sciences at Washington University for its generous support of summer research visits to Japan. I also received financial support from the Northeast Asia Council of the Association for Asian Studies, for which I am most grateful.

Many thanks go to Pamela Kelley and Cheri Dunn of University of Hawai'i Press and Joanne Sandstrom, my copy editor, whose editorial guidance and expertise have been invaluable. I wish also to acknowledge Iwanami shoten, publisher of the Sōseki collected works, for permission to use the images included in this volume. Mr. Eiji Matsuoka of Kinokuniya USA was kind enough to make these arrangements on my behalf.

To Ginger, Danny, and Steve—my Dream Team, who managed to put up with me and Sōseki over these past years—I proudly dedicate this book, with love and gratitude. May we be long on memory, short on melancholy, and ready to enjoy all that life has to offer.

Finally, I wish to thank you, the reader of this book, for your interest and your patience, which I trust will be rewarded in some small measure. Of course I bear full responsibility for all errors of omission and commission, for which I beg your indulgence.

Introduction

The Glass Doors of
Natsume Sōseki

*As I look out from inside my glass doors, certain things
catch my eye.*

*I was reminded of a haiku I'd written long ago: Three
pines in the moonlight, casting uneven shadows.*
—Natsume Sōseki, from *Garasudo no uchi*

If there is such a thing as a Japanese cultural pantheon, Natsume Sōseki (1867–1916) surely occupies a seat of honor. This is the renowned author of *I Am a Cat, Botchan,* and *Kokoro,* a writer who died of a bad stomach and whose work came to epitomize the spirit of the Meiji era (1868–1912). Born at the dawn of the Meiji and surviving its emperor by four years, Sōseki captured an essential quality of that era and of the modern condition itself. Donald Keene may have echoed the consensus view when he proclaimed Natsume Sōseki as the preeminent modern Japanese writer—a stature confirmed by the twenty-year span during which the man's iconic image adorned the Japanese thousand-yen note.[1]

Contemporary tastes in literature run in every conceivable direction, yet Sōseki's work remains both relevant and revelatory nearly a century after the author's death. He devoted the last decade of his life to crafting fiction of extraordinary subtlety and psychological depth. The novels have generated libraries of critical and appreciative commentary over the past century. They continue to attract a broad readership in Japan and are known worldwide in translation.[2] Although long fiction *(chōhen shōsetsu)* comprises the bulk of Sōseki's oeuvre, this was but one of his literary accomplishments. He was a poet of the very first rank, equally adept at haiku and Chinese verse *(kanshi),* and an accomplished watercolorist and calligrapher. He was

1

the leading scholar of English literature in Meiji Japan. And like Mori Ōgai (1862–1922), his great contemporary, Sōseki was a public intellectual who held forth on literary, cultural, and political topics in the print media and on the lecture circuit. The subject of this book—Sōseki's personal writing—displays yet another facet of his literary artistry, while serving as a mirror of the man.

For those preferring high drama and historical moment, Sōseki's reminiscences and reflections will disappoint. In point of biographical fact, and in its various narrative transformations, his is a decidedly mundane life—which seems at odds with the man's stature. A native of Edo, renamed Tokyo in 1868, Natsume Kinnosuke (his given name) was a neglected son of aging parents for whom the new arrival, at this stage in their lives, was both an annoyance and something of an embarrassment. Placed in foster care as an infant, then put up for adoption before his second birthday, Kinnosuke was reclaimed by his natal family some eight years later. The boy, whose real father was a nondescript local official who harbored little affection for his youngest son, did well in school and developed a fondness for theater and traditional entertainments. He showed signs of brilliance as a student in the elite Tokyo academies and was admitted to the prestigious Imperial University, where he studied English. His talents and tastes gradually inclined him toward literature.

Natsume Kinnosuke adopted a pen name—a standard rite of passage for the aspiring writer. He chose Sōseki, a Chinese locution that loosely translates as "gargling with stones."[3] Then, for reasons not entirely clear, he accepted a teaching post in Matsuyama, on the island of Shikoku, then another post in Kumamoto, in even more remote Kyushu.[4] At age twenty-nine, the young teacher was betrothed to Nakane Kyōko, the nineteen-year-old daughter of an official in the legislative House of Peers. It was an arranged marriage, and the couple had little in common—not an unusual state of affairs. A daughter was born, and in 1900, with a second child on the way, the teacher found himself in a select cadre of young scholars chosen to study abroad at government expense. And so at age thirty-three, Natsume Kinnosuke left his family and departed for England, where he would spend two lonely years immersed in literary research while trying to manage on his meager stipend. In London, he experienced bouts of depression bordering on madness.

Back in his native land, Sōseki parlayed his impressive scholarly attainments into a prestigious academic post at the Imperial University. Poised to become Japan's leading authority on British literature, Sōseki privately despaired of ever truly mastering it, and he doubted the effectiveness, and value, of his teaching. In the meantime, he pursued his own literary creations.

Turning from poetry to fiction, he achieved a resounding success with his maiden work, the satirical novel *Wagahai wa neko de aru* (I Am a Cat, 1905). Then, with the enormously popular *Botchan* (1906), a novel loosely based on his experiences in Matsuyama, his literary reputation was established. By this time, the up-and-coming scholar had soured on the academic life, and when offered a relatively lucrative position with the *Asahi shinbun,* a leading newspaper, he left the university to become Japan's first career novelist—an unprecedented move, given the generally unsavory reputation of the popular-fiction writer.

In accord with established practice, Sōseki's work appeared in daily serialization, and only thereafter in book form. In his capacity as *Asahi* staff writer and literary editor, he was not restricted to novels. Having acquired a taste for the personal essay, a genre then known as *shōhin* (small works) Sōseki turned to such writing in the intervals between his serial fiction.

Experimenting with impressionistic description and haikuesque lyrical narrative, Sōseki gradually matured as a novelist. He achieved a major breakthrough with a novelistic trilogy—*Sanshirō* (1908), *Sorekara* (And Then, 1909), and *Mon* (The Gate, 1911)—that explores the world of educated Tokyoites and their essential loneliness. His own life settled into a stable, if tedious, domesticity. Plagued by chronic ill health and displaying a penchant for being difficult, peevish, and moody, the author reflected upon his own melancholy temperament through the lives of his literary alter egos.

Sōseki's reputation steadily grew. He developed a literary following, and his home became a gathering place for fellow writers and younger protégés. Otherwise sequestered in his study and beset by deadlines and unexpected callers, the busy author kept the family—his wife Kyōko, a brood of children, and assorted housekeepers—at arm's length. There were money problems, annoying solicitations, and piles of manuscripts to read. Such was the daily routine as retold in his *shōhin* episodes.

Natsume Sōseki's dyspepsia was both psychological and physical, and he spent his final years in and out of hospitals. In August 1910 he nearly died of a gastric hemorrhage, and the ensuing convalescence afforded a welcome opportunity for quiet reflection and reminiscence. It was around this time that the government sought to bestow a prestigious honorary doctorate upon the author. Wanting no part of such official recognition, he summarily turned it down.[5]

Unable to escape the insistent reminders of his own mortality, Sōseki became preoccupied with death and dying, signs of human frailty, the corrosive effects of modern selfhood, and the fragility of social relationships. He pondered the mixed blessings of individualism—a defining condition of modern society—and labored over the creation of characters who, caught in the grip of egocentrism and self-delusion, were fated to suffer the consequences. A man of deeply reflective temperament, Sōseki was fully aware of his own complex and conflicted nature, and his novels became stages for the pained interactions and psychological ploys that isolate individuals and set them against one another. His literary labors helped create a language for expressing the dislocations and frustrations of modern life. And in the process Natsume Sōseki emerged as Japan's first great psychological novelist.[6]

Sōseki's signature themes are brilliantly evoked in two widely acclaimed works—*Kokoro* (1914) and *Michikusa* (Grass on the Wayside, 1915). Kenzō, the autobiographical protagonist of the latter work, is strongly drawn to the past. He finds himself struggling to grasp its complexity, its specificity. Memory often fails him, but things do come to mind—an old friend, a scene from long ago, a poem, a voice. But the past itself is irretrievably gone. Kenzō frets and broods. Not at all easygoing or sociable, he cultivates a moody self-righteousness in the face of those who intrude upon his private space and offend his sensibilities. He is testy, impatient. His wife and children cannot understand him. He is in poor health as well, and things are rarely as they should be. The human condition, he concludes, is not susceptible to our understanding, much less our control. Himself thoroughly self-possessed, he decries the egotism and self-absorption that he sees all around him.

Finding some surcease in his poetic and artistic avocations, Natsume Sōseki embarked on his next serialized novel—yet another novelistic "anatomy" of a marriage, entitled *Meian* (Light and Darkness, 1916). But his physical condition deteriorated, and he passed away on the evening of December 9, 1916, having finished the 188th installment of this incomplete final work. News of the author's death inspired an outpouring of testimonials and literary eulogizing. His remains were interred in the cemetery at Zōshigaya, in Tokyo—the final resting place of Sensei, the lonely protagonist of *Kokoro* and Sōseki's best-known fictional alter ego.

Writing the Self in Meiji Japan

Natsume Sōseki's personal writings should be placed in the context of *zuihitsu*—a time-honored genre of Japanese literary essay, which in turn owed much to a great Chinese essayistic tradition. One typically points to acclaimed works such as the eleventh-century *Pillow Book* by Sei Shōnagon and the fourteenth-century *Essays in Idleness* by Priest Kenkō.[7] Yet these and other seminal works became acknowledged as canonical only during the

Meiji period, when Japanese literature—*kokubungaku*—was itself being constructed as an academic discipline, in line with Western notions of literary history and theory. A more proximate body of self-expressive writing emerged during the Tokugawa period (1600–1868), when members of a burgeoning literati *(bunjin)* class experimented with various modes of discursive writing, including autobiographical narrative.[8] While generally reflecting the Confucian-centered outlook of the samurai elite, works such as Arai Hakuseki's *Tales Told Round a Brushwood Fire* managed to convey the narrator's personal voice in a convincing manner.[9]

Sōseki and his contemporaries were acquainted with the Japanese literary classics— *zuihitsu* and otherwise—and with the work of their Tokugawa predecessors. But the qualities of modern selfhood that most concerned them were not to be gleaned from such works. Rather, it was to Western sources and inspirations that they would turn.

Avenues of self-expression—intersecting and diverging styles, influences, genres—crisscross the Meiji literary map and complicate its history. In order better to appreciate Sōseki's personal writings, let us briefly examine the larger social and cultural context that fostered the emergence of literary selfhood through reminiscence and reflection.[10]

Backdrop: Cities, Schools, Jobs, Families

The Meiji transformation was accomplished in large measure through industrialization and urbanization. Cities built on Western models would be the embodiment of Japanese modernity and manifest symbols of the "civilization and enlightenment"—*bunmei kaika*—trumpeted early on as a national mission. The erstwhile shogunal center of Edo, with its fortified castle and labyrinthine design, was reinvented as Tokyo—the imperial capital and seat of its new institutions of government, education, finance, and commerce. A national rail system, devised and inaugurated in the early 1870s, would physically unite the nation, enabling those long isolated in rural areas to move elsewhere. Together with the advent of the telegraph, then the telephone, modern transportation and communication radically altered the lives of the mass of the Japanese people.

The Meiji era also witnessed a vast social transformation—the creation of a national citizenry in place of the feudal patchwork of domains and regions and the samurai-centered hierarchy of power and privilege. The modern state required a skilled, educated workforce and a new model of family life. Men got jobs, went to work, and received wages; their wives stayed home and tended to the children and the domestic sphere. The life of city dwellers increasingly hinged upon a money-driven consumer economy and a drive to succeed, but

5

a countervailing spirit of harmony and cooperation was promoted as part of a state-sponsored social doctrine. Here, the notion of *katei*—a new term for the modern household—came to represent the Meiji reformulation of Japanese social relations. At its center was the family unit inhabiting a home, engaging in shared activities, promoting social virtues, and sustaining itself through appropriate domestic economies.

While the "traditional" extended family and its patriarchal dominance continued to be vested with both legal and moral authority, a new value that privileged privacy, autonomy, and "a room of one's own" became prevalent. Meiji literature—and Sōseki's work, in particular—would strongly reflect this tension between the authoritarian ethos, which was sustained by both law and custom, and a nascent individualism that sought to break free from repression and arbitrary constraint.[11]

The Meiji leaders understood that modern education, inspired by Western models and ideals, would be key to their civilizing mission. Boys and girls were to be educated in line with a new egalitarian ethos, but a strong gender bias effectively dictated separate tracks and divergent views of oneself vis-à-vis society. At the educational pinnacle was the university. For years there was only one—the Imperial University in Tokyo, whose graduates would assume positions of prominence. As an early alumnus, Natsume Sōseki in effect entered the Meiji intellectual elite, although he would hold elitism per se in contempt. Through his *shōhin* reminiscence, he would recast school experiences and relationships as a nostalgic evocation of coming of age in the early Meiji.

Backdrop: The *Bundan* and Literary Journalism

By the 1880s, Tokyo was the undisputed center of modern Japan's literary and artistic life—effectively displacing Kyoto, which had long been a mecca for what could now be called "traditional Japan." Aspiring young writers—the so-called *bungaku seinen*—congregated in Tokyo, and for reasons of necessity and shared affinity, they would seek affiliation with the small coteries and salons that appeared—and in many cases just as quickly disappeared—at the turn of the century. Getting published was, of course, the shared goal, and the sine qua non of a literary career. Hence, the coteries, centering upon a dominant figure who served as editor and literary arbiter, typically produced a periodical that would showcase the work of the respective circle. This putative literary community—the aggregation of writers, coteries, and literary adjuncts (publishers, editors, illustrators, journalists, etc.)—is referred to as the *bundan*. As an institution, it has been likened to a guild system, which organized the activities and careers of writers through the journalistic orientation of its constituent groupings.[12]

In contrast with the present-day situation of Japanese writers, who are essentially free agents in the literary marketplace, aspiring Meiji writers were understandably drawn to the coterie system. Here the notion of *oyabun-kobun* (parent-child) has been applied to exemplify a master-disciple reciprocity that *bundan* coteries are said to have fostered.[13] This is a problematic notion, which threatens to play into convenient stereotypes of a uniquely Japanese group dynamic, thus obscuring the agency of complex economic and social forces and the way these forces changed over time.[14] A nuanced historical and institutional understanding of the Meiji media is of the essence here.

With the 1890s, the scope of literary journalism expanded. Major publishers entered the literary field, as did the newspapers. (Sōseki's move to the *Asahi* is a watershed in this development.) Commercial publishing expanded on all fronts, and the small-circulation coterie magazine—together with the coterie system per se—became increasingly marginalized. Bookstores flourished, and the reading public had a wealth of options. Within a decade, the mass-circulation periodical would become a mainstay, and the writerly career more than ever hinged upon access to the new print media. Inhabiting what amounted to an ecological niche within a rapidly modernizing society, Meiji writers were well attuned to the "networking" aspect of this society and to the rules and conventions that governed the buying and selling of books and manuscripts.[15]

Chatting in Print

One noteworthy development was the appearance in literary periodicals of personal accounts by name writers. Individuals were interviewed on set topics, and their remarks were transcribed in shorthand notation by the interviewer and later converted into a *danwa* (literary chat). An informal conversational style became a staple of the Meiji *bundan*.[16] Encouraged to speak to their readers on personal as well as literary matters, some writers flatly refused to be drawn into what they regarded as a demeaning publicity stunt. Gradually, though, the boundary separating the public and private sphere was effectively blurred, as was the distinction between writer and journalist. By the end of the Meiji period, the old coterie readerships were being replaced by a media-driven national readership.[17] Writers served as editors and critics, careers were sustained by manuscript fees and honoraria, and everyone was beholden, to a lesser or greater extent, to a business model whereby writing would appear in print, on time, and in the proper format. Sōseki's literary career, underwritten, in effect, by the Tokyo Asahi corporation, is illustrative of the new paradigm. And his own published *danwa* contributed to the *bundan* "chatroom" ambience.

Romanticism, Naturalism, and Modern Selfhood

To mix several religious metaphors, modern selfhood can be said to have possessed a holy grail significance within the Meiji *bundan,* and it can equally be likened to a Zen paradox that bedeviled and bemused writers and intellectuals. Given the interest in literary expressions of selfhood, the appeal of Western-inspired movements that elevated the subjectivity and autonomy of the individual was inevitable. Romanticism *(rōmanshugi),* in its many forms and genres, found fertile soil within the *bundan.* Pioneering efforts by Mori Ōgai and Shimazaki Tōson, drawn respectively from German and British models, have ranked among the early entries into the Meiji literary canon.[18]

Another mid-Meiji landmark was the appearance of an unprecedented work of fiction—*Ukigumo* (Drifting Cloud, 1886–1889)—by a little-known writer named Futabatei Shimei (1864–1909). Subsequently touted as Japan's first modern novel, *Ukigumo* featured a brooding, introspective protagonist—Utsumi Bunzō—who would become a prototype of literary interiority and subjectivity.[19] "Bunzō" is an eponym of sorts, signaling a dominant trait of introversion and ineffectuality among Japanese literary protagonists—callow young men, painfully self-conscious and socially awkward, who struggle to bridge the gap between self and other—typically in the form of ill-starred romantic encounters.

Futabatei's work heralded another important development as well—the search for a modern literary language, known as *genbun itchi*—that would replace the hodgepodge of outmoded literary forms and ornate styles that had held sway for centuries and that impeded the emergence of a truly national readership. Futabatei experimented with variants of *genbun itchi* in *Ukigumo,* and the work in effect challenged other writers to rethink their own narrative techniques. Sōseki's novels—especially his later work—can be said to represent the culmination of *genbun itchi* as a common goal of the Meiji *bundan.*[20]

Japanese romanticism had its heyday in the 1890s before giving way, as the standard account goes, to the so-called naturalist school *(shizenshugi).* This new movement, associated with the writings of Tōson and Tayama Katai (1871–1930), enjoyed a brief heyday in the first decade of the twentieth century. Initially inspired by Zolaesque notions of a "scientific" literature that would offer a dispassionate, objective view of social conditions, naturalism was creatively "misread" within the *bundan.* What emerged was a literary credo of subjectivity, which attributed authenticity to ostensibly unvarnished, sincere confessions of inner torment.[21] Notwithstanding the widespread disdain aimed at the naturalists' tendency toward tawdry self-exposure, a certain confessional impulse took root within the *bundan.* As we will see, Sōseki's *shōhin* should be understood within this context.

Psychology, *Shōhin*, Memory

Unlike the naturalists, who were attempting to "be themselves" through a crafted artlessness, Sōseki sought a narrative means of constructing a psychological persona that would simulate the ongoing shifts of mood and attention, the associational triggers and synapses, and the complex introspective voicing that marks the interface between an individual and his world. An interested student of Western psychology, which was among the academic disciplines that comprised the new curriculum of higher education, Sōseki put his keen understanding of human cognition—conditioned by his own deeply introspective temper—in the service of his literary craft.[22] As argued by Howard Hibbett and others, it was the acuity of Sōseki's ongoing self-examination that enabled him to craft protagonists with such fluent interior voices.[23] His achievement was a discourse of "thinking out loud"—of reflecting on one's circumstance, pursuing lines of association to remembered encounters and episodes, and musing upon the meaning of it all. As a literary complement to the novelistic mainstream, the personal essay, in series, would allow for a free discursive movement through remembered episodes and seemingly random reflection.

Again, such literary ephemera abounded in the late-Meiji media, occupying a group of vaguely synonymous genre categories that encompassed the lyrical, impressionistic, confessional, and philosophical essay. These shared what can be termed an "authenticity effect"—a sense of authorial presence, even in overtly fictionalized episodes.[24] Sōseki's work in this vein was assigned to the *shōhin* category, which roughly corresponds to the Western notion of belles lettres.[25] Derived from a prominent Chinese essayistic genre of the Ming dynasty,[26] the *shōhin* literary vignette was resurrected in the early years of the twentieth century as part of the *bundan*'s embrace of the personal voice. Sōseki was but one of many writers drawn to what had come to be regarded as a congenial mode of literary expression.[27]

It should be noted that *shōhin* is merely one of a number of modern essayistic styles employed by Meiji writers. In contrast with the explicitly personal voice expressed through *shōhin* and related subgenres, there emerged a major category of essayistic writing that fostered objective, analytical expression and critical inquiry. Sōseki published many such essays, marked by a dispassionate, intellectual discourse, throughout his career. In sum, however, the modern Japanese essay form—*kindai zuihitsu*—clearly reflects the strong current of literary selfhood and self-expression, in all of its psychological dimension, that took hold within the Meiji *bundan*.[28] And again, the widespread adoption of the personal voice relates to the contextual factors noted above—an expanding literary journalism, the institution of a modern national curriculum, and a discourse of individualism that played out in the social, political, and economic lives of the Japanese citizenry. Also, expanding opportunities for travel, both within Japan and overseas, beginning with the 1890s helped foster a new genre of modern travel writing *(kikō bungaku)*, which became an important vehicle of literary self-expression.

Sōseki published his *shōhin* episodes, both individually and in series, as literary intermezzi in between the novelistic serializations, which spanned 1906–1916. An early inspiration was his tutelage with the poet Masaoka Shiki. This began with haiku composition but extended to *shaseibun*—a category of literary sketch mastered by Shiki that entailed closely observed renderings of the visual field. In Sōseki's hands, this mode of narrative sketching would be applied to personal reminiscence.[29]

The first noteworthy work in this vein, *Bunchō* (Java Sparrow), appeared in June 1908. It concerns the sad fate of a pet bird taken into the Natsume home. The story, with its minutely detailed depiction of the small bird and its curious habits, marks the first appearance of the slightly querulous first-person writer-narrator, who would be a mainstay of subsequent *shōhin*.

What followed this realistic portrayal of the writer in his domestic milieu is arguably the most inventive—and surely the best known—of Sōseki's personal writings—*Yume jūya* (Ten Nights of Dream, 1908). These richly imagistic and surreal dreamscapes, readily subject to psychoanalytical interpretation, have emerged for some as keys to the author's inner life.[30] This, in turn, has obscured their literary artifice, which reflects the author's concern, in his earlier fictional and essayistic writing, for coalescing the introspective voice of his narrator and a vivid imagistic landscape.[31]

Literary Études: *Eijitsu shōhin*

The *Dream* serialization was well received, and the editor of the Osaka *Asahi* requested something along the same lines. Sōseki responded with a more ambitious series, entitled *Eijitsu shōhin* (Spring Miscellany, 1909).[32] This is a true miscellany—a mélange, in twenty-five episodes, of fictive and personal vignettes.

One set of episodes, reflecting the domestic realism of *Bunchō,* is set in the home and presents various family tableaux. We read of visits by literary cronies, a spunky girl next door who exacts her small revenge on a neighborhood bully, the harried writer at his desk on a wintry day when the baby won't stop crying, the children marching through the house dressed up in mommy's clothing. At a gathering of the literary circle, an eccentric young man pays an unexpected visit. He has brought along a pheasant, which he insists on stewing and serving as a communal dinner.

There are overtly fictional episodes as well. One tells of a woman who goes to the theater and witnesses a fallen-down drunk shouting down the crowd of bystanders. A habitué of curio shops buys a dust-covered Mona Lisa, which he ends up selling to the trashman. There is an old man who reluctantly parts with a cherished scroll—a family heirloom—to get enough money to purchase a marker for his wife's grave and a schoolteacher in the provinces who is reminded of his dead mother.

A set of related episodes concern the author's experiences in London. There is an eerie, Poe-like quality to several of these—macabre accounts of being alone in the forbidding foreign metropolis, consumed by the fog and losing oneself in a sea of strange faces. Sōseki's narrator betrays a sense of racial inferiority, casting himself as the impecunious Oriental, short of stature, surrounded by a race of tall Aryans.

With the London episodes, Sōseki demonstrates an affinity for literary melancholia. The city, with its dark streets and suffocating fog, becomes the stage for a stifling, rankling self-obsession. The artistic effect here is striking, irrespective of any claims one might make regarding the underlying psychopathology. But the London reminiscences are not uniformly dark and depressing. The final *Eijitsu* episode centers on the Shakespearean scholar William Craig, with whom Sōseki had a weekly tutorial. The portrayal of the tightfisted, absentminded professor is comically irreverent yet strangely moving.

A Writer in the Colonies: *Mankan tokorodokoro*

Following the *Eijitsu* project, Sōseki would not again experiment quite so freely with modes of storytelling—autobiographical or otherwise. His next major venture into personal writing would be a travel journal—*Mankan tokorodokoro* (Here and There in Manchuria and Korea, 1909)—a record of the author's month-long trip. Having been invited by Nakamura Zekō, director of the Southern Manchurian Railway and an old boyhood friend, Sōseki is taken on a grand tour of Japanese-run factories, offices, and warehouses. He meets the upper crust of the colonial administration, runs into familiar faces, decries run-down hotel facilities, and balks at the food.[33]

The touring author, taking in the alien terrain of the Manchurian countryside, embarks on a series of surreal encounters—an army of coolies hauling huge bags of soybeans, Sisyphus-like, up the stairs of a giant storage facility; a chance visit to a local opium den; an old Chinaman (the equivalent pejorative term is used) run over by a careening carriage, lying injured and bleeding in the road. In short, this is not a pleasure trip—and Sōseki's account draws to a close before he crosses into Korean territory. *Mankan* tells of a sickly man on a difficult journey, wondering what he is doing in this desolate land—the fog-shrouded streets of London transformed, as it were, into the Manchurian wasteland.[34]

An Anatomy of Memory: *Omoidasu koto nado*

Whatever else can be said regarding his tour of the colonies and its literary reportage, Sōseki's trip did wreak havoc with his delicate stomach, and it was during the subsequent period of hospitalization, which lasted eight months, that Sōseki composed his next *shōhin* series—*Omoidasu koto nado* (Recollections, 1911). Written from a hospital bed, the thirty-two episodes reflect upon illness and convalescence. This is a serious, at times intense, work—an amalgam of diary-style narrative and philosophical reflection. In keeping with the title, and in line with the earlier *shōhin* experiments, the narrator ponders memory and its intrinsic imperfections. We move from utterly mundane concerns to musings on life and death, remembrances of youth, and learned commentary.

Proceeding chronologically, *Omoidasu* centers upon the dramatic events of one fateful day—August 24, 1910—when the author nearly died of an attack of cerebral anemia *(nōhinketsu)*. This event has entered the annals of Sōseki biography as *Shuzenji taikan*—the crisis at Shuzenji. Hospitalized until February 1911, Sōseki took to writing about his long confinement. Playing with the very act of recollection, he recounts his daily routine—his food intake, the round of medication, the day's visitors. The sickroom itself is an object of reflection and an enclosed frame of reference, emerging as a kind of sanctuary.

The author's "living experience of death" posed large philosophical questions, which are broadly explored. The raw data of memory, which prove insufficient and flawed, are augmented with journal entries made during the Shuzenji stay. And gaps in his own account are filled in with citations from his wife's diary. Memory, in other words, has become a collaborative act, and despite concerns regarding one's tenuous claims to knowledge of the past, Sōseki's acts of remembrance are coherent and impressively detailed.

The *Omoidasu* series, by turns cynical and cheerful, mundane and pensive, intimate and scholarly, weaves many strands of reminiscence. Yet its most salient feature lies not in the prose narrative but in the poetic postscript with which each episode ends. Consisting of both haiku and *kanshi,* these verse codas provide an exquisite lyrical synopsis of the respective episode while pointing to the author's deep and abiding poetic sensibilities.[35]

Inside Glass Doors: *Garasudo no uchi*

Sōseki's final *shōhin* collection, serialized in the *Asahi* a year before his death, is a culmination of his literary personalia. Entitled *Garasudo no uchi* (Inside My Glass Doors, 1915), this collection of thirty-nine episodes is flanked by his two novelistic masterpieces, *Kokoro* and *Michikusa*. The authorial narrator, speaking in many voices, essentially recapitulates the key themes that mark his mature fiction.

The reader is once again ushered into the author's book-lined study as he reflects upon his present situation and relates episodes from the past—a past regarded from what seems a great distance. He recalls an old boyhood friend, Kii-chan, in connection with some antiquarian books the friend sold to him. There are the high-school classmate remembered for his intuitive brilliance and a pair of ne'er-do-well cousins who would come by the house to make merry and sponge off the family. The narrator recalls his oldest brother, a sickly young man who ended up having an affair with a geisha before dying of a lung disorder. There are wistful memories of the old neighborhood in Babashita, just down the road, with its quaint shops and rusticated charm, its narrow lanes and dark bamboo groves—all done in by the inexorable course of modernization.

Sōseki's parents are at best a marginal presence, evoking ambivalent feelings. The father emerges as an austere, petty old man. The mother, who elicits an instinctive if disembodied affection, is remembered with difficulty. Imagistic fragments remain—a pair of eyeglasses, a well-worn blue kimono. A gesture of affection is reserved for a maid, her name and appearance long since forgotten, but whose special act of kindness is vividly recalled. Struggling to conjure up some pattern from the patchwork of ephemeral traces, the narrator muses on the fragility of memory, on our imperfect connection with the past.

Episodes from the more recent past are related in considerable detail. One concerns the family dog, Hector, and his sad demise. Another tells of a woman, in suicidal despair, who comes by to seek counsel. Tapping into a vein of self-parody, Sōseki writes of victimization by actual burglars and by the more insidious kind—predatory reporters and pestering readers.

The *Garasudo* episodes are woven together by the introspective voice of their authorial narrator as he traverses the landscape of memory. Reminders of death and dying abound. Friends and relatives are gone, yet he remains—a bemused observer, a reluctant survivor. The mind itself seems incapable of retrieving anything more than scraps of the past. The totality of things is beyond one's grasp. People—oneself included—do strange things, hurtful things, and one cannot ultimately do much to improve upon the human condition.

But the world within glass doors affords, as well, a safe haven and a measure of solace. From this quiet space, one can observe the clamorous world outside—with its wars, its political turmoil, its clash and clatter. The minimalist credo of the small, the slow, and the understated strikes a responsive chord, calling to mind an aphorism famously associated with Natsume Sōseki—*sokuten kyoshi,* which means something to the effect of "follow the dictates of heaven, forsake the self."

Sōseki's literature, in its exploration of psychological states and problematic relationships, both reflects and epitomizes a crucial aspect of Japanese literary modernity. And the interior monologue that engages his characters—and his *shōhin* narrator—bespeaks an emblematic quality of loneliness and disillusionment associated with the age itself. As I've suggested, convincingly personal accounts are readily accepted as autobiographical data, whereby the figure of a troubled protagonist is identified with the author himself.[36] But larger questions are raised here. How is any narrative read as "psychological"? How do narrative cues—interior monologue, crafted dialogue, plot contrivance, imagery, and so forth—yield the effect of psychological substance and depth? Similar questions can be asked, too, of the specific visual cues in a painting or photograph that create an impression of wholeness, of individuality.

Applied to Sōseki's personal writing, "psychological effect" points to acts of memory, to a narrator "caught in the act" of remembering—or attempting to remember. Then again, the *shōhin* genre itself grants a virtual license to reminisce, and notwithstanding the higher wisdom that recognizes the impossibility of a genuinely retrievable past, and of memory as its reliable agent, we are driven to recapture and reinvent that which is lost.[37] For Natsume Sōseki and his colleagues, much would be lost in the course of their lives. The Meiji itself—the look and feel of its earlier years—would become an object of retrospection, be it clinically detached or ripe with nostalgic longing. Modernity, and the institutions that helped create it, would be both blessing and curse.

Then again, the *shōhin* reflections are not uniformly ponderous and dark. Many are breezy sketches of the here and now, or of some passing fancy. Through Sōseki's "figures of thought," the reader is brought into the narrative reenactment of being reflective. And while there are many objects of reflection, one is drawn to the presence of a thinking, feeling person who is both rooted in his world, in all its imperfection, and open to the whims and fancies of the moment.

Concerning This Book

Literary studies have been marked by a certain Balkanization of theoretical positions and "discourse domains" that have effectively excluded the general reader and rankled the specialist. Our quest for the scholarly high ground has tended to obscure the pleasures of reading that beckoned us in the first place and that we presumably try to foster in our students. Non-Western literatures have been relatively late in adapting prevailing theory, and there has been a healthy resistance of late to the willy-nilly application of theory in order to establish one's bona fides in the academic market.

It is my hope that this book will be both accessible and enjoyable. Its constituent chapters will center on the themes and concerns articulated above, and each will incorporate illustrative episodes drawn from the *shōhin* collections and paired with interpretive commentary.[38] As the title makes clear, memory and melancholy will figure as recurrent motifs. And a concerted effort will be made to situate the writer and his work in the relevant contexts—historical, social, economic, as well as cultural.[39]

Chapter 1 will examine Sōseki's literary retellings of his experiences in England. The textual selections will demonstrate the author's variations on the theme of loneliness and instability, which comprise what I've termed a rhetoric of melancholy. Testimony from those familiar with Sōseki's experiences will shed light upon his state of mind during those two years abroad. Chapter 2 shifts to Sōseki's literary reminiscences of—and memorial to—the Tokyo of his childhood. Selected *shōhin* episodes will highlight the intersection of memory and nostalgia in the construction of a landscape that, together with one's youth, has long since vanished. Pursuing Sōseki's reflections on the Tokyo of his early years, chapter 3 will present accounts concerning family and friends, which are marked by an ebb and flow of precise detail, hazy recollection, and a muted nostalgia.

With chapter 4, the focus of Sōseki's reminiscence shifts to family, and one's role as husband and father. Here, depictions in both the *shōhin* and the autobiographical fiction point to an uneasy modus vivendi with one's domestic circumstance and an ongoing tension between egocentrism and empathy. By way of contrast, chapter 5 consists of episodes that present Sōseki's writer persona as he muses upon his career and the larger world as seen through the glass doors of his study. The themes of loneliness and introversion explored in chapter 1 are revisited here through accounts of individuals who make demands upon his time and intrude upon his private space.

Providing a corrective to the "isolate" persona, with its intimations of misanthropy and self-obsession, chapter 6 turns to Sōseki's many literary affiliations. Selected *shōhin* episodes recall early mentors, *bundan* colleagues and protégés, and assorted eccentrics and oddballs. A journalistic category of memorial reminiscence will be studied as a vehicle for reflections upon prominent literary lives and, inevitably, one's own mortality.

Chapter 7 reflects back upon Sōseki's literature of reminiscence and goes on to explore the manner in which this iconic figure has himself been remembered and reappropriated over the years by family members, literary people, and the popular media. A postscript will present some personal thoughts on Natsume Sōseki and on the course of this book project.

As I hope to demonstrate, Sōseki's personal writings provide a kaleidoscopic view of the author's private and public faces and illuminate his larger concerns as a novelist and culture critic. But quite apart from this, and from the *shōhin*'s value as source material for the biographer and literary historian, I wish to convey an appreciation for the art of the personal essay, a genre richly deserving of its place in the sun.

One more thing, in connection with the editorial aspect of this project. Having culled Natsume Sōseki's *shōhin* collections, I've assigned the selected episodes to this or that chapter of the book in line with the above schema. (All of the *Garasudo* and *Omoidasu* episode titles are my own; none were titled in the original. But the *Eijitsu* episodes were titled, and the episodes I've included bear the translated titles.) What has been thus sacrificed is the integrity of the source works—the original ordering of episodes, with its shifting voice, mood, image, and theme—in short, the artistry of assemblage and sequencing. As with other Japanese literary miniatures—haiku, most famously—Sōseki's *shōhin* accounts are embedded with others of their kind, with which they relate in a kind of aesthetic synergy. Regrettably, something of this higher-order artistry has been lost here. I trust that something equally worthwhile will have been gained.

Finally, I should note that all translations from the *shōhin* collections are my own. But for each excerpt, I have cited the corresponding translation drawn from works published over the course of my writing and research.

Kurt Vonnegut once remarked that writing a book is akin to driving at night. The headlights illuminate only a short piece of road, but you end up getting where you need to go. Vonnegut's observation epitomizes the process that has eventuated in this book.

London Underground

A Rhetoric of Melancholy

The novel *Michikusa* opens with a brief passage of interior monologue that introduces the protagonist and at the same time identifies him as the author's autobiographical proxy:

> Exactly how many years, Kenzō wondered, had he been away from Tokyo? He had left the city to live in the provinces and then had gone abroad. There was novelty in living in his native city once more; but there was some loneliness in it too.
>
> The smell of the alien land that he had left not so long ago seemed still to linger about his body. He detested it, and told himself he had to get rid of it. That he was also rather proud of it, that it gave him a certain sense of accomplishment, he did not know.[1] (*Michikusa* 1, 1915)

Thirteen years after the fact, the author returned to the scene of the crime, so to speak, to craft a literary persona who feels tainted by his prolonged sojourn among the aliens and whose pained reminiscence will deeply color the ensuing tale. In the interim, how did the author reflect, in his personal writings, on the "alien experience" that he revisited, yet again, in his final completed novel? And how did those who knew him in London remember the reclusive scholar in their midst?

Sōseki returned to Tokyo in January of 1903, but he never truly left London behind. Critics such as Etō Jun have held that the two years in England would largely determine the shape of his subsequent work. Nevertheless, what he managed to produce during his stay abroad—that is, aside from the accumulated mass of research notes upon which his scholarly career would hinge—was a meager assortment of sporadic diary entries, essays, and correspondences.

It was in the years following his return that he would recount—in an intermittent narrative retrospection—what befell the thirtyish educator who left behind a pregnant wife and child and sailed away to England, as a Monbushō (Ministry of Education) scholar, and what faced him upon his return home. Much of what we know of Sōseki's day-to-day life in London is from the testimony of others. But even his wife, who attempted, in her own memoir, to provide an authoritative account, had to dig for information.[2]

Despite his sterling credentials, the young teacher was initially reluctant to make the journey to this far-off land. Furthermore, there were misunderstandings about his course of study. Monbushō officials had expected him to pursue research on the English language, although there were no specific terms stipulated. Natsume Kinnosuke opted instead to study literature. Despite having provided no formal instructions or letters of introduction, the ministry held their scholar accountable for his activities. But he was irked by their demands and resentful of the meager stipend they were providing, and he ultimately failed to respond to requests for information.

The young man came to see himself as a stranger in a strange land. He lived alone in a succession of London boardinghouses, reading book after book and making elaborate notes in a crabbed scrawl. There was only sporadic communication with his wife. Rather than take university courses, he settled for a weekly tutorial with a somewhat eccentric Shakespearean scholar. He obsessed over money and how to stretch the little that was available— much of it spent in the local bookstores. As he refined his understanding of English literature, Kinnosuke cultivated a profound distaste for its society and people.

The saga of these years of virtual exile in London strongly resonates among Japanese—and others—for whom the prospect of being set adrift on foreign soil with none of the usual safety nets can be a horrific prospect. Such experience has a larger context—that of Meiji nation building and the educational and moral agenda that reinforced it. Much was expected of those fortunate enough to experience *yōkō*—travel and study in the West. As a brilliant university graduate and rising star in the Meiji intellectual firmament, Natsume Kinnosuke was in effect on a mission—to survey the terrain of English literature and become a ranking scholar in the field. This he would accomplish, in spite of money problems and gnawing doubts concerning his ability to master the literature that he so slavishly studied.

The London years have generated an impressive biographical literature. Books and monographs have mapped out every inch of London real estate that the author traversed and reconstructed his social network, such as it was.[3] Compelling evidence indicates that the experience of living alone and poor in this great Western metropolis had driven the man to the brink of madness—and perhaps beyond. The *kodoku* persona of alienation and disaffection—Sōseki's "London Underground," in other words—may be said to have certain British roots.

As noted above, the London stay generated a miscellany of personal writings. Aside from his correspondences and some undated notes and fragments, Natsume Kinnosuke made regular journal entries from late October 1900 until November 1901, when they end abruptly. There is not a single entry for 1902. Apropos his mental state, the July 1, 1901, entry stands out: "I've been terribly out of sorts lately. The most minor things will get on my nerves. It may be that I've got some nervous disorder *(shinkeibyō)*."[4]

A revealing series of essays appeared in May 1901, under the title *Rondon shōsoku* (Letters from London). These essays, in their representation of Natsume's state of mind some six months into his stay, prefigure subsequent retellings of the London experience.[5] Note the following excerpts:

ON HAVING TO MAKE DO WITH A MEAGER STIPEND
Here I am practicing every type of economy and living in such a wretched place. One reason is that I have a strong sense of not being the same person I was in Japan, but a mere student. Another thing is that, since I have gone to the trouble of voyaging to the West, I want to buy as many books as possible relating to my speciality to take home. So I have forgotten about having my own house and employing maids.... People will perhaps laugh at my being cooped up, as they might say, in a slum like Camberwell, but there is no need for me to be bothered about such things. I may be living in a dive, but I have never kept company with prostitutes or conversed with streetwalkers. I cannot vouchsafe my inner heart, but at least my actions are becoming of a virtuous man. Even if I say it myself, my conduct is exemplary.

OUT ON LONDON STREETS
Once outside, everyone I meet is depressingly tall. Worse yet, they all have unfriendly faces. If they imposed a tax on height in this country they might come up with a more economically small animal. But these are the words of one who cannot accept defeat gracefully, and, looked at impartially, one would have to say that it was they, not I, who look splendid. In any case, I feel small. An unusually small person approaches. Eureka! I think. But when we brush past one another I see he is about two inches taller than me. Then a strangely complexioned Tom Thumb approaches, but I realize this is my own image reflected in a mirror. There is nothing for it but to laugh bitterly, and, naturally, when I do so, the image laughs bitterly, too....

19

Most people are extremely busy. Their heads seem to be so teeming with thoughts of money that they have no time to jeer at us Japanese as yellow people. "Yellow people" is a well-chosen term. We are indeed yellow. When I was in Japan I knew I was not particularly white but regarded myself as being close to normal human coloration. But in this country I have finally realized that I am three leagues away from a human color—a yellow person who meanders amongst the crowds going to take in the plays and shows.

But sometimes there are people who surreptitiously comment on my country of origin. . . . In a park I heard a couple arguing whether I was a Chinaman or a Japanese. Two or three days ago I was invited out somewhere and set off in my silk hat and frock coat, only for two men who seemed like workmen to pass by saying, "Now there's a handsome Jap." I do not know whether I should be flattered or offended.[6] (*Rondon shōsoku* 1901)

The pained self-consciousness and manifest sense of racial inferiority anticipate the figure of the lone walker in the city in subsequent *shōhin* episodes.[7] But the first London reminiscence upon returning to Japan would place the author upon a bicycle. Crafted as a series of journal entries entitled *Jitensha nikki* (Bicycle Diary, 1903), the work presents its hapless narrator on a veritable collision course with Western civilization. Consider the following excerpts:

Oh, how terrible this bicycle business is! I eventually succumbed [to my landlady's urgings] and reluctantly went to Lavender Hill, where I was supposed to ride my bicycle or, rather, where I was supposed to fall off the bicycle. . . .[8]

A certain day of a certain month: Holding my bicycle, I wait at the top of a slope and slowly let my eyes roam around the far distance below. My intention is to wait for the coach's signal and then come galloping pell-mell down the slope. . . . Whether the British government, hearing that an Oriental celebrity would be practicing falling from a bicycle, had specially ordered the Public Works office to build this road we will never know. But in any case, as a road for bicycles, it is beyond reproach. . . .

Ordered to ride, I start trundling down like the wind from the top of the slope. . . . Now I encountered something extraordinary—about fifty schoolgirls coming in procession from the opposite direction. . . . Both my hands are occupied. My back is bent. My right leg is flung into the air. Even if I tried to get off, the bicycle would hear nothing of it. Desperate, and with no alternative, and in a bent posture all of my own creation, I narrowly manage to squeeze along the side of the female army. Whoosh! Yet no sooner have I caught my breath than the bicycle has already descended the slope and is on flat ground. However, there is absolutely no sign of it stopping. Rather, it turns in the direction of a policeman standing at the crossroads opposite and rapidly gallops toward him.... The bicycle, intent on bringing about a senseless double suicide, impetuously dashes toward the pavement. Eventually I run up on to the pavement from the road, full tilt, then proceed to crash into a fence, rebound three yards, and narrowly stop a distance of three feet from the policeman. "You appear to be in a spot of bother, sir," said the officer, laughing. To which my reply is "Yes, I am."[9]

Since surrendering to my landlady and being subjected to bicycle torture, I have had five major falls and countless small falls. I've crashed into stone walls, grazed my shins, collided with trees and had my nails torn off. I have fought a desperate war, but in the end it has all been for nothing. For one, this woman is someone who makes fun of people indiscriminately.... And her younger sister fulfills the role of inspecting any change of expression by keeping an unblinking eye on my yellow face. Subjected to the exquisite torments of these two old women, my sense of suspicion has only deepened, and my sense of ill treatment has increased day by day. In the end it's time to close the door and simply resign myself to having a face that is unavoidably yellow.[10] (*Jitensha nikki* 1903)

Composed shortly after his return from the scene of these bicyclist pratfalls, Sōseki's diary-style account (which might be subtitled "tales of an unreconstructed klutz") is a clever vehicle for an ironic sensibility that would soon be the talk of the town (Tokyo, that is), in the form of the famous *Wagahai wa neko de aru*. The fine comedic touch here belies the fact that the bicycling adventure was a form of physiotherapy recommended by the Japanese researcher's doctor and his solicitous landlady as well, both of whom were concerned about the gentleman's mental state.[11] The comic figure of the rogue Oriental biker unleashed upon the local citizenry is undercut by the pose of victimization, helplessness, and—once again—racial inferiority.

In 1905, Sōseki published two more London essays. The first, entitled *Rondon tō* (The Tower of London), is an account of a visit to the famous tourist destination shortly after he arrived in London.[12] Written in the midst of his serialization of *Neko*, while Sōseki was teaching at the Imperial University, the essay touches on the Tower's architecture, its bloody history, and memorable artwork depicting its famous victims. Clearly moved by the expe-

rience (precisely five years earlier), and by the dark history that the site calls
to mind, Sōseki turns to philosophical speculation upon the mental state of
those locked in the Tower, awaiting execution:

> Having been born, one must live.... All people must live. Those bound
> in the hell of this Tower, as well, accorded with this great truth and had to
> live. At the same time, they confronted their own doomed fate. With every
> passing minute, with every second, the question must have remained—
> How may I continue to stay alive?... The markings that remain on the
> Tower walls are the ghosts of that tenacious will to live.[13] (*Rondon tō* 1905)

The younger Sōseki, still in relatively good health, is moved by the
memento mori that he recalls in his mind's eye. As yet, the dead could only
be imagined. But as he grew older, and his advancing infirmity became a
relentless reminder of his own mortality, the notion of death grew at once
more personal and more deeply inscribed in his literature.

The Tower essay, though, ends on an anticlimactic note, with an account
of what happened when the new arrival to London returns from his touristic
excursion:

> Arriving at my lodging-house in a trance, I tell my landlord that I
> have visited the Tower today.... When I mention the epigraphs on the
> walls, he remarks with an indifferent air, "What, those scribblings?
> Waste of time, and they completely spoil a perfectly pretty place.
> And besides, the scribblings of criminals are not to be trusted. Lots of
> forgeries there, you know." Then I tell him about meeting the beautiful
> lady and how she fluently read obscure passages that were absolutely
> indecipherable to us. But the landlord, in a disdainful manner, says,
> "So what if she did? Everyone reads a guidebook before setting off.
> Being knowledgeable is nothing to be surprised at. And you say she's
> a great beauty? Well, there are lots of beautiful women in London. If
> you don't watch out, you'll be getting yourself into trouble."... After
> that I decided not to speak to anyone about the Tower of London.
> And I made a point not to return there.[14] (*Rondon tō* 1905)

The jaded landlord is quick to disabuse the credulous Japanese boarder of
his naïve notions concerning the Tower and its legends. It's a nice bit of local
real estate, he notes, but its history can be had in any guidebook. And as for
those London beauties—watch out! Sōseki may well have been sufficiently
chastened not to return to the Tower, but the essay stands both as an inter-

esting guidebook in its own right and a window upon the author's "London persona."

Another tourist destination, the Thomas Carlyle museum, had more specifically literary associations for Sōseki, who as a student had been an avid reader of Carlyle's works. His visit would inspire an essay, entitled *Kārairu hakubutsukan* (The Carlyle Museum, 1905), which retraces the official museum tour:[15]

> The higher we go [in the house,] the more unearthly my feelings become. When we reach the third floor I feel a vague sense of happiness. Or, rather, I have a feeling of indescribable strangeness. This is the loft....All the rays of light that filter into this attic space enter from directly overhead, through the single pane of glass beyond which is the sky, which leads out upon the entire world....
>
> It was Carlyle's plan to build this room and to turn it into his study. When it was completed he shut himself away here, only to realize for the first time the drawback of his plan. This is an uncomfortable place to be in summer, what with the heat, and in winter, due to the cold. The guide recites this much and looks back at me. Somewhere in that perfectly round face is the flicker of a smile. I nod without saying a word.
>
> For what purpose did Carlyle trouble himself with this scheme of a room close to the sky? As his writings show, he was somebody who had a touch of lightning about him. It seems his irritability did not allow him to ignore the many noises that mercilessly surrounded him so as to absorb himself in his books. The piano, the dog, the rooster and parrot—every single sound affected his delicate nerves and caused him such extreme agony that in the end he was made to seek refuge in this third-floor attic, as close to the sky and as far from people as possible....
>
> [We go downstairs,] and with each level we descend I have the feeling of approaching a lower world. It feels like a skin of meditation is peeling off. When I descend the stairs and lean against the bannister at the bottom and stare out at the road, I have once again become an ordinary man.[16]
> (*Kārairu hakubutsukan* 1905)

The essay has little to say about Carlyle the writer or the man. What interests the visitor, instead, is the house itself, located on Cheyne Row, which he refers to as a "hermitage." Fancying himself the first Japanese to have set foot in the place, he is escorted around the premises by "a plump woman of about fifty." They finally arrive at the sanctum sanctorum—Carlyle's private retreat on the top floor, a refuge from the clamorous world below, as described in the passage just quoted. Understandably keen on witnessing the actual environs in which other writers plied their trade, Sōseki would go on to craft a *shōhin* persona enclosed within his own study, a private space from which to freely reflect upon his world.[17]

Incidentally, Natsume Sōseki could hardly have imagined that the site of his fifth and final lodgings in London, at 81 The Chase, would be honored with a Blue Plaque, designating it as a historical landmark—the first London site to commemorate a Japanese.[18]

Bungakuron

For the Meiji intellectual and literary historian, the significance of Natsume Sōseki's years in London lies in the fruits of his research labors. Misery and melancholy, however these are to be understood in Sōseki's case, can be dismissed as the price one pays for such dedicated toil in the scholarly vineyards.

Of the assorted fruit, none is more substantial than *Bungakuron* (Theory of Literature, 1907).[19] This difficult and often tedious work, written in the formal *bungotai* (literary) style, is in effect a distillation of Sōseki's London researches, cobbled together from the notes he used for his English literature courses at the university.[20] The work is predicated on a deceptively simple empirical formulation, which construes a literary work as the sum of two variables—F (the focal impression/percept/concept) plus f (the emotional, affective counterpart to F). Sōseki's $F + f$ theorem, expounded in the first chapter, is elaborately explicated and expounded over the course of well over five hundred pages.

Bungakuron has come to be regarded as a pinnacle of Meiji literary scholarship, and it is enjoying a resurgence of scholarly interest.[21] Yet there is unmistakable irony in the fact of its publication at the very point when the author bade farewell to academia and embarked on his *Asahi* career as writer of fiction. Sōseki himself did not hesitate to cast a sardonic eye on the book, which he referred to as the "deformed corpse" of his erstwhile academic career.[22]

Doubly ironic is that what is best known of this imposing work of literary scholarship relates not to the theoretical exposition per se, but rather to the book's preface, which presents the background circumstances.[23] Written in November 1906, the preface concerns the London years and the author's struggle to pursue his literary research. The following excerpts, often cited as psychobiographical evidence, speak frankly—and bitterly—about the experience:

FIGURE 1. Natsume Sōseki's fifth and final London residence, at 81 The Chase. It bears the commemorative Blue Plaque. (Author photo)

The two years I spent in London were an utterly miserable two years.[24]
In the company of English gentlemen, I was like a poodle loosed among
a pack of wolves. I led a truly pitiful and wretched life. They say that the
population of London is five million. I can assert unhesitatingly that I
barely managed to eke out an existence in that city, my circumstance akin
to the single drop of water lost amidst five million oil drops. The owner
of a freshly laundered, sparkling-clean white shirt will most certainly be
upset when he discovers ink stains on it. What a pathetic figure I must
have seemed to those good English gentlemen—this alien ink stain of a
Japanese, wandering about Westminster like some beggar, for two solid
years breathing in thousands upon thousands of cubic feet of that great
city's fetid air, with its choking miasma of man-made soot and smoke....

The English regarded me as a nervous wreck.... Following my
return to Japan, word got out that I was still a nervous wreck, that I
remained out of my mind. Even relatives of mine appear to have affirmed
this.... However, when I reflect on the fact that my condition has enabled
me to write *Neko,* and to publish my *Yōkyoshū* collection and *Uzurakago*
as well, I consider it only right and proper to express my deepest gratitude
to these mental disorders.... I can only hope and pray that this madness
will never forsake me.[25]

Written under the author's personal signature (Natsume Kinnosuke), the
Bungakuron preface drips with sarcasm and spite—a rather inauspicious pre-
lude, one might say, to the magnum opus that it is meant to introduce. But
the author had burned his bridges, and he appears positively to delight in
performing his little masquerade as Oriental smudge on the lily-white garment who embraces his putative madness as an ally, a precious muse.[26]

Yet despite the scant affection Sōseki felt toward the London of the here
and now, he had a remarkably sophisticated knowledge of the *historical* London, which after all had figured significantly in his research agenda. The fruits
of this research can be gleaned in a later work, in effect a companion to *Bungakuron,* entitled *Bungaku hyōron* (Literary Critiques, 1909). Based on extensive lecture notes for his university course on eighteenth-century English
literature and society, the book contains a wealth of details on London life,
manners, and society. Here the author holds forth on the status of women, on
clothing and hairstyles, popular entertainments, coffeehouses and bars; and
he comments with enthusiasm and authority on its great writers, artists, and
intellectuals.[27] Again, one is struck by the contrast of such fascination with
the city as revealed through historical and literary texts and the vituperation
aimed at the city as personally experienced.

London in *Eijitsu*

Having included London in his narrative repertoire, Sōseki would revisit it in subsequent *shōhin* contexts. One set of reminiscences would be incorporated into the *Eijitsu* collection.[28] A "miscellany-within-a-miscellany," the seven constituent episodes concern life at the boardinghouse; the weekly tutorial with Craig, the Shakespeare scholar; a brief excursion to Scotland; and strange happenings out on the streets of London. Of these, the street scenes jointly recreate the melancholy atmosphere of the earlier writings. What follows are excerpts from Sōseki's three-part exercise in dystopian discourse—an eerie urban phantasm that will mirror the alienation and despair of his "underground" persona.

Castaway on London Streets

A WARM DREAM

The wind as it strikes against the tall buildings finds its natural course obstructed, and in an instant it branches like lightning and comes blowing down in diagonal streaks, down onto the passersby and the pavement below....

Everyone on these London streets walks quickly past. Even the women hurry by, holding on to their skirts and positively pounding their high-heeled shoes against the pavement. It's a wonder the heels don't break off. Every face I see has the same urgent, harried look. All of them—men and women alike—keep their eyes fixed on the road ahead, obsessed with reaching their destination. Nothing can stop them....[29] It's as though these people are unable to endure the act of walking and cannot bear being outside, as though their very dignity as human beings hinged upon finding immediate refuge under a roof somewhere.

I plod along, at my own pace, thoroughly depressed at the thought of being here in this city.... The imposing gray buildings block out the sun, casting their shadows on the suffocating streets below.... The human beings are mere specks of shivering black, as they make their way along a narrow strip of the great canyon floor. And I, among their vast number, am the most sluggish, the most infinitesimal.... Moving slowly, so slowly, I, too, am being buffeted about by the wind gusts that whistle through the dark, walled-in streets and all but propel me into the building.[30]

Safely inside, I circle all the way around the long corridor, then up several flights of stairs. Coming upon an imposing door, I push upon it gently, and at once it swings open, soundlessly, and I find myself deposited inside a great gallery. Below me is a spectacle of dazzling luminescence. I could barely keep my eyes open before acclimating myself to its intensity. Turning around, I notice that the door has closed. And I notice, too, how warm it is inside—positively springlike.

At length I am able to take in the scene before me—a mass of people, wherever I look. Yet they are quiet, demure, composed. Such a crowd of people, in such close proximity, and no sign of strain or discomfort. Indeed, their very presence seems mutually comforting. I look up at the great domed ceiling—rich, ornate colors and a gorgeous, radiant gilt decor that is truly breathtaking. Before me is an encircling balustrade, with nothing beyond—a great void. I approach the balustrade and, craning my neck, peer down into the void. Far below, I can make out a space filled with people—a mass of small human figures, yet each one remarkably vivid and distinct—as though painted onto a canvas, with a rich palette of hues. A veritable sea of humanity, quietly undulating with a steady, wavelike momentum.

Then, all of a sudden, the spectacle of this rippling human mass vanishes. Pitch darkness descends, from the great dome to the depths below. Thousands of human souls who had sat shoulder to shoulder, now buried in the darkness—and not a single sound to be heard. It is as though their very existence had been snuffed out, leaving neither shape nor shadow—only a hush stillness.[31]

IMPRESSIONS

As I left my flat, . . . carriages and coaches of every description were coming and going—teeming, like some multicolored cloud. I stopped for a moment to take in the spectacle of this great sea of conveyances moving all about. Where were these people coming from, I wondered. Where were they bound? Just then a tall man approached from behind and took me bodily by the shoulders, moving me aside as he rushed past. I seek a way out, but where is one to flee? Tall people to the right of me, tall people to the left of me. The one who'd pushed me aside is himself pushed aside by another. No one utters a word. The crowd simply forges ahead.

It was then that I truly realized what it meant to be drowning in a sea of humanity. The sea is vast, beyond comprehension, yet remarkably quiet. And, alas, one cannot escape. Obstructions and obstacles abound. With a human wave approaching from the rear, one moves quietly forward. Seemingly controlled by nothing more than a slender thread of fate, I fall in line with tens of thousands of anonymous souls, as if by some prior arrangement, and march forward in unison, one step at a time.

As I walk, I have a sinking feeling. It occurs to me that my flat is located in a four-story building that looks exactly like every other building in this vast city of four-story buildings. How in the world am I supposed to find my way home? . . .

In this forlorn state, I am jostled and shoved by the throng of tall people. At a loss, I turn down this street, then that street, and at every turn I sense that I'm heading that much farther in the wrong direction. Caught in this mind-numbing mass of humanity I felt an inexpressible sense of loneliness.[32]

FOG

I get out of bed, pull up the blinds, and look outside. Everything is shrouded in fog. Not a thing is visible. . . . I go outside, and the only things that come into view are within a range of ten feet. Walk another ten feet, and yet another panorama materializes. The world reduces to a ten-foot radius, and with each step this ten-foot world gives way to another, renewing itself yet again. And with each such renewal, the world one has just passed through yields to the passage of time and vanishes. . . .

I took care of some business at Victoria and then walked along the river by the Tate Gallery. By the time I arrived at Battersea, the leaden, grayish elements suddenly closed in, and everything was dark. Like a river of liquid coal flowing around me, the thick fog presses in upon my eyes, nose, and mouth. My overcoat is so damp it feels plastered to my body. The air is a dense, soupy miasma. With every breath I feel suffocated. Moving my legs is like treading the floor of some dungeon.

Rendered all but insensible in the midst of this oppressive, dank world, I come to a stop, virtually paralyzed. I sense that crowds of people are passing me by, but one wouldn't actually know this unless a passerby happened to jostle you as he went on his way.

Then I catch sight of something—a dim, yellow light, a bean-sized beacon suspended somewhere in this great sea of fog. Bestirring myself, I move in the direction of this tiny landmark. I come upon a shop window. Inside, a gas lamp is burning—light enough for me to notice human beings inside, doing what people normally do. What a sense of relief.

When I pass through Battersea, though, I lose my bearings. . . . I am stopped in my tracks, standing alone in the dark, straining for some clue. I hear footsteps approaching from my right. But they stop, some twenty feet from where I stood, then move off in some other direction. The sound grew faint, then gave way to total silence.

Here I am, stranded in the middle of nowhere, in pitch darkness,
wondering how I'd ever be able to find my way home.[33] (*Eijitsu* 15, 1909)

The streets of London are presented in these atmospheric, spectral episodes as a malevolent organism threatening to devour the peripatetic narrator. The first of these, "A Warm Dream," was inspired by a visit to the theater—a performance of *Twelfth Night,* to be exact.[34] The narrator, exquisitely
conscious of himself as a stranger in a strange land, is overwhelmed by the
phalanx of resolutely advancing human shapes, as he slowly moves toward his
destination.

Once inside the theater, though, the gloom and darkness of the city streets
give way to dazzling light and brilliant display. The mass of black figures con-
fronted outside are now rendered as a great canvas of colored shapes, each
sharply defined, yet belonging to an otherworldly collectivity, which sways
and swirls in wave-like unison—a veritable sea of humanity. Then, just as suddenly as the dazzling spectacle of color and shape is revealed, darkness restores
the world to emptiness and silence. And with that, the curtain will rise.

The next episode, aptly titled "Impressions," amplifies the sense of one's
alien presence in this nightmarish city and the utter isolation and confusion that follow. Caught in a swirling human maelstrom, the hapless narrator
is struck by an "inexpressible sense of loneliness" *(iubekarazaru kodoku),* an
expression that conveys the underlying tenor of the London experience. Haga
Tōru has remarked on Sōseki's construction here of an urban dystopia as
experienced by the peripatetic narrator, who is disoriented and debased by his
attempts to navigate the streets of this "bizarre town" *(fushigi na machi).*[35]

In the third episode, "Fog," Sōseki employs a familiar symbol to portray his narrator's hopeless situation. The fog—this palpable "river of liquid
coal"—erases all sense of location, of meaning; it erases even the *human* flow
that would at least provide some orientation. Alone, cast adrift in the impen-
etrable darkness, Sōseki's narrator aptly symbolizes the alien's sense of utter
depersonalization. These, to borrow from Dostoyevsky, are his "notes from
underground."[36]

Haga correctly points to *Eijitsu* as a collection of literary experiments,
which draw upon the *shaseibun* impressionism favored by Shiki. I would
emphasize the sense in which these London episodes stand as a modernist
treatment of city as dystopian space, a spectral phantasm, and the individual as
castaway—a lost soul in this alien realm. Sōseki's narrator, alone and undone,
all but revels in his *kodoku* identity. But this in turn serves as a vehicle for an
imagistic and sensory phenomenology of the city and its streets, the people
and their society. The sensitized narrator channels the flow of visual impres-

sions—the patterns of light and shadow, color and shape. Sōseki's *shaseibun* impressionism, which fostered this play of color, artistic composition, and their narrative figuration, merges with the modernist construction of "urban phantasm" in these episodes.

In *Imagined Cities,* a study of the novelistic depiction of city space and the urban experience, Robert Alter notes certain distinctive features of his "imagined cities": self-reflexivity (a concern for the interior view of a character's consciousness, rather than plot dynamics per se); fragmented narrative structure, and the fragmentary nature of the reality presented; a "phenomenology of urban life"—the experience of the city as a concatenation of emblematic patterns, shapes, phenomena of swarming and teeming, fog, and the compromised view; and the anxiety and paranoia induced by one's prolonged exposure to fragmented, obscured, spectral spaces.[37] All of these tally with Sōseki's evocation of London in the above *shōhin.*

The author would briefly revisit the London experience toward the end of *Omoidasu koto nado,* at the point where his narrator, about to leave the Izu Peninsula town of Shuzenji and return to Tokyo, is reflecting on the peace and tranquility of his long convalescence:

> Years ago, when I lived in England, I came to despise the country with
> a passion. My unbridled hatred of England could rival even that of
> Heine. Yet when the time came to leave, I looked out upon this teeming
> metropolis of London, this swirling maelstrom of alien souls, and
> somehow sensed that the sooty, fetid air that enveloped them contained
> a kind of vapor that was fit for me to breathe. I lingered on, standing
> alone in the midst of that vast city, looking off into the skies.[38] (*Omoidasu*
> 32, 1911)

The remembered experience of London as Dantesque inferno persists, in spite of one's having somehow established a modus vivendi. As before, the memory of the city betokens an unquiet spirit and the haunting specter of one's past.

In a sense, though, the most poignant account of the London experience, and the turmoil that would await him upon his return, is found in *Michikusa,* as it recasts the situation in the Natsume household during that period. Hemmed in by painful memories and gnawing self-doubt, Kenzō reflects guiltily upon the privation his family had to endure while he was away:

> Immediately on returning to Japan, Kenzō had begun to be short of
> money. By the time he had settled in a new house in his native Tokyo after

31

years of absence, he didn't have a penny to his name. . . . The government had sent his wife an allowance every month, and he was thus able to leave her behind with a clear conscience. . . . But very soon the truth dawned on him, and he was shocked. During his absence, his wife had worn out all of her clothes and had been forced to restyle some of his. . . for her own use. The bed mats had hardly any stuffing left in them. The counterpanes were tattered. And her father had had to let her live in this state, unable to help. He had taken risks on the stock market after losing his position, and his modest savings had dwindled almost to nothing.[39] (*Michikusa* 58, 1915)

Kenzō then recalls his wretched life in London, where he lived "like a frightened mouse in a cell-like room that faced the north." And he remembers how he had to economize:

Once he bought a sandwich on his way back to his lodgings and munched it as he wandered about aimlessly in a large park. In one hand he held his umbrella, with which he tried to ward off the rain that blew in at a slant; in his other hand he held the slices of bread with the thinly cut meat between them. It was very difficult to eat like that, and more than once he hesitated before a bench, wondering whether he should sit down. But the benches were all soaking wet. Sometimes he would open a tin of biscuits in his room and chew the dry, crumbly things until they felt wet enough to go down his throat. If he had had some hot water, it would not have been such an ordeal.[40] (*Michikusa* 59, 1915)

Kenzō's confused and torn view of himself—composed of equal measures of disgust and pride—is nowhere better expressed than in the passage with which this chapter began. But we should recall that these proxy reminiscences were fashioned late in life, and as part of the larger autobiographical project of the novel. In other words, they must be seen alongside the many elements of Kenzō's character as presented in *Michikusa*.

Sōseki's London: A Parallax View

The London experience has become a fixture of the Sōseki mythos. And it figures prominently in the history of Western literary sojourns, which would serve as a vital apprenticeship for many Meiji writers, helping to foster the development of modern Japanese literature overall. For Sōseki, the experience yielded a trove of literary gleanings, together with a deep ambivalence toward

Western society and values. The scholarly accomplishments are undeniable, as is Sōseki's disparagement of them. In like manner, the author's retelling of the London years is by turns inventive and self-pitying, with disgust and revulsion as a common refrain.[41]

But there are other views of Sōseki in London—accounts by relatives and friends who could bear personal witness. In her memoir, for instance, Kyōko bitterly recalls the London years, from her vantage point in Tokyo, as a time of privation and dependency. And things would only get worse upon her husband's return, when she would have to deal with his abusive treatment and violent tantrums.[42]

Those who knew Natsume Kinnosuke in London had different stories to tell. Nagao Hanbei (1865–1936), a railroad official, lived in the same boardinghouse—but in a larger room than his Japanese acquaintance, and in much more comfortable circumstances. Natsume was clearly bad-off, as Nagao recounts, having little disposable income beyond the money he spent on books. One day Natsume came by and nonchalantly requested a loan of twenty pounds. Nagao agreed, but felt constrained to ask whether this was actually a loan or whether it would be treated as an outright gift. "No, this money is on loan. I'll definitely repay you!"

Nagao relates having returned to Japan—minus the loan repayment. Back in Tokyo, he happened to run into Natsume one day, out on the streets, and the man immediately brought up the matter of the twenty pounds, which he insisted on paying back. "It's not really necessary. Can you afford to part with that amount?" "Yes, I can." And the very next day Natsume came by with the money. "He was a very scrupulous *(kichōmen)* person, to a fault!"

A different perspective is provided by another fellow boarder, Watanabe Shunkei (1879–1958), one of a small circle of Japanese businessman who lodged together and actively socialized with one another.[43] As Watanabe relates, Sōseki (whom he refers to as Sensei) did not have much to do with the other Japanese boarders:

> Sensei was generally locked away in his room, pursuing his researches, and we knew not to intrude.... When he was bored, though, he would occasionally ask me and Watanabe Tarō up to his room on the third floor for a chat. The furnishings were spare—only a single chair, so the two of us were left standing. Sensei would bring by two big piles of magazines and books and have us use them as chairs. The room, after all, was absolutely crammed with books—piled onto his desk, on the floor, on the mantelpiece—everywhere!

We also got together on several occasions to compose haiku. Sensei, of course, would be in charge. We did worry about his health, though, what with his being alone and studying all the time, so we'd take him along with us to the theater, to give him a break. . . .

Thereafter, Sensei grew all the more involved in his researches and hardly left his room. I was unaware that he'd become subject to depression *(shinkei suijaku)*. In any event, I was to leave London in November, prior to which I went to bid farewell to Sensei, but he was not in. . . .

It's generally accepted that Sōseki sensei hated London and spent two miserable years there. Certainly there was a negative side to his stay, but it was not all depression and gloom. I for one witnessed otherwise.[44]

Natsume, seishin ni ijō ari

The association of Sōseki's London stay with isolation and mental anguish is strong, as evidenced by the reminiscences of others who knew him there. Okakura Yoshisaburō (1868–1936), younger brother of the famous art historian and culture critic Okakura Tenshin, wrote in 1936 of his overseas acquaintanceship with Sōseki. Both had been sent to England as Monbushō scholars, and they spent time together in the early summer of 1902.[45] By then, as Okakura relates, Sōseki was deep into his literary researches and so hemmed in by the accumulated books that he couldn't even contemplate making a move from his Clapham lodgings.

Okakura recalls the day later that year when he received a telegram from Monbushō headquarters: *Natsume, seishin ni ijō ari. Fujishiro dōdō kikoku seshimubeshi* (Natsume is mentally unbalanced; have him return to Japan, together with Fujishiro). He tells of acting as intermediary, under the ministry's directive, in having Fujishiro Teisuke monitor Sōseki's activities once he arrived in London from his research stay in Germany, then accompany him back to Japan.[46]

For his part, Doi Bansui (1871–1952) had known Sōseki at the Imperial University, where both graduated from the English department. Doi himself went overseas, in 1901, at his own expense, and settled in London. His reminiscence is contained in a detailed letter sent to Natsume Kyōko in February 1928. In it, he remarks on his association with Sōseki in September 1902, when, out of growing concern for his friend's state of mind, he moved into the Clapham lodgings to see the situation firsthand. More so than Okakura, it was Doi who understood how serious things were—noting that he found his friend in a terrible emotional state *(mōretsu no shinkei suijaku)*. And it was he who was subsequently assumed to have been the one to alert the Monbushō to the man's psychological deterioration.[47]

As noted above, Sōseki addresses the "madness" question at the very end of the *Bungakuron* preface, in which he expresses his "deepest gratitude to these mental disorders," which have served as his literary inspiration. "I pray," he adds, "that this nervous disorder of mine, this madness, will never forsake me."[48] *Michikusa* is proof that Sōseki's prayers had been answered. Here, the author would revisit the family crisis that ensued upon his return to Tokyo in 1903, through the troubled moods and reflections of his literary alter ego, whom he casts as follows:

> Kenzō felt as though his head was stuffed with crumpled paper. His irritability was such that sometimes he thought he would go mad unless he gave vent to it. Once for no reason at all he kicked a pot of flowers that belonged to the children off the veranda. It was a prize possession of theirs, something their mother had bought them after days of begging on their part. The sight and sound of the red pot smashing as it hit the ground gave Kenzō some satisfaction. But when he saw the broken stem and the torn flowers he was momentarily overcome with sadness at the useless, cruel thing he had done. These pitiful flowers, he thought, had seemed beautiful to the children, and now their own father had destroyed them.[49] (*Michikusa* 57, 1915)

Kenzō is clearly disturbed, yet Sōseki does not elaborate upon his "acting out." Years later, in her own reflections upon that time, Kyōko would provide concrete details as she recounts her husband's emotional fits, which began around June. He would throw things all about, terrorize the children, and attack the maids. It reached the point where Sōseki ordered his wife, who was pregnant at the time, to leave the house. Fearing for her children's safety, she did precisely this, in July of 1903. It was around this time, as she notes, that her husband was diagnosed by the psychiatrist Kure Shūzō as suffering from *shinkei suijaku*—a chronic disorder, according to Kure, with predictable periods of relapse.[50] Kyōko notes that this diagnosis actually came as a relief, insofar as she now recognized that her husband was not some willful maniac, but suffered from a disease. Rethinking the situation, she and the children returned home early in September. Alas, her husband showed no signs of recovery. He ranted and raved, accusing people of conspiring against him. Kyōko somehow managed to hold the family together, though, and with the spring of 1904 the situation improved.[51]

Kyōki: Madness, Modernity, Sōseki

Disorientation, dehumanization, alienation, descent into madness—these are handmaidens of the modern condition, and their ecosystem, so to speak, is the city. The equation of city life and pathology—both physical and psychological—is a hallmark of the high literary modernism of the early twentieth century.

As Karatani Kōjin has argued, modern Japanese literature—*kindai bungaku*—was strongly conditioned by advances in medical science and a concern—a fetish, perhaps—for objectivity, empiricism, and fact.[52] From this perspective, individuals were easily reducible to a constellation of symptoms and syndromes, which could be "read," interpreted, and appropriately treated. For the modern writer (especially those in the naturalist coterie), the aim was not diagnosis and treatment of others, but rather *self*-diagnosis—which is to say, exploring inner states and constructing a narrative representation of pained interiority. Anxiety, disturbance, madness—here is the mother lode of *kindai* literary symptomatology. Given the *bundan* concern for authenticity and unembroidered personal disclosure, it is only natural that the reader would be disposed to interpreting such accounts as case histories.

Beginning with the London years, and the widely known *shinkei suijaku* diagnosis that ensued, the life and writings of Natsume Sōseki have, for some, fused into a uniform clinical profile. This would be true, as well, for many of his famously "disturbed" contemporaries.[53] One can speak here, in other words, of a psycho-biographical determinism that traces in the life and writings a process of physical and psychological decline, triggered by the trauma of the London years, which progresses through stages of advancing debility and despair. There is ample evidence of emotional crises in 1903 and again in 1913. And the theme of madness and mania certainly recurs in much of Sōseki's writing.[54] Moreover, Sōseki the culture critic points ruefully to the rampant individualism and egocentrism of the modern age—the madness, as it were, of contemporary life.[55] Yet the author also understood, as evidenced in the concluding section of his *Bungakuron* preface, that one could convert the dross of emotional instability into the precious metal of literary creation—the process of sublimation, in Freudian terms.

Did Natsume Kinnosuke go mad in England? The evidence suggests that the answer may be yes.[56] But it is all too tempting, and facile, to conflate armchair psychology and literary analysis. It can be argued that *Neko* and *Michikusa*—the alpha and omega, so to speak, of Sōseki's autobiographical fiction—channeled the "madness muse" of the author's London experience.

But what does this explain regarding the shape and sense of these literary creations?

In 2002, Natsume Fusanosuke visited London in connection with an NHK television production commemorating the centennial of his grandfather's return from his stay in England. A noted professional cartoonist, Natsume was to be interviewed, with relevant city sites as backdrop, regarding Sōseki's life in London at the beginning of the twentieth century.[57] As he relates in his memoir, *Sōseki's Grandson* (*Sōseki no mago,* 2002), Fusanosuke had little interest in Sōseki the man, the author, *or* the details of his London experiences. Growing up, he had mainly heard about the famous relative from his father and his Uncle Shinroku, both of whom had talked about what a miserable parent he had been. But as the disaffected grandson took in the dark, gloomy city and toured through the cramped flat in Clapham Commons, he felt a surge of empathy for the man. Being cooped up in his little room, he reflects, reading and scribbling away for sixteen months—this would have driven anyone crazy![58]

Babashita Traces

Memories and the City

M emory defines us. And we in turn give definition and meaning to our memories. The temper of our times serves as a constant reminder of how crucial memory is to our most basic conception of who we are and how we live. We forget things, and this awareness, however exasperating it may be, in turn reminds us that memory exists—as a fragile, contingent, and magical act of mental prestidigitation.

On Memory and Modernity

As a subject of scholarly research, memory has migrated from its home base in philosophy and psychology to the farthest corners of the disciplinary map, and it now occupies the research agendas of fields as disparate as biochemistry and neurophysiology, history, law, economics—and, most emphatically, literary and cultural studies. The transformation of remembered thought into writing—be it in the form of diary entry, essay, or novel—is a fascinating bit of alchemy. It is most certainly not a routine transaction. Lab scientist and poet alike understand that memory is anything but a lockbox of indelible replications of the past, accessible with the ease and immediacy of a neural mouse-click.[1]

For the cultural historian, memory has emerged as a sine qua non of modernization theory, where it figures in conceptions of nation building and the formation of collective identity. Eric Hobsbawm's well-traveled notion of invented tradition has inspired a broad-based rethinking of how modern societies deploy reconstructed elements of cultural practice and essentialist rhetoric to bolster a sense of shared identity among an otherwise dispersed and disparate citizenry. The process entails creating the illusion of time-honored communal ritual and belief through the strategic erasure of the historical circumstances of their very creation.[2]

Collective memory as a tool of political and economic manipulation is a concomitant of our age, standing at the intersection of contending global and local forces.[3] The strategic possibilities of memory were clearly understood, too, by the architects of the Meiji restoration, who sought to strengthen the new nation by enshrining "ancient traditions"—especially those centering on Shinto mythology and the divinity of the emperor. As Carol Gluck and others have demonstrated, Japan's modernization was built upon an ideology of national uniqueness and exclusivity, embodied in a mythicized concept of *kokutai,* or "national essence," that aimed at galvanizing the Japanese people as loyal and tractable imperial subjects. Thus, while the state vigorously promoted progress and advancement, it simultaneously sought to inoculate the people against the radical destabilization that industrial development, urbanization, and "massification" of modern life was already in the process of engendering.[4]

The creation of memory as modern discourse would lie at the very heart of the Meiji modernization. Writers and the print media would be an engine of memory construction. Embodying the lived experience of Japan's rapid transformation, writers were challenged to fashion new ways to conceive of, and recount, the past—a past that grew ever more remote and strange in the face of changing circumstances. Writers would bear witness, through the creative agency of words.

What is more, Meiji literature, mirroring the physical location of its writers, would be markedly Tokyo-centered. This would entail a gradual break with the Edo past and a reconfiguration of urban locales.[5] Inevitably, perhaps, writers explored ways to incorporate aspects of urban life—the life they knew—into their work. Tokyo itself—its neighborhoods, its shrines and stores, rivers and bridges—emerged as a dominant literary subject, a character in its own right. And the ever-changing face of the city would be duly inscribed in literary texts.

A standard critique of modern civilization invokes notions of displacement and alienation—the anonymity of urban existence, the struggle to forge a sense of identity and meaning in a vacuum. As noted in the Introduction, European literary expressions of interiority and self-awareness effectively migrated to Meiji Japan, where they circulated among Tokyo writers and intellectuals.

Enter Sōseki, whose novels, in tandem with the *shōhin,* would comprise a discourse of interiority and a commentary on Japan's modern temper. At the same time, his is a literature of the city—the living city of Tokyo, with its cast of urbanites. At its heart, though, is the intersection of the individual and one's past, mediated through memory and reflection.[6] As we have come to understand, narrated memory is a cocktail of invention and actuality—ingredients that appear mutually exclusive but indeed defy separation. Memory, then, is perhaps best understood as an indispensable catalyst for an ongoing refashioning of one's sense of self. The prominence of reminiscence in Meiji literature—and Sōseki's work, in particular—is an index of the very dislocations that would provoke a quest for meaning and order through recalling the past.

Memory, Childhood, and Place

It is a commonplace yet crucial observation that the physical transformations wrought upon the landscape—and in the Meiji case, these would be breathtaking in their scope and pace—were paralleled in their figuration and metaphoric representation. Meiji history, so closely identified with urban and industrial development and the "leveling" technologies of transportation and communication, is marked by deracination and relocation. Writers such as Sōseki and Nagai Kafū, who grew up in early-Meiji Tokyo, would construct scenes from childhood cast in rusticated, almost primeval settings—a strangeness commensurate with the gap between the transformed urban present and the "distant" past of one's early years. A literature of nostalgia would emerge as an all but obligatory counterpart to the juggernaut of progress. For Kafū, evoking the look and feel of an early-Meiji Tokyo that retained the aura of its Edo roots became something of an obsession, and it rivaled the revulsion he felt toward the modernization project in its architectural and urban-design realization.[7] For him, late-Meiji Tokyo was a monstrosity, a pathetic imitation of the great Western capitals.

Closely tied to the nostalgic mode of reminiscence as corrective to the defamiliarized present is the mythos of village roots—an invented tradition of *furusato,* a timeless "Japanese-ness" rooted in the hinterland and centered on the putative virtues and spiritual purity of communal life.[8] A corollary to this utopian realm, located somewhere over the rainbow and well beyond city boundaries and the toxins of urban life, is yet another Meiji "invention"—namely, childhood. Analogous to the village qua untainted, prelapsarian paradise, childhood stands as the age of innocence.[9]

Sōseki: Memories and the City

The peaceful village, the innocent child—these casualties of Japan's modernization would be transformed into literary themes and tropes. But they did not resonate equally among Meiji writers. An inveterate city-dweller,

Natsume Sōseki was unable to draw upon memories of a happy childhood spent in a nurturing community. In his fictional world—notably, *Kokoro* and *Michikusa*—the past is suspect terrain, a source of anxiety and uncertainty. And the present offers no sanctuary from gnawing doubt. Both past and present are identified with the same city. Yet the city is equally a barrier separating what was from what is.

The subtitle of this chapter is an homage to an exemplary work of literary reminiscence—*Istanbul: Memories and the City,* by Orhan Pamuk, the 2006 winner of the Nobel Prize in literature. Pamuk's city is Istanbul—a place, and a state of mind, that is movingly evoked through memories, photographs, and personal reflection. Sōseki's city, at the time of his birth, was Edo. A year later it would become Tokyo. As was the case with many of his contemporaries, Sōseki and his literature would be inextricably tied to the city. And so were the memories he shared with his readers.[10]

Recalling the Old Haunts

The standard account of Natsume Sōseki's upbringing tells of an unhappy childhood spent in multiple households, an upbringing that bred a chronic distrust and insecurity. In his *shōhin* reminiscences, the author is largely reticent on the subject of his childhood and early upbringing. His fictional surrogates—Kenzō, most notably—will be struck by some image, scene, or thought that sets in motion a train of association to scenes and episodes from the past. The remembered past may be rich in detail and incident, but it will have meaning only in relation to the moment, and manner, of its recollection.

Born in the Babashita district of Edo in 1867, in the final year that the Tokugawa shogunate would claim this city as its capital, Sōseki would go on to witness the dramatic transformation of his birthplace—a microcosm, in effect, of Japan's epochal modernization during the Meiji period. His reminiscences underline the centrality of place, and the memory of place, to one's conception of self, and the poignancy associated with the loss of old landmarks and the dislocations wrought by the modern age. The following account draws on early memories of the city seen from the perspective of the author's declining years.[11]

BABASHITA

The house in which I was born was located in the Babashita district, not far down the road from where I now live. To call this area a district, though, is somewhat of a misnomer. As a child, I could only think of it as a small backwater outpost, entirely run-down and desolate.... There were several stores and shops in the area, for the most part built in the old "storehouse" style. The Omiya pharmacy was one of these, located up the road on the right-hand side. Where the road bottomed out, the Kokuraya sake shop, with its wide frontage, could be found.... There was also a maker of wooden implements and a blacksmith shop. And on the Hachiman-zaka road, there was the vegetable market, whose roof covered the broad expanse of dirt flooring....

And as with every town and village in Japan, we had our local tofu shop. An oily-smelling rope curtain marked the entrance, and the water running through the gutter out front was surprisingly clear—the sort of thing you might find in Kyoto. Not far beyond was the Seikanji temple. Beyond its main gate, painted in red, stood a dense bamboo grove, which obscured everything inside the temple precincts from the view of passersby. But the sound of the temple bell, which rang at intervals throughout the day and into the night, has remained with me ever since. From the time of autumn, when mist and fog prevailed, and on into winter, with its biting winds, the somber *gong-gong-gong* of the Seikanji bell would chill me to the core, as though hammering some sad, cold thing into my very being.[12] (*Garasudo* 19, 1915)

I can still recall, as though an illusion of sorts, the *yose* entertainment hall located next to the tofu shop. Whenever the image crosses my mind, I'm struck by a queer sensation—my memory having perhaps been dulled by the incongruity of a *yose* hall in a backwater such as ours—as I gaze with incredulous eyes toward the distant past.... Back then, before the building was converted into a normal residence, I'd head to the hall, with its dark sign hanging drearily out front, and buy a ticket with money my mother would provide.

I went to hear a particular storyteller perform his *kōshaku* tales.[13] I believe the man's name was Nanrin, or something of the sort.[14] Curiously enough, this Nanrin seems to have been the sole entertainer at our local *yose*. It must have been quite an undertaking for him to get to our area on foot, from wherever he might have lived. Things have changed so dramatically since then, of course, with the improved roads and residential planning. I recall that the audience would never exceed fifteen or twenty patrons. This, at any rate, is how I've come to picture things in my mind. But I cannot convince myself that the reality accorded with the product of my imagination....

To get from our house to any area worth going to, you had to pass through tea fields, bamboo groves, rice paddies—with no sign of human habitation along the way. The closest shopping district worthy of the name was in Kagurazaka, and getting there required a considerable effort. True, I'd been habituated to the necessity and didn't feel especially put out. But there was a particularly daunting stretch—a dark path lined with great, old trees, the gaps between them overgrown with stands of bamboo. The path was so densely wooded that even in midday it remained utterly dark and gloomy, as though the sun had been eclipsed by dense clouds. Setting out for the busier parts of town wearing only one's everyday wooden clogs would surely be courting disaster. I'll never forget how treacherous the footing could be; and even worse than rain or snow was when the ground would thaw.

Fire, too, was an ever-present danger, even in our secluded area. I vividly recall the tall fire ladder erected at an intersection, and the alarm bell suspended from the top—a token of the old days. I can clearly picture the little eatery located near that ladder, with the odor of piping hot vegetable stew,[15] its steam wafting through the shop curtain, merging with the evening mist outside. An altogether unforgettable scene, which in fact inspired a haiku that I composed years ago, when Shiki was still alive: All in a row / Alarm bell tower and those / Tall trees of winter.[16] (*Garasudo* 20, 1915)

KIKUI-CHŌ

Kikui-chō is the name of a small district not far from where I currently live.[17] I was born there. I have more than a routine knowledge of the area, but having moved from place to place over the years, I discovered that Kikui-chō had changed so much. It now extended all the way to Negoro.[18]

Since the name Kikui-chō had been so familiar to me as I was growing up, it failed to inspire the nostalgic aura that might conjure up memories of the past. But as I sit here alone in my study, adopting a pensive pose and giving free rein to my thoughts, I find myself drawn to Kikui-chō. And for a while my mind will linger on the name—on the characters that form it and on that which the name evokes.

It is unlikely that the area existed very far back into the Edo period. I'm unaware exactly when in the Meiji it was formally established, but I do know that my father is the one who named it. You see, the Natsume family crest incorporates the characters for chrysanthemum [*kiku*] and well [*i*]—hence their combination as *kikui*.[19] This is how I recall the story, although I can't be sure whether I heard it from my father or someone else.

Having relinquished his old Edo post of local headman and for a time serving as local ward chief, Father may have availed himself of the perquisites of office in being the one to select the name of this new district.[20] In any event, he was very proud of his position of authority. And while I used to regard this seeming vanity with a jaundiced eye, at this point in my life it merely evokes a smile.

What is more, Father also took it upon himself to name the long, sloping road that we would have to climb when heading south from our home. This he coined Natsumezaka (Natsume hill), borrowing the family name. But while the name Kikui-chō has survived intact, Natsumezaka has lost its "Natsume" designation and is merely referred to as "the slope." Then again, someone came by recently and remarked on having come across the original name—Natsumezaka—on a map of the area. So it may be that the name Father chose is still in use after all.[21]

Many years passed from the time I left Tokyo to my returning in 1907 to settle here in the Waseda area. Before we moved, I happened to be walking around the area one day—perhaps in the course of house hunting or on my way back from an excursion somewhere—when by chance I passed near the Kikui-chō house. Catching a glimpse of the old roof tiling, I thought it odd that the place should still be standing. I continued along my way without stopping.

It was after we moved to Waseda that I walked back to Kikui-chō to have a better look at the old house. It seemed as though nothing had changed. But to my surprise, a boardinghouse sign hung from the gate. I was hoping to see the Waseda rice paddies, but the land had been developed for residential use. I then went to visit the Negoro tea plantings and bamboo groves, but not a trace was to be found. Everything had changed; how could I even know whether I'd gone to the actual site? And so I lingered there, lost in thought. Why should the old house alone still be standing, like some derelict wreck from the past, while everything else was gone? Better for the thing to simply fall apart once and for all.[22]

Time is the great leveler. Passing by the old neighborhood last year while out on a walk, I noticed that the old house was gone—demolished—and in its place a new boardinghouse was being built. In the meantime, a pawnshop had gone up next door, in front of which stood some trees and shrubbery enclosed by a straggly fence. Three pine trees caught my attention. Though pruned and trimmed into a freakish shape that barely hinted at their former appearance, something about those trees looked strangely familiar. I was reminded of a haiku I'd written long ago: *Three pines in the moonlight, casting uneven shadows.*[23]

I returned home, wondering whether the haiku pines were those trees standing by the site of the old Kikui-chō house, or perhaps some other trees.[24] (*Garasudo* 23, 1915)

The reminiscing author, whose boyhood was largely spent with his adoptive family, presents a pastiche of image and episode recalling the environs
of his natal family. Time is indeed the great leveler. A measure of the urban
transformation wrought during the Meiji, the old Babashita neighborhood is
remembered as a remote village, cut off from civilization by dark, forbidding
woods. The only human presence here is the *yose* performer, whom the narrator struggles to recall. Some of the local stores and shops are recalled, but
what strikes one is the melancholy tone elicited by the sound of the temple
bell and the pervasive gloom of that old, rusticated district.[25]

With this episode, the narrator adopts a meditative mode—seated in the
study, chin propped on his hand. The old neighborhood comes to mind in connection with his father, the vain, small-minded local official who bequeathed
a name on a map and little else of substance. Almost everything is gone, done
in by the ravages of time. The old house has been destroyed—just as well, as
the narrator reflects on life's evanescence. Built late in the Tokugawa, it has
undergone a gradual demolition in the course of remembered visits—a process of decay and dismemberment with powerful echoes of human mortality.
The most poignant connection with the past may be the three pine trees that
he notices, which he associates with a haiku he'd written many years earlier—
memory encapsulated in seventeen syllables of verse. And the fugitive traces
of a distant past, rendered with a curious mix of detachment and nostalgia,
stand in sharp contrast to the clamorous present of the reminiscing author in
his twilight years.

Sōseki's alter ego, Kenzō, is equally attuned to the transformations
wrought upon the remembered sites and scenes of childhood, as he revisits
areas he'd known as a child:

> Kenzō felt quite lonely as he left his sister. He walked vaguely in the
> direction of his house, knowing that his familiarity with Tokyo geography
> would get him to his destination eventually. After a while he found himself
> in a very busy quarter which had that cheap, dirty look peculiar to newly
> developed areas. There was nothing in the surrounding scene that he could
> recognize, despite the fact that he had certainly been to this part of Tokyo
> before. Over the ground from which all vestiges of the past had been taken
> away, he walked like a man lost.
>
> There had been rice paddies here once, with straight footpaths
> running between them. Visible on the far side of the paddies were the
> thatched roofs of farmers' cottages. He could remember seeing a man
> seated on a bench somewhere around here, his sedge hat beside him,
> eating jelly. Nearby had stood a large paper mill. One followed the path

around the mill and came to a little stream with a bridge over it. The banks were built up high with stones, so that the stream seemed much farther below than one had expected. The old-fashioned signs on the bathhouse at the foot of the bridge, the pumpkins lying in front of the grocer's next door—these had often reminded the young Kenzō of scenes from Hiroshige's prints.

Now everything was gone like a dream; all that was left was the ground he stood on. "But when did it all go?" He was shocked to see how a place too could change—as though until then he had imagined that only people changed....

People really didn't change very much, he thought; they only decayed. They were not like this place, which had not only changed beyond recognition but gained new vigor in the process. As the contrast struck him, he could not help wondering: And what about me? What will *I* be like in the end?[26] (*Michikusa* 69, 1915)

These episodes call to mind the modernization of Tokyo as perhaps the most tangible marker of the Meiji transformation—which is to say, the sense of deracination produced by relentless urban development and the erasure of entire neighborhoods and districts. By the time Sōseki embarked on his literary career, the city had expanded, and new construction had consumed the vestiges of old Edo. Kenzō's sense of dislocation, which puts him in a pensive mood, contrasts with that of the narrator of *Koto no sorane* (Hearing Things, 1905), an early experiment in fiction. Though living in Tokyo, he is beset by a looming supernatural presence—an otherworldliness not yet expunged by the gradual disappearance of the old neighborhoods. The spectral landscape that the author inscribes upon the Tokyo of this 1905 story would disappear in his later novels, to be replaced by wistful memory and a haunting sense of loss.[27]

Yet even with the late Meiji, many outlying Tokyo neighborhoods had yet to be transformed by urban development. Some writers, drawn to the pastoral mode, would write the city as an idyllic topos, still marked by natural beauty and communal harmony.[28] For others, the very disappearance of such qualities would conjure a nostalgic longing for lost innocence, on the one hand, and a gnawing sense of estrangement and dislocation, on the other. For Sōseki, the transformation of modern-day Tokyo over the course of the Meiji decades conjures up both dark forebodings and cheering reminiscence. Among the brighter moments recounted in the *Garasudo* collection is the following episode:

ENTERTAINMENTS

The memories that remain of my old home tend to be dominated by images of rustication and remoteness, which harbor a distinctly plaintive and wintry pathos. Hence my astonishment when I heard stories from my older brother, just the other day, about our sisters having been kabuki patrons at the time! Could this have been true, I wondered. For me, any notion of gaiety and stylish amusement in connection with our family was hard to reconcile with my overwhelmingly somber image of that world.

Back then, the theater houses were all located in Saruwaka-chō.[29] Since ricksha and trolley transportation was not yet available, the trip from our house in Babashita all the way to the theater district, near the great Kannon temple in Asakusa, was a major undertaking. I learned that our sisters had to get up well before dawn to prepare for their journey. Since unattended women might be subject to some unpleasantry, they'd have a serving man with them as a precaution. The threesome would make their way to Ageba, along the Kanda River, where a small excursion boat had been reserved for them by the rental agent there.[30] How eagerly they must have anticipated their evening at the theater, as the boat made its way, ever so slowly, to Yanagibashi, at a point just before the Kanda flows into the Sumida River.[31] Yet this was by no means journey's end—which affords me further opportunity to reminisce upon those days long ago, when the pace of life was slower and more relaxed.

From Yanagibashi, the boat would enter the Sumida and proceed upriver, under the Azuma bridge, as far as Imado, where, according to my brother, our sisters would debark at the Yūmeirō.[32] They would walk from there to the theater and, following some refreshments at the adjacent teahouse, would at long last be shown to their seats.

The sisters would invariably reserve the choicest seats, which in the older-style kabuki theater were elevated above the rest of the audience, thus affording an advantageous position for the stylish patrons, bedecked in the height of fashion, to attract the envious gaze of one and all.[33] In fact, those of an especially ostentatious persuasion would vie with one another for these seats. During intermission, they would be invited to visit with one or another of the actors in their dressing room, their favorites being Tanosuke and Tosshō.[34] Escorted there by a man in the actors' entourage who was decked out in a patterned kimono and formal *hakama* skirt, they would have the actors personally inscribe their fans as souvenirs—something to show off, no doubt, and available only to those who could afford the price.

The return trip, at night, took them back along the same route they'd traversed earlier. Out of concern for the young ladies' safety, the serving man would carry a lantern. The threesome would not arrive back home before midnight. Thus it took almost twenty-four hours—from dead of night to dead of night—for my sisters to be able to take in a single kabuki play.

Hearing my brother's account, I could scarcely believe that this had anything to do with my own family.[35] (*Garasudo* 21, 1915)

Unable himself to conjure a cheerful recollection of the old days, Sōseki relies here on the secondhand reminiscence of his older brother. This impressively detailed account, set in the final years of the Tokugawa period, points to the status of kabuki as the preeminent Japanese performing art and to the allure it held for the sisters. Yet the focus here—the dramatic element, in effect—is the trip to and from the theater, rather than the play itself. Again, the narrator is basking in the afterglow of his brother's account, which affords the opportunity to savor someone else's past.

Natsume Sōseki had an ambivalent attitude toward kabuki; he was never much of an aficionado. Rather, as a boy he developed a taste for the reciters' art—a rich tradition of tales and episodes recounted in the *yose* halls that abounded.[36] This interest would develop, later in life, into a serious engagement with *yōkyoku*—the performative art of chanting classic Noh texts.[37] As we will see, Sōseki would have occasion to recall his own failed attempts to get a musical passage just right. But the *Garasudo* reminiscences center on the boyhood fascination with *yose* entertainers and the feel of the old performance spaces.

YOSE

As a boy, I'd often go to hear the storytellers at the Isemoto, a *yose* hall in Nihonbashi, located directly across from the present-day Mitsukoshi Department Store....[38] At that time I was not with my family in Babashita. But despite my more favorable living situation, at least in terms of location, it still seems odd that I'd have such abundant free time to take in the performances. Be that as it may, the Isemoto, unlike the run-of-the-mill *yose* hall, was designed to convey an impression of refinement—an impression quite possibly colored by my reflecting back upon a very distant past....

The regular patrons of this particular *yose* hall had time on their hands and money to spare. They would be decked out in lavish style, adopting a pose of studied nonchalance—casually plucking out nose hairs, for instance, with a little tweezers they'd have with them. The easy, carefree ambience of those afternoons put one in an idyllic mood, inspiring images of nightingales singing from the plum trees in the garden.

During intermission, a man would circulate among the patrons, selling tea and cakes. The cakes—some ten in number—were contained in shallow, rectangular wooden boxes arranged within easy reach of the clientele. It was understood that payment for what was consumed would be placed directly into the box.

For the young boy taking it all in, these little customs and rituals seemed both unusual and interesting. But when I consider the current state of affairs in our *yose* halls, where one can no longer savor such ease and intimacy, I wax ever more nostalgic for those days, and the wonderfully gentle and mellow atmosphere that prevailed.

Of the various storytellers who would appear, I recall one in particular—Tanabe Nanryū, who was known for his bizarre interjections and utterances—*nonnon, zuizui,* and the like. Apparently he'd gotten his start as the *yose* footwear attendant.[39] But his repertoire of *nonnon*'s and *zuizui*'s were evidently all the rage back then, even though not a soul knew what they meant....

Nanryū died long ago. And most of his fellow reciters are gone as well. But I know precious little of the *yose* world since then, and haven't the faintest idea whether any of those individuals who gave me such pleasure in my childhood may yet be among the living.[40] (*Garasudo* 35, 1915)

This episode, which took place during the boyhood years spent with the Shioharas, shares with the kabuki episode a curious disregard of the actual performance—with the exception of Nanryū's weird utterances. Instead, the narrator lingers on the theater itself and its ambience. Employing a lexicon of "slow/easy/mellow" adjectivals, he underscores the many delights associated with *yose,* a nostalgia elicited by association with the physical site and the comings and goings of its patrons. Here was a virtual oasis in an otherwise barren cityscape.

Sōseki's fond recollection of childhood visits to the *yose* halls was likely reinforced by his friendship with Masaoka Shiki, who was also a devotee of *yose.* It only stands to reason that Sōseki's fiction would contain numerous references to *yose* entertainments and characters who have a fondness for them.[41]

School Memories

The Meiji Charter Oath of 1868 proclaimed the creation of a modern educational system as central to Japan's nation-building mission. Education would be the lifeblood of Meiji society. In the ensuing cultural modernization,

49

school emerged as a stage upon which the drama of modern social circumstance would be enacted in literary form. Natsume Sōseki and his contemporaries, the first generation of Japanese to enjoy the fruits of modern education, would draw upon long years of personal experience as students and teachers in creating their literary portrayals of life in the Meiji era.[42]

Much of Sōseki's fiction—notably, *Botchan* and *Sanshirō*—is set in schools, and plot revolves around the interaction of students, teachers, and administrators—a microcosm of the larger society and a gallery of assorted character types. Schools would provide an ideal setting for the unfolding drama of friendship, enmity, success, and failure. Despite a strongly segregated educational system, in which the state, in loco parentis, promoted careerism for boys and womanly virtue, under the rubric of *ryōsai kenbo,* for girls, avenues for fraternization existed at the higher levels, where new horizons of experience—romantic and otherwise—could be explored.[43] Yet the Meiji schools, in line with official dictates, reinforced the gender divide at precisely the same time that notions of freedom, equality, and individualism were gaining currency. These were desiderata among Meiji youth, but there were obstacles to achieving them—as was the case, all the more so, under the restrictive shogunal regime.

The incongruity here is reflected in the typical novelistic plotline that concerns the unfulfilled amorous longings of ineffectual young men who are drawn to spirited, attractive women but fail to convert emotional impulse into action. Literature, in other words, served as an arena for the contest between old and new visions of state, society, and individual.

A word regarding the educational experience as presented in Sōseki's personal writings. In the first place, his was a decidedly elite urban education. As for the school system itself, the Meiji *chūgakkō* (middle school) corresponds to our best high schools; its *kōtōgakkō* (higher school) system, whose students were in their late teens and early twenties, corresponds to our top undergraduate institutions. University (*daigaku*) was the very pinnacle of the educational pyramid, equivalent to our elite graduate schools. Until 1897, there was only one—Tokyo Imperial University, which was founded in 1877.[44]

Students were expected to endure privation and adversity in their quest for an education; indeed, the figure of the *kugakusei*—the impoverished student—is a familiar presence in *kindai* literature and in Sōseki's *shōhin*.[45] The reminiscing author recalls episodes later in his school career, from the perspective of early adulthood. Evidently reluctant to adopt a child's point of view, he only occasionally writes of boyhood experience.[46] Instead, his *shōhin* provide occasions to recall older friends from school through dramatized episodes that reflect upon friendship and its small rituals.

KII-CHAN

I had a good friend in school named Kii-chan. He lived with an uncle in
Naka-chō, a considerable distance from our house, and so it was difficult
to visit each other regularly. As a rule, he'd come to visit me, since I was
not one to go out, and I could always count on him to come by. Actually,
we would meet at a tenement house that my family was renting out to a
person named Matsu, who ran a stationery shop.

Kii-chan had evidently lost his parents, which at the time didn't seem
at all unusual. I don't recall having ever asked him about it, and thus I
knew nothing about his connection with the Matsu family. It was only
much later that I learned the details. It appears that Kii-chan's father had
held some official post at the mint and was imprisoned on a charge of
counterfeiting. He died in jail, and his wife left Kii-chan with her former
husband's family and went off to marry this Matsu. And so it stood to
reason that the son would occasionally come to see his mother....

One day Kii-chan came by to see me at home—at the time, the
entranceway [*genkan*] was serving as my room. He'd brought over two
books to show me. They were old manuscripts, handwritten in *kanbun*.
I leafed through the books, as though I had some idea what they were all
about. In fact, I couldn't understand a blessed thing. But Kii-chan was not
one to press me on whether I could make out any of it.

"These happen to be the work of none other than Ōta Nanpo
himself.[47] A friend of mine would like to sell them, and I thought you
might be interested. What do you say?"

"Ōta who?" I had no idea who this was.

"He's also known as Shokusanjin. You must've heard of him—a really
famous writer!"

In my benighted ignorance, I'd never heard the name Shokusanjin,
either. But judging from Kii-chan's enthusiastic endorsement, I could only
conclude that the books had genuine value.

"What will you take for them?"

"He says he wants fifty sen. How does that sound?"

Thinking things over for a moment, it occurred to me that I might be
in a position to try some bargaining.

"I'll give you twenty-five sen."

"It's a deal!"

Kii-chan took my money and proceeded once again to expound
earnestly upon the many virtues of these books and their author. Being
thoroughly in the dark on this score, though, I was in no position to
derive much pleasure from his assurances. Oh well, I thought, I probably

won't come out on the losing end. And later that night, on this single note of satisfaction, I put the books on my desk and went to bed. If memory serves, they turned out to be a two-volume collection of essays entitled *Nanpo yūgen.*[48] (*Garasudo* 31, 1915)

The very next day, Kii-chan stopped by to see me.

"Umm...It's about those books I sold you." He hesitated, his nervous gaze fixed upon the two books sitting on my desk.

"What about the books?"

"Well, as it turns out, my friend's dad got wind of what happened and he had a fit. So I'm supposed to get the books back. That's why I'm here. Look, I don't like having to do this any more than you do—after all, I *did* hand them over to you, fair and square. But I'm really in a bind."

"So you're here to take back the books, is that it?"

"I wouldn't put it quite that way. If it's all right with you, I'd appreciate it if you'd agree to return the books. The fact is, they're worth a lot more than twenty-five sen, I'm told."

This last remark clearly revealed to me the uneasiness—the sense of guilt—that lurked behind my satisfaction at having gotten such a bargain. In other words, I was angry both with myself, for my deviousness, and with my friend for having accepted the twenty-five sen to begin with. How could I cope with both sources of anger at the same time?

I made a sour face and remained silent.

Allow me to note that this attempt at analyzing my psychological state as a child is based on the retrospection of an adult, which makes it rather easy to express things with a degree of clarity. The young boy experiencing this situation would have had no such understanding. The only thing I was aware of at the time was the sour face I'd put on as my initial response. Naturally, Kii-chan would have understood nothing beyond this. Parenthetically, I confess to experiencing such moods even today, as a mature adult, and this has given rise to no shortage of misunderstandings on the part of those around me.

"Twenty-five sen really *is* too cheap, you know," Kii-chan said, looking me right in the face. In a flash, I grabbed the books from the desk and handed them over to my friend.

"Here, take 'em back!"

"Sorry, really. Anyway, they didn't actually belong to my friend. He was sneaking off with some of his dad's old stuff and selling 'em on the sly for spending money."[49]

I continued to pout and made no response. Kii-chan took the twenty-five sen from his pocket and placed it in front of me.

"I won't take your money."

"Why not?"

"What difference does it make? I won't take it, that's all!"

"Look, this is getting us nowhere. It's only a couple of books you're returning. So take the money and let's be done with it!"

I couldn't stand it anymore.

"These are *my books!* I bought them and they belong to me!"

"That's true. You have a point. But my friend is in trouble and his dad is up in arms and..."

"That's why I'm giving 'em back. But I won't take the money."

"Stop talking nonsense."

"Look, I'm giving you the books. They belong to me, but if you want 'em, I'm giving 'em to you. So why not just take them already?"

"All right, then, if that's the way you want it."

And so it was that Kii-chan left with the two books, and for no reason whatsoever I'd also lost twenty-five sen in the bargain.[50] (*Garasudo* 32, 1915)

This episode, which comprises two *Garasudo* installments, concerns a friend named Kuwabara Kiichi, of whom little is known.[51] It is interesting that the memory of this supposedly close friend should be so conspicuously unfriendly and that it should be so vividly dramatized. Together with other *Garasudo* episodes, the reminiscence reads much like a parable, underlining the corrosive effects of selfishness, opportunism, and wounded pride. And at its root lies money and the complications that arise on its account.

The Kii-chan episode thus presents a cross-section of traits associated with Sōseki's protagonists and with his own *shōhin* persona—peevishness, pettiness, and righteous indignation. Yet at the same time his narrator is able to stand back and reflect upon psychological motivation and narrative point of view, aware of his having constructed this episode "from the retrospection of an adult." While the episode reveals little about the friend who reneged on the transaction, it says a good deal about the low threshold for misunderstanding and hurt feelings that marks so many of Sōseki's literary relationships.

Another *Garasudo* episode draws a more detailed—and admiring—portrayal of a somewhat older friend, whom the author would have occasion to meet later in life.

ŌTA TATSUTO

Ōta Tatsuto was one of my closest friends at the Tokyo First Higher School.[52] Not having had many companions at that time, it naturally developed that the two of us got together quite frequently. I'd visit him around once a week. Ōta had lodgings in Masago-chō. One year during summer vacation, I invited him every day to go swimming at the pool in Ōkawa.

Ōta hailed from the Tōhoku region of northern Japan, and he had the distinctively slow, easy manner of speech characteristic of its people. To my mind, it beautifully captured his personality. Though I recall many arguments that we had, I never once saw him get enraged or lose his temper. That alone would have warranted the respect and affection that I felt toward him.

Ōta's was a gracious and generous nature, and he had an amazingly keen intellect—far sharper than mine. He would always be pondering questions beyond my comprehension. While pursuing his original aim of entering the university's science division, he read widely in philosophy and related areas. I still recall borrowing his copy of Herbert Spencer's *First Principles* [1862].

The two of us would go out together for leisurely walks on fine autumn days, chatting about whatever came to mind as we strolled aimlessly under crystal-clear skies. It was quite common for us to take in the sight of small, yellow-tinged leaves fluttering down from branches overhanging the walls of the homes along the way, despite there being no breeze. On one such occasion, Ōta happened to take note of this trifling occurrence. "I've got it!" he exclaimed in an excited whisper. For someone like myself, who was quite incapable of comprehending such a scene as anything more than the beauty of autumn colors moving through space, Ōta's sudden exclamation, which betokened imponderable mysteries, struck me as uncanny.

"Enlightenment is a very strange and marvelous thing," he mentioned later on, in that calm and composed manner of his, as though speaking to himself. I was unable to utter a single word in response.

Ōta lived the impoverished life of a student. He cooked for himself in a small room near the Kōgenji and would often have me over for a spartan meal. . . .[53] Following graduation, he took a position in a provincial middle school. I felt sorry for him. Professors at the university who didn't really know him may have thought this to be perfectly suitable. Ōta himself took it entirely in stride. There followed a series of school appointments, in both Japan and China. He is currently principal of the middle school in far-off Karafuto.[54]

Just this past year, Ōta stopped by for a visit during a stay in Tokyo. We hadn't seen one another in many years. Having been handed his calling card, I went to the parlor and took a seat so as to properly receive my guest. No sooner did Ōta enter the room and see me sitting demurely on the cushion than he remarked, "Rather prim and proper, aren't we?"

"Yes, I suppose you're right," I responded, before I even realized what I was saying. How strange that such a casual affirmation of Ōta's little barb should so effortlessly trip off my tongue. Truth be told, it left me feeling bright and refreshed. (*Garasudo* 9, 1915)

As Ōta took his seat across from me, the first thing we did was have a good look at one another. It seemed to both of us that something of our appearance long ago still remained, as if a token of a precious dream. But this perception, as though a fabric woven out of feelings from both past and present, took on an unsettling blurriness and lack of clarity. It was impossible for either of us to overcome the inexorable power of time and recover that which was gone. There was no alternative but to turn toward this strange world of the past, which had come to fill the wide gap between our parting long ago and this reunion.

Ōta had been an apple-cheeked young man, with unusually prominent eyes and the plump facial features one associates with women. He had retained these features—the eyes were still round, the cheeks red, the face still chubby. But things had changed.

I showed off my moustache and sideburns. In turn, he patted the top of his head, which was balding. My own hair had grayed in the interim.

"When you get as far north as Karafuto, there's really nowhere further to go, is there?" I gibed.

"I suppose you're right," he remarked, and proceeded to talk about life on the remote island, which I'd never visited. I've forgotten the details, except for his having mentioned how wonderful the summers are.

The two of us went out together, for the first time in many years. Over his frock coat, Ōta wore an Inverness, which flapped around as we walked. We got on a trolley, and as he held on to the strap to keep his balance, Ōta took out of his pocket something wrapped in a handkerchief.

"What might that be?"

"A chestnut bun."

He'd evidently taken the bun, which had earlier been set out as a refreshment at my house, and stashed it in his handkerchief! This took me by surprise.

"So you took that bun from the house?"

"It would appear that I did."

Having made fun of my surprised reaction, Ōta placed the wrapped-up bun back in his pocket.[55]

That evening, we took in a play at the Imperial Theater. The tickets indicated that we were to use the north entranceway in the theater. When I mistakenly headed toward the south entrance, Ōta corrected me. This gave me pause.

"Yes, it seems that the gentleman from Karafuto has the superior sense of direction," I retorted, then turned back and headed toward the designated entrance.

Ōta claimed to have been familiar with the layout of the Imperial Theater. But when we'd finished our dinner and headed back to our seats, he made the common mistake of confusing the first- and second-tier doors. Now it was *my* turn to laugh.

I noticed that Ōta would occasionally take out his gold-rimmed spectacles and glance over the program, then leave them on to watch the play.

"Aren't those reading glasses? You mean they work for distance viewing as well?"

"*Cha bu duo,*" he answered, using a Chinese expression I didn't understand.

"It means 'no big difference,'" he explained.

On the way home from the theater that night, we parted company as Ōta got off the trolley, eventually making his way back to Japan's remote, frigid northern extremity. Whenever I recall him, it strikes me that his given name, Tatsuto—which connotes wisdom and depth of character—was truly heaven-sent.[56] Yes, this good and wise man is still serving as principal of a middle school in the far north, locked in a world of snow and ice.[57] (*Garasudo* 10, 1915)

The subject of this two-part *Garasudo* reminiscence—identified in the original merely by the letter O—is presented both in the context of the earlier friendship at the preparatory school and through his unexpected visit nearly thirty years later. Through this play of past and present, and the brief reflection on how powerfully we are drawn to thoughts of the past, Ōta emerges, albeit within a small compass, as an exemplary character. He is somewhat reminiscent of K, Sensei's impoverished student friend in *Kokoro*. Both are admired for their superior intellect and uncanny intuitive sense. What is more, in the "reunion" episode, Ōta embodies a trait near and dear to Sōseki—namely, that of not standing on ceremony.[58]

But of particular interest is the scene where the two friends are out for a stroll during a fine autumn day, when all of a sudden Ōta, watching the leaves fluttering down, exclaims "*satotta!*" (Now I understand!). Having witnessed his friend's experience of transcendental awareness—which uncannily fore-shadows a well-known scene in Shiga Naoya's short story, *Kinosaki nite* (At Kinosaki, 1917)—Sōseki's *shōhin* narrator can only look on uncomprehendingly.[59] All of this is simply beyond him.

In this regard, it bears noting that despite the great fuss made over Sōseki's alleged Zenish enlightenment, epitomized by the *sokuten kyoshi* epigram with which he has been identified, his literary protagonists would remain mired in doubt, uncertainty, and relentless self-absorption. Here one is reminded of Sōsuke, the protagonist of *Mon* (The Gate, 1910). Having made his way to a Zen monastery in Kamakura, Sōsuke struggles with the *zazen* meditation regimen, only to find his path to enlightenment blocked.[60]

In the above episode, the friend's unexpected visit elicits a much more mundane recollection of their evening at the theater, marked by some good-natured joshing and banter—a sign of mutual affection that survived the long hiatus in their relationship. And no sooner has the friend appeared, out of nowhere, than he is back in the frozen northlands.

Sōseki's remembered friendships are curiously devoid of private disclosure, despite the occasional gesture of affection. These are essentially *adult* friendships, recalled in later adulthood. Nonetheless, such episodes are of interest to the literary biographer and Meiji historian—especially the references to Meiji student life. Let us turn to several reminiscences that more directly relate memories of Meiji school days.[61] Among his school-related *danwa*, an early one, published in 1906, recounts experiences in middle school. It speaks both to Sōseki's manner of recalling his past and to the journalistic agenda that lay behind it.

FAILURE

There was only one middle school in Tokyo back then. I don't recall the name. I was around thirteen when I entered, and the school was much smaller than today's middle schools. There were two separate curricula. One was oriented around English-language study, which would prepare students for matriculation to the college [*daigaku yobimon*]. I was enrolled in the other program, which offered no English. After several years, though, I'd had my fill of middle school and transferred to the Nishō Academy, which offered a traditional Chinese-oriented curriculum of *kangaku* studies.[62]

Nishō was truly in deplorable shape—the classrooms were filthy, the tatami was black with age and falling apart. And there were no desks! We'd go into class and sit down anywhere at all. I recall that our turn to explain the texts was decided by a traditional Chinese-style lottery system. Classes began at around six or seven in the morning. It was just like the old *terakoya* schools of the Tokugawa—a throwback to an earlier age. But the tuition was low—only some two yen per month. And there was no boarding expense since I was commuting from home.

As a youngster I greatly enjoyed *kangaku.* I was always reading Chinese books. Nowadays I work with English literature, but back then I positively hated English. You see, my older brother, who was studying English, tried teaching me. But he was hot-tempered and irascible, and I couldn't stand learning from him. We only made it to the second book of the *National Reader* series.[63]

Despite my interest in *kangaku,* it didn't seem wise to pursue a career in Chinese studies, given the new modern spirit that had swept the nation. And so I decided to enter the university, although I had no idea what I'd like to study. Since I hadn't gotten far enough with my English—which was a requisite for college admission—I would need an intensive language course to prepare for the entrance examination.[64] And so I entered the Seiritsu Academy in Surugadai. For an entire year I worked hard on English. I became obsessed with it and ended up selling off all of my Chinese books. Meanwhile, I made great progress, and my English proficiency improved dramatically. Thus, in the summer of 1884 I was able to enter the *daigaku yobimon* college.[65] Here I was reunited with several of my friends from middle school, who'd been enrolled in the English curriculum and were thus able to gain entrance ahead of me.

I'd struggled to be accepted into the college, but once admitted I became terribly negligent in my studies. The students were divided into two groups—the serious ones and the slackers—and there was little fraternization between the two. My fellow slackers and I were dedicated to screwing around and shirking our studies. The grinds looked down on us as a bunch of good-for-nothings, and we regarded them as mere grade-grubbers. We pursued our indolence with a passion, convinced of our superiority.

The *yobimon* was a five-year program of study, the first three years of which were oriented around math and science—and the science texts were all in English. Our English reading skills were frankly superior to today's standard. But we were a hellish lot, compared to which the students today are positively meek. We were always up to some prank or another. For instance, we'd surreptitiously stoke the heating stove that stood next to our Chinese studies instructor and watch as his face turned red. This was great fun. And in math class, while the teacher would be facing the blackboard, explaining some equation or another, one of us would sneak up with a piece of chalk and write something on his back—an off-color word or some doodle. Or else we'd darken the classroom and scare the teacher when he came in. This is how we amused ourselves.

In the meantime, my second-year grades were quite poor, and when it came time to take final examinations, I was having serious stomach problems and couldn't sit for them. At the time, the school itself was in the process of expansion and overhaul, and what with all the confusion that ensued, I wasn't permitted to take a make-up exam.[66] All of this set me to thinking. I was aware of the circumstances that had worked against me. But it dawned on me that I had to bear some of the responsibility. I had to first earn the trust of the teachers and staff if I was to make anything of myself. This would mean applying myself to my studies. I'd wasted my time up to that point, and it was up to me to set things right. And so I accepted a failing grade that year and resolved to repeat the course of study.

What a remarkable turnabout! Subjects such as math, which had totally perplexed me at first, were now easy to understand. I ended up being quite a whiz at science. As for English—while I could read and translate with relative ease, I had serious difficulty with oral expression. I just couldn't find the words to convey what was on my mind. But I refused to believe that my thoughts had to remain locked inside my head, and so I resolved to work on my spoken English. When I got the hang of just letting fly with the words and not fretting about accuracy, my proficiency in the language improved quite dramatically.

In other words, failure became an opportunity to better myself in many ways. Failure was precisely the medicine I needed. Who knows what sort of future would have lain in store if I'd chosen to remain a third-rate student, idling away my time.

And so I repeated my second-year course, then moved on to third year.[67] I decided to learn French. And I also chose to study architecture, for reasons that are interesting in retrospect. Spurred by childish fantasy, I'd thought of myself as an eccentric, someone who'd never fit into mainstream society. But if I were to choose a respectable profession, I might be able to get by without having to change my basic nature. The key, I thought, was to find a calling that would enable an eccentric such as myself to ply one's trade and earn society's respect. This is what led me to consider a career in architecture.

One more thing. In view of my penchant for things artistic, architecture seemed a likely outlet for creative expression, aside from its more practical appeal. Well, several classmates with whom I was close were kind enough to question this decision, in no uncertain terms.[68] At the time I had great plans in mind—pyramids, monumental projects. It was my friend Komeyama who cautioned that I was getting carried away, that the grand schemes I'd conjured up were totally impracticable. "Your ideas will never see the light of day in this country," he assured me. "Forget about architecture and do literature instead. *Here's* where you can leave a real legacy—through works that might well last hundreds—even thousands—of years."

Komeyama was right. My interest in architecture as a career was based entirely on narrow self-interest. He pointed me to a higher calling. And so I rethought things once again and resolved to study literature.[69] Since I needed no further instruction in either Japanese or Chinese studies, I decided to major in English literature. And this is the path I've followed up to the present day. Truth be told, I've gotten rather bored with the status quo and have felt the urge to change careers, but I'm afraid it's too late for this sort of thing. At the outset I envisioned great things for myself— I'd study English literature and eventually produce my own literary masterpiece—in English, no less! But that was long ago.[70]

Sōseki's account, in response to a journal solicitation in connection with a feature on middle-school reminiscence, appeared precisely at the point of his transition from university professor to newspaper novelist. Hence, the fatalistic tone at the conclusion belies the actuality of his circumstance. Be that as it may, this exemplary tale of transformation from hellion to model student, by virtue of learning from one's mistakes, reflects the journal's express aim of providing edifying material for the nation's youth. The moral exhortation aside, such episodes shed light on the experiences and lifestyle of Meiji students.[71]

Sōseki responded to several subsequent solicitations from youth-oriented journals. The first is a six-part reminiscence on his school years, intriguingly entitled *A Consistent Lack of Effort: My Years at School*.[72] While revisiting the material covered in the previous *danwa*, the author stresses the devil-may-care attitude he took toward much of his schooling.[73] One final school-related chat appeared in the April 1910 issue of *Shinkokumin*.[74] This time, the focus is on providing advice on writing to his young readers. Here, Sōseki recalls aspects of his own schooling that early on fostered an interest in writing. For one, he emphasizes the importance of his training in Chinese, noting how his fondness for *kanbun* was fostered within his family. And he remarks on his deep interest in *kanshi*—poetry in Chinese.[75]

Reminiscence on the Road

Sōseki would take a different tack in the context of his travelogue, *Mankan tokorodokoro,* in which he includes several school-related reminiscences inspired by chance encounters with old friends. Not beholden to a didactic agenda, he provides a more candid—and entertaining—tale of life at school. The first such account is in connection with one Hashimoto Sagorō—a professor of agriculture visiting Dalian at the time, who unexpectedly called on Sōseki at his hotel.[76] The *Mankan* narrator reflects on their acquaintanceship:

> Back in 1884, we shared a room at the Shinfukuji Temple in Koishikawa, where we cooked our meals together. For a mere two yen a month, we could pay for our lodging, eat beef every other day, and have good-quality rice.... Hashimoto and I were studying at the Seiritsu Academy, preparing for exams to enter the *daigaku yobimon*.[77] He was more advanced in math and English than I was.
>
> On the day of the exam, I stared at the algebra test and couldn't make heads or tails out of it. Totally at a loss, I quietly signaled to Hashimoto, who was seated nearby, to give me a hand. Thanks to him, I managed to pass. But as it turns out, my friend, who'd provided the answers, failed miserably![78] (*Mankan* 13, 1910)

Noting Hashimoto's relaxed, easygoing demeanor—quite at odds with the exam-related anxieties, and the likelihood of one's future hanging in the balance—the narrator goes on to reflect on how the *yobimon* group dealt with the stress:

> Around ten of us took up lodgings in the Suetomiya, a boardinghouse in Kanda. We resorted to all manner of tomfoolery, wanting to display our open contempt for studying, and all but declaring our sworn mission to avoid it. Thus, we hardly ever prepared for class, and just managed to squeak by, a semester at a time. We were *this* close to flunking out. When called upon in English class, for instance, we'd come up with some gibberish by way of a translation of the passage in question. In math class, where you'd have to work out problems at the blackboard until you got them right, I'd be up there for an hour at a time, staring at the numbers and letters on the board without a clue. We'd go to class, lugging our algebra texts, wondering what tribulations would be in store for us that day.
>
> Those in our little clique were nicely clumped together at the bottom of the class rankings.... Our test scores were awful; yet, just at the point of being given the heave-ho, we'd somehow manage to stage a comeback. All of this, you understand, was a point of pride with us. We disdained those at the top of the class, writing them off as a bunch of pathetic grinds and grade-grubbers.[79] (*Mankan* 14, 1910)

Cheating and slacking off may have been de rigueur among mid-Meiji schoolboys, but such behavior may come as a revelation in connection with Natsume Sōseki. More is revealed in yet another *Mankan* reminiscence, which concerns Satō Tomokuma. Another erstwhile classmate at Seiritsu and *yobimon*, Satō happened to be serving as chief of police in Port Arthur when Sōseki made his trip.[80] The *Mankan* narrator reminisces on the day he first set eyes upon Satō:

> I arrived at Seiritsu one rainy day and was waiting in the entranceway
> for classes to start when a bizarre-looking fellow—a mail carrier, by all
> appearances—showed up at the school. Totally barefoot, he was done up
> in an oil-paper raincoat and a large wicker rain hat. And for some ungodly
> reason, he was carrying an iron kettle. Still, one expected him to do his
> duty and deliver the day's mail. But the fellow, without uttering a word,
> briskly made his way into the building and straight into the classroom.
> This was none other than Satō. I never did find out, by the way, what he
> was doing with that kettle!
>
> Satō became a boarder at the school. By and by, in one of our
> occasional attacks on the school's kitchen, in retaliation for the slop they
> passed off as food, Satō sustained an injury to his forehead.[81] For a while,
> he went around with a white bandage wrapped around his head, in a style
> that put one in mind of some valiant warrior. I remember well the dashing
> figure he cut—all on account of his having been beaten up in the school
> kitchen![82] (*Mankan* 21, 1910)

Typically dismissed as an embarrassment among Sōseki's works, *Mankan* did serve as a vehicle for reminiscence, insofar as the author's colonial "tour of inspection" enabled him to renew old school ties, which he relates in passing—a welcome respite from his grueling and unpleasant trip through alien territory.

What emerges from these and related episodes is a sense of the clique that formed at Seiritsu and *yobimon*, and how his early friendships would be serendipitously revived. Again, these are memories of early adulthood. There is only a single *shōhin* episode, from the *Eijitsu* collection, that relates to his early schooling:

KIGENSETSU

It was a south-facing room. Thirty children, their backs to the incoming light, looking at the blackboard. Thirty dark heads of hair, row upon row of them. And then, from the hallway, their teacher enters the room.

The teacher was short and thin, with large eyes, and from cheek to chin a slovenly growth of beard. The collar of his kimono, which just touched the stubbly chin, was dark with dirt and grime. This, and the unkempt beard, and the fact that the teacher never scolded anyone made him the laughingstock of the entire school.

By and by the teacher picked up a piece of chalk and wrote three kanji characters on the blackboard—*ki gen setsu*—which spelled out the word for Empire Day. Hunched over their desks, the children, thirty dark-haired heads in unison, set to work on their compositions. Although short of stature, the teacher drew himself up to his most impressive height, looked out upon his young charges, and left the classroom.

Just then, a student sitting in the middle of the third row from the rear got up from his desk, went up to the teacher's table, and picked up the chalk that had just been used. To the astonishment of his classmates, he went up to the blackboard, drew a thick chalk line through the character for *ki* that the teacher had drawn, and replaced it with a different kanji, using bold strokes.[83] The student returned to his desk, and before long the teacher returned to his classroom. He noticed what was on the blackboard.

"It appears that someone has substituted the other character for *ki*," he said, looking out at his students. "But they *both* happen to be acceptable." No one said a word.

The boy who'd corrected the teacher was none other than myself. It is now 1909, many years having passed since this little incident. Yet I've never been able to rid myself of a certain remorse for what I'd done. Would that my victim had been our principal, whom we all feared, rather than the disheveled and hapless Fukuda *sensei*.[84] (*Eijitsu* 17, 1909)

This vignette, originally published to help commemorate the national holiday of its title, contrasts the willful, irreverent child, who makes so bold as to correct the teacher, and the reminiscing adult, who wishes he'd picked on someone his own size. The figure of the teacher, reduced here to a simple caricature, harkens back to Sōseki's lampoons of teachers and literary folk in *Neko* and *Botchan*, and it anticipates the *Eijitsu* portrayal of Professor Craig, the Shakespearean scholar with whom Sōseki studied while in London.

As with the *Botchan* protagonist, whose qualities of impetuosity, guileless-ness, and moral integrity stand as thinly veiled self-reference, one can detect here similar qualities attributed to the author's boyhood persona. The frame then shifts to the adult narrator, who shares his *own* feelings of remorse in retrospect.

Finally, let us turn to the reminiscent narrator of *Omoidasu koto nado* as he relates an episode that begins with the very end of his long years of schooling:

THE FORTUNE-TELLER

Following graduation from university, I took up residence in a temple in Koishikawa.[85] As it turns out, the priest at this temple did fortune-telling on the side, and I'd regularly see his equipment—the divination block and sticks—set up in the room adjacent to the dark, gloomy entrance foyer. Now, insofar as this wasn't a formal business enterprise with a sign out front, the priest would at best see four or five clients a day. And entire days would pass when the telltale sound of the divining sticks was not to be heard at all.

Not being one to place much store in fortune-telling, I had virtually nothing to do with the priest. Indeed, I got by for quite a while without any contact whatsoever. My only connection with the man was overhearing him from time to time in the adjacent room advising his clients—a marriage consultation, say, when he'd encourage parents not to oppose the couple's plans.

Then, one day, I found myself actually chatting with the priest. As he gradually shifted the conversation to subjects near and dear to him—the divination of facial features and auspicious directions—I asked, half in jest, if he wouldn't mind predicting my future.[86] The priest fixed his gaze upon my face and said, "Nothing especially bad will happen to you."

Nothing especially bad—I took this to mean that nothing especially *good* would happen, either, and that I was fated to lead an ordinary, humdrum existence. I remained silent.

"I can also tell you," the priest added, "that you won't be present when your parents die."

"Is that so?"

"And you will go west, far to the west—I see this, too."

"Is that so?"

"And I advise you to grow a beard, and do it soon."

He concluded with one more word of advice—to buy a parcel of land and build a house on it.

I resisted the temptation to point out that if I were in any position to buy land and build a house, I certainly wouldn't have to rent a room in *this* place! Still, I was curious to know the connection between growing the beard and building the house, so I asked the priest to comment on this.

"If we divide your head into upper and lower halves," he remarked, with a most serious expression, "the upper half, in your case, happens to be too long, and the lower half is too short. It's off balance. Growing a beard, you see, restores the balance. Your face will gain stability; it won't be distorted."

What utter nonsense, I thought. He's telling me that my future, my fate, is governed by the physical contours of my head and that he can help me improve upon my ill-starred deformity!

"Yes, I see."

It so happened, though, that less than a year later, I traveled to Matsuyama—to the west. Then I moved to Kumamoto, which is further west. And from there I traveled to London, heading much further west— just as the priest had foretold. My mother died when I was fourteen. We were both in Tokyo, but I was not with her when she passed away. My father, too, died in Tokyo. I would receive word of his death, by telegram, during my stay in Kumamoto. And so the priest had been right on the mark with this prediction as well. As for the beard—ever since that time I've scrupulously observed my daily shaving routine, which may well account for the fact that I own no real estate!

It is true, though, that when I took ill in Shuzenji, a stubbly growth started to sprout on my face, and in less than a week it had become quite prominent. I was soon sporting an actual beard, from cheek to chin. It had taken some seventeen years, in other words, for the priest's suggestion to bear fruit. My wife wanted me to let the beard grow, and I went along with her request.

Soon, I was incessantly stroking and preening the hair on my face. And before long, I could no longer tolerate the squalid appearance—my head buried under a scraggly growth of hair, and an unkempt beard that was oily, grimy, and generally disgusting. And so we had a barber come by and set to work with his razor—not an easy assignment, given that I was flat on my back.

In the end, the beard was gone. And with it any qualification I might have to become a property owner. The people around me all clapped and cheered and told me how young I looked. My wife, though, seemed disappointed when she saw my fresh-shaven face, remarking "Oh, so you've had it all cut off." Over and above her husband's recovery, it would seem, my wife wished for her own home and plot of land. I do believe that if someone were to guarantee that in exchange for keeping the beard I'd get the house and property, that is precisely what I would have done.

Thereafter, I returned to my normal shaving routine. Sitting up in bed early in the morning, I'd happily stroke my clean-shaven face while looking out at the mountaintop just visible between the *shōji* screens and the roof across the way. For the time being I'd given up on becoming a property owner. But it may be that I'd merely deferred this as a pleasure to be savored in old age.

KANSHI

Dreaming traveler wakes to singing birds
Mountain rain at night gives way to morning sun
Atop the lonely peak, a solitary pine
Radiant in the crimson light of dawn [87] (*Omoidasu* 28, 1911)

This clever anecdote, a corrective to the darker tones of the *Omoidasu* collection, plays on comic reversal—the idiocy of fortune-telling, which in this case turns out to have been [comically] correct. The account moves on to the subject of facial hair, a recurring motif in the *shōhin*, and the momentous consequences, in light of the priest's oracular pronouncement, of shaving or not shaving.[88] Choosing to relinquish his chances of property ownership, the freshly shaven narrator, bedridden with a debilitating illness, is able nonetheless to savor such beauties of nature that can be glimpsed from his sickbed, and even to anticipate a long life.

What begins, within the small compass of this episode, with a memory drawn from one's youth takes us on an interesting narrative journey before returning home, as it were, in the form of a poem of transcendent beauty.

Sōseki's memories of the early Meiji will be pursued, in the following chapter, from the vantage point of family reminiscence. As a means of bridging these two related chapters, I wish to conclude this one by calling attention, once again, to the invention and embroidery that underlie all retellings of lived experience. Reminiscence, tapping into our creative resources at a fundamental level, is the very soul of art. The immediacy of remembered events and the emotions they evoke are powerful, striking deep chords. Through the magic wrought by the teller of tales, we share in worlds of human experience made out of words.

CHAPTER 3

Shōhin Episodes

In Search of a Meiji Upbringing

As noted in the Introduction, Meiji writers explored new modes of self-expression and literary discourse, modes that reflected a complex synergy between imported Western models and existing genres and styles. Poetry and fiction emerged as productive avenues for experimenting with persona and voice. But autobiography in the Western literary mode—which is to say, a coherent recapitulation of one's life—generated little interest. Likely models—Benjamin Franklin's autobiography, for instance, along with Rousseau's *Confessions*—were known within the Meiji *bundan*, but they failed to inspire much in the way of imitation or adaptation.[1]

Natsume Sōseki represents the *bundan* norm, in other words, in not having produced an autobiography. Rather, he wrote of himself episodically, in the form of hundreds of *shōhin* vignettes, over a decade's span. The resulting reminiscence entails two complementary elements—the reconstitution of a scene or episode drawn from past experience and a reflection upon the past from the vantage point of the narrative present. To speak of "self-expression" in the abstract is to overlook the role of narrative invention: a story is selected among the many possibilities, and its narrator employs dramatization, dialogue, figuration, and mood in the telling.

Past and present, the youthful persona and the older storyteller—these exist in a shifting complementarity. There is no simple, singular "self," no simple, singular "past." But as readers of personal reminiscence, we are naturally curious. What *is* revealed here? we ask. What sort of portrait can we conjure? Is there evidence of an inner life?[2] If so, what sort of life *is* it? Or are Sōseki's literary morsels just that—a pastiche of small talk, interesting on a superficial level but ultimately lacking substance and coherence?

From the perspective of our own media-driven taste for the graphic, intimate, tell-all confession, the *shōhin* reveal next to nothing. It is tempting to conjecture that the unhappy circumstances of the author's upbringing may explain the seeming reticence. Prevailing social norms and literary conventions presumably played a role, but these are notoriously difficult to tease out. Ultimately, we may lack any reliable criteria for judging the "depth" or "authenticity" of a self expressed in words or a past reconstituted in a series of short episodes. But let us first examine the evidence, in the form of *shōhin* episodes that recall scenes from one's youth and family members who have passed on—remembrances of one writer's upbringing in the early years of Meiji Japan.

AZUMAYA

Descending the gentle slope in front of our house, one comes upon a little bridge that spans a stream. Just across this bridge, on the left, is a small barbershop. I've had my hair cut there only once. The shop's glassed-in door is normally covered with a white muslin curtain, which hides the interior from passersby. And so when I stopped in for my haircut and took my seat in front of the mirror, I did not recognize the barber's face at all. As soon as I entered, he threw down the newspaper he'd been reading and greeted me. I couldn't help but feel that we'd met somewhere before. And so as he went around behind me and began snipping away with his scissors, I took the opportunity to start up a conversation. Just as I'd suspected, the barber mentioned having had a shop next to the post office in Teramachi.

"I should tell you how indebted I am to Mr. Takada," he said, referring to a cousin of mine.[3]

This took me quite by surprise.

"You know Takada?"

"Not only do I know him—he used to be one of my best customers!" The choice of words was unusually polite, coming from a barber.

"Takada died, you know."

"What? You don't say!" The barber raised his voice in surprise. "What a shame! Such a fine man. When did he pass away?"

"Just recently. About two weeks ago, actually."

The barber proceeded to tell me various things he remembered about my cousin.

"Ah, yes. Life just passes us by, sir. Seems like yesterday, but it's been almost thirty years now."

I wasn't sure what the man was getting at.

"You know—since he moved to that place near the Kyūyūtei restaurant."

"The two-story house?"

"Yes, it did have two stories. Well, when he moved in, presents started arriving from all over. Things certainly were lively. By the way, it was after that, wasn't it, when he moved to that place in the Gyōganji temple precincts?"

I had no answer for him; this was so long ago I'd totally forgotten.

"They say the area has completely changed. Then again, I haven't had any reason to go there myself."

"*I'll* say it's changed! It's become a regular red-light district!"[4]

Come to think of it, I'd always noticed a confusion of square lanterns displayed along the narrow lane leading toward the temple, as I would pass through Sakanamichi. But I was never so given to playing the prodigal that I might do a precise calculation, and so the barber's account came as somewhat of a surprise.

"You don't say. But now that you mention it, I'm pretty sure you can see a sign for the Tagasode, or some such inn, as you pass through the area."

"Yes, there are so many of those places. But the change is only to be expected. After all, it's been almost thirty years. As I'm sure you'll recall, sir, there was only one geisha house within the temple precincts—the Azumaya. The entrance was directly across the way from Mr. Takada's place." (*Garasudo* 16, 1915)

Yes, I remembered the Azumaya well. It was indeed directly across from my cousin's house. His family and the geisha were well enough acquainted to exchange greetings when their paths crossed. Back then, my older brother Einosuke used to hang around my cousin's place.[5] Einosuke was a total wastrel. He'd gotten into the nasty habit of stealing things in the family's possession—hanging scrolls, swords—and selling them on the cheap. At the time I had no idea why he'd come to roost at my cousin's. But in retrospect, he may have been kicked out of the house on account of his outrageous conduct.[6]

In addition to Einosuke, there was a cousin on my mother's side, Shō, who would also spend time at the Takada house. The three fellows could usually be found sprawled out on the floor or relaxing on the veranda, regaling one another with their own brand of foolishness. From time to time, one of the geisha in the house across the way would call out to them from the bamboo-latticework window. As though awaiting their cue, the gang would try to entice them.

"Come on over. We've got something you'll like."

Since the geisha were free during the day, they'd occasionally make their way over, just to be sociable. I was a bashful lad of seventeen or thereabouts. And so if I happened to be present at such times, I'd retreat to a corner and not say a word. On one occasion, though, I joined in on a visit to the Azumaya, where the group of us played cards. The loser had to treat everyone, which meant that I got to eat sushi and sweets at someone else's expense.

Around a week later, I returned to the geisha house, together with my ne'er-do-well older brother. Cousin Shō was on hand, too, and things got very lively.

"Let's play cards again," said a young geisha by the name of Sakimatsu, glancing in my direction. I was decked out in a formal-looking *hakama,* which belied my actual financial situation.

"Sorry, I don't have a penny on me."

"That's all right," she responded. "You can use some of mine."

As we chatted about this and that, it occurred to me that the girl must have something wrong with her eyes, since she was incessantly rubbing her red-tinged eyelids with the sleeve of her lovely robe.

I would later hear from my cousin that Sakimatsu was rumored to have found a steady patron. His family referred to her by the more informal "Osaku." It thus occurred to me that I'd likely have no further opportunity to meet her. But as things turned out, I would run into Osaku once again. This was a good deal later, when I stopped at the Tokyo Emporium, near the Zōjōji, with my friend Tatsujin.[7] There she was, looking every bit the refined housewife, in contrast to my own unimpressive student outfit. And by her side was her patron.

The barber's mere mention of the Azumaya, a name rich in associations, was enough to bring forth this reminiscence of times past.

"By any chance do you happen to recall a geisha at that house by the name Osaku?"

"I should say I do. She's my niece!"

This came as quite a surprise.

"What about her current whereabouts?"

"She died, sir."

"You don't say! When was that?"

"It was a very long time ago. Around 1890, I'd say. She'd gone to Vladivostok, actually, together with her gentleman. He was connected with the consulate there. Well, it was shortly after they arrived when she died."

Back home, seated at my desk inside the glass doors, it crossed my mind that the only ones left alive were myself and the barber.[8] (*Garasudo* 17, 1915)

Sōseki constructs many of his reminiscences out of such "happenstance" encounters that yield unexpected news and breathe life into old memories. Much is revealed in this casual chat with the barber, whom the narrator barely knows.[9] A train of association leads to the geisha house, the Azumaya, which serves to trigger further associations, and word of yet another player in this little drama who had passed away. Incongruously, two virtual strangers learn from one another of these deaths, and the narrator, having returned to his private study, is left with the realization—sad, perhaps, or merely resigned—of having survived while those others are gone. As we will see, the memento mori episode, of which this is an example, would be a mainstay of Sōseki's literary reminiscence.

As a family remembrance, though, what bears noting is the contrast between the shy young man and the dissolute older brother and cousin, brought together thanks to the attractive young ladies next door. But this, too, is a rather thinly clad caricature, with no affectionate overtones. Rather, the tale shifts to the Azumaya geisha, Osaku, whom the narrator chanced to meet in later years—and then to the revelation that she is none other than the barber's niece, who ended up dying in Russia.

Of the many interwoven threads in this episode, the figure of the dissolute relative would be revisited in a subsequent *Garasudo* reminiscence:

MASU

I wonder why my cousin Masu had fallen so low in the world.[10] When I knew him, he worked as a mailman. Shō, the younger brother, was at loose ends and would appear at our place to sponge off of the family....

Masu, too, was a regular visitor, if only to see his younger brother. Every month or so, he'd bring a little something—a bag of rice crackers or the like—as a respectful gesture to my father. They say he had lodgings somewhere near Shiba, or Shinagawa. But since he lived the devil-may-care bachelor life, he was free to spend the night at our place whenever he pleased. There were times when he'd be about to leave, and my older brothers would gang up on him and not let him go. These brothers— Einosuke and Wasaburō—were at the time taking courses at the Nankō Academy, in preparation for entrance into the university.[11] In the evening, they would set up their desks in the entranceway and prepare the next day's lessons. Their study habits differed remarkably from today's students'. My brothers would carefully go over every paragraph of the assigned reading— Parley's *History of England* was a standard text—closing the book after each paragraph and quietly reciting it from memory.[12] When the study session was over, it was time to get hold of Masu. In due course, cousin Shō would join in on the fun. And even Daisuke, my eldest brother, by nature a moody and dour sort, would put in an appearance if he felt up to it. When all were assembled, they'd start in on Masu:

"You deliver mail to foreigners, right?"

"Sure I do. I may not exactly enjoy it, but it is my job, after all."

"How's your English?"

"Well, if it were any good, I sure wouldn't be doing *this* for a living!"

"But don't you have to say things to them—like 'Here's your mail'?"

"Look, I don't need to use English. Foreigners are speaking Japanese these days."

"Are you serious? You mean they can actually say things in Japanese?"

"They sure can. There's this Missus Gadzooks. She can say 'You-very-good-thank-you'—in perfect Japanese!"[13]

Having gotten a good laugh out of this teasing and bantering at Masu's expense, they'd start in on him again.

"What was it she said, Masu?" Time and again they'd try baiting him with the same question. They'd do their best to wear Masu down, but he'd finally stop playing their game, displaying a bitter smile. And so the fellows would move on to some other caper....

By the time I grew into adulthood, Masu had stopped coming by the house. For all I know, he may have died. If he were still alive, I imagine that he'd have gotten in touch. Then again, if he has in fact died, I know nothing of the details.[14] (*Garasudo* 26, 1915)

In this amusing episode, Sōseki's circle of family ne'er-do-wells expands to include cousin Shō's older brother. But the "fun with Masu" jocularity is tinged with a certain melancholy air. Masu is cast here as a *fugūsha*—a hapless sort, who is pressed into service as a jester for the amusement of students in need of diversion following a hard day of book learning. The notion of delivering mail to foreigners counts as high comedy, and Masu is pressed to do his imitations of "Missus Gadzooks," the "talking gaijin." But the joke was actually on him. And his fate, as the narrator speculates, is anyone's guess.

Brothers

Of note in the above episode is the depiction of the brothers' study habits, which provides an interesting perspective on early-Meiji schooling. The detached view is not without reason. A late returnee to the Natsume family fold, Sōseki understandably lacked a store of memories—fond or otherwise—of his siblings. The sisters are recalled chiefly in the context of their visits to the kabuki, occasions depicted with a studied curiosity. The three older brothers, who are equally remote figures, make a somewhat more lively appearance in the *shōhin,* as the above episodes suggest, albeit in a fragmented manner.

Sōseki would have occasion to recall these brothers in the context of his Shuzenji convalescence, as recounted in *Omoidasu koto nado:*

MY DEAD BROTHERS; MYSELF IN THE MIRROR

I lost two older brothers when I was young. They had both been ill and bedridden for extended periods, and by the time they died, the ravages of disease were clearly etched upon their features. Yet the hair and beard that each sported, left unshorn throughout their respective illnesses, remained thick and vibrant, gleaming with a black-lacquer sheen, until the very end. The beards, though, were a sorry sight, having grown out into a wild and bushy disarray. I still recall the bold look of one brother's beard—what a sad and eerie contrast was this token of robust manhood with the awful emaciation and pallor that had consumed my brother as he approached death.

For my part, I'd spent many days, following the near-fatal episode, in that strange liminal state hovering somewhere between life and death. Once the crisis had passed, one of the first things I did, out of a desire to confirm that I was in fact still alive, was to look at myself in the mirror. And there, reflected in the unforgiving glass, was the very image of my brother, dead these many years—bones protruding, skeleton-like, from sunken cheeks; the sallow complexion, deathly pale and cold; the lifeless eyes, unmoving in their sockets; the hair and beard in wild profusion.[15]

Unlike my brothers, though, whose hair had been jet black when they died, mine was liberally streaked with gray. This only stands to reason, since neither had yet reached middle age. Perhaps this is the more noble, manly way to die. When I thought of myself, beset by graying hair and encroaching old age, obsessed with staying alive at all costs, how embarrassingly spineless I felt in comparison with those who resolutely face death in the very prime of life. Looking at myself in the mirror, I detected an expression of sad resignation, tinged with a certain shame in having outlived one's allotted time.

In his *Virginibus Puerisque,* Robert Louis Stevenson wrote that no matter how old we become, we never entirely lose the spirit of our youth. I could envision the moment long ago when I came across this passage, and how deeply it moved me. And I found myself longing to return to those happier days of the past. Stevenson himself suffered from chronic illness, yet he maintained his cheerful disposition to the bitter end, and so he bore faithful witness. Then again, Stevenson died at a relatively tender age. Had he lived on into his sixties or seventies, one wonders whether the positive outlook would have persisted. . . .

Should one bow to the inevitable and cross gracefully the threshold of age, or conceal the graying hair and linger on in the realm of youth? The choice did not cross my mind as I stared at the mirror. Nor could it have, given that my diseased state distanced me from the world of young people.

Before my illness, I went out to dine with a friend. Staring at my shortened sideburns, he asked whether I'd been having them trimmed shorter out of concern for the encroaching gray. I must have seemed spry enough to be asked such a question. But having taken ill, I came to accept the gray hair as a token of my acceptance of things as they are. Now that I've recovered, it remains to be seen whether I will maintain the sober, resigned sense of self or seek to retrieve the youthfulness that preceded my illness. Will I pursue Stevenson's path or choose instead to honor the gray hair?

Those caught in limbo between an active life and old age must surely appear ridiculous to young people. But today's youth will one day find themselves straddling this world and the grave, unable to decide which way to turn.

KANSHI

The happy youth upon a chestnut steed
Astride a silver saddle, brushing aside the willow branches
But now the tree-shaded stream has vanished far away
And a bright moon shines upon silver strands of hair [16]
(*Omoidasu* 31, 1911)

Nearing the end of his *Omoidasu* musings, the narrator is reminded of two older brothers—Daisuke (1856–1887) and Einosuke (1858–1887)—and the cruel irony of their untimely death in the very prime of life. The memory of their thick, luxuriant black hair, even when they were in the final stages of consumption, is posed against his own unseemly figure reflected in the mirror—haggard, wasted away, all but dead. But, somehow, still alive.

Interestingly, it was years earlier that Sōseki, still a student, had chosen to write an essay on this very subject—*in English*. With a remarkable command of the language, he reflects, in a voice of lyrical melancholy and romantic sentimentality, upon the death several years earlier of his brother Daisuke. The essay is marked by an emotional unburdening conspicuously lacking in the subsequent *shōhin* reminiscences.[17]

In the *Azumaya* episode above—a later *Garasudo* reminiscence—the one brother, Daisuke, is remembered as a cold, remote figure given a new lease on life by a geisha; the other, as a chronic ne'er-do-well. Here, though, the brothers are vested with a sort of tragic nobility through the fact of their early demise and the image, tinged with pathos, of their disease-ravaged countenances incongruously matched with the thick black hair and beard. Yet compared to the openly expressive student composition, written in 1889, the reminiscing narrator here remains curiously unmoved by the figure of two dying brothers. Rather, he juxtaposes their image with the harrowing reminder of mortality that stares back at him from the mirror, then pursues a new train of association—one that calls to mind Robert Louis Stevenson. This kindred spirit—who died of a cerebral hemorrhage at age forty-four following a life spent chronically ill—was nonetheless endowed with an indomitable spirit and, as noted above, a childlike lightness of being that enabled him to surmount the ravages of disease. Himself at the very age when Stevenson died, Sōseki ponders the question of whether this self that he has become will persist until his own dying day or whether there might be another self—in the Stevenson mode—that he could assume. What remains is the solipsistic gaze that reveals only visions and versions of oneself.

Sōseki would have one more occasion to recall his brother Daisuke, in the concluding section of *Garasudo*:

DAISUKE

I regarded Daisuke more as a parent than a brother, given the considerable difference in our ages. He was quite handsome, with fair complexion and an impressively straight nose. But his facial features were marked by a grave, solemn aspect, and he struck one as being unapproachable. I could hardly imagine being on intimate terms with him, a sense that was powerfully reinforced whenever he'd get angry with me.

Daisuke was at the Kaiseikō Academy in the early years of Meiji, when the old *kōshin* system, which had sent promising young men from the *han* domains to the academy, was still in place. Young people today could scarcely imagine the atmosphere there, which retained much of the flavor of late-Tokugawa society.

Among his experiences at the academy, Daisuke told about the upperclassman—years older than he—who sent him a love letter.[18] For someone raised in Tokyo, where such customs did not prevail, my brother surely found this a very troubling situation. He mentioned his awkwardness and embarrassment whenever he happened upon this older student in the bath.

By the time he left the Kaiseikō—forced to drop out because of his lung disorder—Daisuke had become painfully stiff and punctilious, so much so that even my parents kept him at arm's length. Moreover, at home he displayed a cheerless, melancholy expression—a symptom of his illness, perhaps—and generally kept to himself.

But things were to change. The stiffness relented, the hard edges softened. Daisuke started going out in the evening, dressed up in dashing *chōnin* style.... Souvenir fans from the fashionable restaurants would be casually tossed into the parlor. As if this weren't enough, he'd sit himself down next to the hibachi and start acting out popular kabuki scenes. The family, however, appeared generally unfazed by these goings-on. I merely maintained my pose of indifference.

Daisuke ended up dying of consumption. This was in 1887. The funeral was held, followed by the prescribed ritual observances. And just when things were returning to normal, a woman came to visit the house. Wasaburō received her in the parlor, and she began inquiring about Daisuke.

"Your brother never did marry, did he?"

"No, he remained single his entire life."

"I'm relieved to hear that. But someone in my position can't survive without a patron, so what's one to do..."

The woman, who had come all the way from Kōshū,[19] asked about the location of the temple where Daisuke's remains were buried. She then departed. This was the first I'd learned of my brother's affair with a Yanagibashi geisha.

From time to time I've thought that it might be interesting to meet this woman and talk with her about my brother and their relationship. But she would have aged, and her heart would be as desiccated and wrinkled as her body. If this were the case, would such a person really want to see the younger brother of her former lover? No, it would be all too painful to bear.[20] (*Garasudo* 36, 1915)

In this episode, Daisuke figures in several intriguing aspects of early-Meiji society—homosexual advances at the academy, Edo-style theatricals and parlor games, and the all-but-obligatory geisha. Viewed, however, from a retrospective gap of almost thirty years, the brother is presented here as an enigma for the questing narrator. How to account for the strange transformation from morose invert to sybarite, in the Edo *iro otoko* style?[21]

Enter the Yanagibashi geisha, who with perfect dramatic timing appears at the house at some point following Daisuke's demise to inquire about him—and just as suddenly departs. She would certainly have a story to tell, but the narrator rationalizes his decision not to contact her—which forecloses any possibility of uncovering the brother's past. And the geisha herself becomes yet another "mystery woman," whose ephemeral comings and goings in the *shōhin* narratives point to avenues in life that one will neither locate nor traverse. Even within his own family, Sōseki's narrator remains a passive observer.

Sōseki was clearly not on close terms with his brothers; what little pathos one detects in these accounts has to do with the memento mori of their untimely death. In life he hardly knew them. Given such thin strands of remembrance, how much more can one expect of the author's recollection of his parents, toward whom he had every right to harbor guarded sentiments?

Remembering the Father

Raised in separate families—natal and adoptive—Sōseki's *shōhin* narrator would recall a childhood where place and locale inspired more vivid memories than their human inhabitants. His biological parents figure here and there, but they tend to be cast as stage properties belonging to the old home and its environs. Concerning the father, we have seen in chapter 2 a glimpse of a petty local official recalled with scant affection. Concerning the adoptive parents, the Shioharas, there is virtually no *shōhin* reminiscence. But the father, in his incarnation as Shimada, looms large in Sōseki's autobiographical novel.

The biological father appears, in assorted unflattering poses, here and there in the *shōhin*. The following account is drawn from an earlier *Garasudo* episode.

THE FATHER'S HOUSE
Our family had no samurai roots. My father was a so-called *nanushi,* a local official who had inherited this position from *his* father.[22] The position itself entailed a good deal of socializing, some of it evidently quite lavish. What little I recall of my father is of a bald old man. But they say that in his youth, he had a flair for vocal entertainment, having studied one of the then-popular *jōruri* styles.[23] And there was talk, too, of a lady friend in the pleasure quarters who'd been the recipient of his favors.

What is more, I learned that my father owned rice fields in Aoyama, and that the proceeds from the harvest were sufficient to feed the family. My older brother vividly recalls the ceaseless sound of rice hulling at harvest time. Even I remember people back then referring to our house as *"genka"* [entrance foyer]. As a child, I didn't get the gist. But it likely meant that ours was the only house in the vicinity that could boast such a relatively imposing entranceway.[24] I can still recall the things that were hanging up in the entranceway—the three special devices used back then to apprehend criminals, and an old-style lantern used on horseback.[25] (*Garasudo* 21, 1915)

This largely secondhand account of the father—much at odds with what Sōseki had known growing up—recalls the Daisuke episode above. Both point to subsequent revelations concerning dalliance in the pleasure quarters. Yet the notion of the bald old man having once been a dandy and a womanizer evokes little wonderment. After all, this sort of thing was virtually de rigueur among Edo and early-Meiji townsfolk with sufficient means.

In the end, the father remains a remote and unsympathetic object of curiosity, and it is rather the old Babashita house that evokes the clearest recollection. Reduced to caricature, the father is available for further comic treatment, as in the following account of a burglary in the Natsume home.

INTRUDERS

Just the other day I heard of a burglary that took place in our house long ago. The incident evidently occurred before my elder stepsisters were married, which would place it around the time I was born.[26] Those were turbulent times, with the imperial loyalists and the shogunal supporters arrayed in staunch opposition.

One night, so the story goes, my eldest sister, Osawa, had just finished relieving herself. Opening the door to go out and wash her hands, she noticed something glinting at the base of the old plum tree that stood in a corner of the narrow courtyard. Without lingering to ponder the situation, Osawa immediately shut the door and stood there on the veranda, stock still, trying to make sense of the strange light she'd just seen.

My sister's face, you see, left an indelible impression on me as a child. And whenever I recall her, the image comes to life with amazing clarity. But what I see is my sister after she'd married and blackened her teeth.[27] I can't quite picture her as a young woman in her prime, engaged in this little drama on the veranda of our house. The only image I can conjure up from my youth is of my sister's broad forehead, her swarthy complexion, the small though prominent nose, and her large, double-lidded eyes. And her name, Osawa—what a lovely name.

As my sister stood there, mulling over the situation, it occurred to her that there might be a fire. Fearing the worst, she again opened the door to have a look—when all of a sudden a glinting sword appeared out of the darkness and was thrust into the small passageway. Astonished, Osawa drew back. And just at that moment, a group of masked men rushed into the house, with swords drawn and carrying searchlights. There were about eight of them.

The intruders made it clear that they hadn't come with any violent intentions and that no one would be harmed if we did as they said. Then they approached Father and demanded money to help support their cause.[28] Father said he had none on hand, but the intruders were equally adamant.

"No sense holding out on us," they warned. "We've heard about you at the Kokuraya, the sake shop on the corner. Let's have the money!"

With great reluctance, Father produced several gold coins, which he presented to the men. But they made no move to depart, evidently displeased with the monetary yield.

"Let them have what you've got in your purse and be done with it," advised my mother, who until then had been sound asleep. The purse was said to have contained some fifty *ryō* in silver coins.

After the thieves made off with their haul, Father had some harsh words for my mother, roundly scolding her for telling them about the purse. Following this incident, Father arranged for a secret compartment to be installed inside one of the wooden pillars in the house, to keep spare cash and valuables out of harm's way. But items worth hiding were in short supply, and the house would be spared further intrusion by masked bandits. And so with the passing years, no one knew which pillar housed the secret compartment.

As the story goes, the thieves had words of praise for the Natsume household as they left the scene of their break-in that night. This was a well-guarded house, they supposedly remarked. But the individual who'd steered them to our place—Hanbei, the proprietor of the neighborhood sake shop—wound up with a number of nicks and scratches on his head. It appears that each time he insisted that there was no money in his shop, the thieves refused to believe him, and one of them would take a little swipe at his head with the tip of his sword. But Hanbei would not relent.

"Look, you won't find any money here. But the people who live just behind my place—the Natsumes—they've got plenty." In the end, his persistence paid off. They didn't get a thing from him.

I heard this account from my wife, who in turn heard it from my older brother.[29] (*Garasudo* 14, 1915)

Here the account is thirdhand—related by his wife, who in turn had heard it from Sōseki's older brother.[30] The tale reconstructs a bit of Natsume family lore, whose context is the high drama of Japan's *bakumatsu* period—a turbulent period during which shogunal supporters struggled with imperial loyalists. This transformative epoch in Japan's modern history has generated a wealth of historical and personal accounts. The dramatization that marks *this* incident, in contrast with episodes where the narrator wrestles with his memory to piece together a coherent account, likely reflects the manner in which the story was related by Sōseki's wife. But here again, the focus is on the more mundane, but nonetheless telling, family interaction. The account has been fashioned in advance, and is thus a "borrowed" reminiscence. But the narrator, as he begins recounting the twice-told tale, pauses to reflect on his older sister, Osawa, whose image, forged in childhood, has lost none of its clarity, and for whom he expresses fondness, albeit at a considerable remove.

The story concerns a group of armed men who break in and demand money—at which point Sōseki's father appears. Granted a somewhat larger role than usual, the father is caricatured as a peevish skinflint and victim of his own pettiness—a projection, in effect, of Sōseki's *self*-caricature. His money is stolen, thanks to the double betrayal of Hanbei, who steered the thieves to the Natsume residence, and his own wife, so quick to have him part with the remaining cash. And his bright idea of constructing a secret compartment to hide the family valuables will have been in vain. Indeed, the location of the compartment itself, as the tale is told, would be forgotten.

The extent of Sōseki's embroidery upon the story as told to him is of course impossible to ascertain. But the victimization theme, here given a nice comic twist, is a frequent refrain in the *shōhin* and elsewhere. This theme will concern us at greater length in chapter 5.

Shimada

If it can be said that Sōseki effectively erases his biological father from the domain of personal reminiscence, his adoptive father, Shiohara Masanosuke (1839–1919), is resurrected in the fictional guise of Shimada Heikichi, who plays a key role in *Michikusa*. Shimada is seen almost exclusively from the point of view of Sōseki's alter ego, Kenzō, for whom the man is both a nagging presence in the here and now and a haunting reminder of one's unhappy past.

As Kenzō stops to reflect upon this man who was his adoptive father, the sequence of remembered episodes becomes a composite reminiscence of childhood, based upon the author's personal experience. The reminiscence begins as follows:

Kenzō could remember clearly how as a child he used to trot alongside Shimada on their many outings together. . . . Shimada also bought him many of those goldfish with the beautiful long tails. And whenever Kenzō saw an illustrated children's book that he liked, Shimada would unhesitatingly buy it for him. Kenzō even possessed a miniature suit of knight's armor, authentic to the last detail, that fitted him perfectly. . . . But despite the clarity with which he could recall those childhood scenes, he was quite incapable of coloring them with any of the affection he might then have had for Shimada.[31] (*Michikusa* 15, 1915)

Kenzō goes on to recall, in vivid detail, scenes from his life with the Shimadas—formative experiences that disturbingly reflect upon his own character. He is first drawn to the image of an empty house:

His memory carried him down a trail at the end of which stood a large, square house. In it were wide stairs that led to the second story. The upstairs and downstairs seemed to his eyes exactly the same. The inner garden, surrounded on four sides by verandas, was a perfect square. Strangely enough, no one lived in this house. . . . Kenzō could not remember who was looking after him then. But judging by the awareness of the boy in those scenes, he must have already begun living with the Shimadas. (*Michikusa* 38, 1915)

Not long after, the Shimadas had entered his awareness as his parents. They were living in an odd house in those days. The main entrance was at one end of the house. You turned right when you came out, and went up three stone steps beside the wall of another house. You were in a small alley, about three feet wide, which opened into a busy street. . . . (39)

Shimada was miserly enough, but his wife Otsune was worse. Some time later, when he had been returned to his original family, Kenzō became accustomed to hearing about her miserliness. . . . While living with her, though, he was unaware of her notorious vice. . . . Yet Shimada and Otsune spent a surprising amount of money on Kenzō. Thus, so mean in other respects, the couple pampered this child that had been given to them. (40)

The Shimadas were inwardly uneasy about Kenzō, and constantly demanded reassurances of affection from him. On cold winter evenings as they sat huddled around the brazier they would ask him, "Who is your father?" And Kenzō would point at Shimada. "All right, who is your mother?" Kenzō would look at Otsune and point. The interrogation would not yet be over; only partially satisfied, they would go on to ask, "But who are your *real* father and mother?" The boy, with obvious reluctance, would once more point his finger at one and then the other. Somehow this gave the two pleasure, and they would smile happily at each other....

The couple did everything in their power to make Kenzō exclusively theirs. They regarded him no doubt as their possession by right. And the more they pampered him, the more possessive they became. He did not mind so much being owned physically, but even his childish heart grew fearful at the thought of becoming emotionally enslaved to them. (41)

It was not long before Kenzō's character was affected by their behavior. He had originally been a rather meek child. But gradually his meekness came to be replaced by an incorrigible stubbornness, and he was in the end turned into an utterly spoiled brat.... (42)

In the meantime, strange things had begun to happen between Shimada and Otsune. One night, Kenzō awoke to find the two reviling each other at his bedside. He was taken aback, and burst into tears. After this, hardly a night passed without their quarreling. Their voices became louder and louder, and finally they went beyond mere exchange of words.... (43)

Some time later, Shimada went out of Kenzō's life completely. Then the house by the river disappeared too, and Kenzō found himself living alone with Otsune in a strange apartment at the back of a large grocery. Time had been kind, and he could remember nothing about the place except that it smelled of boiled soybeans.... Their life together did not last long.... One day she disappeared, and he found himself back again with his real parents.[32] (44)

Kenzō's musings on those years spent as the Shimadas' adoptive son comprise seven consecutive episodes of the novel—among the most sustained reminiscence in all of Sōseki's work. The account begins with evocative details regarding the locale—an empty house, a wooded grove, a pond—sights and scenes arranged in geometric precision and in precise relation to one another, yet entirely devoid of human presence.

The scenes unfold before the rapt gaze of the adult, who literally "pictures" his childhood. The adult is watching the resurrected images of his past—much as one might dust off the old movie projector and screen eight-millimeter footage of one's neighborhood, long forgotten, but now thrust before one's eyes in a brightly colored simulacrum of the real world.

While appearing to construct a child's point of view, the account is ultimately an artifact of adult retrospection and reasoning. The child, and the past in which the child lived, are nowhere to be found. The scenes evoke not so much presence as absence. Where, Kenzō seems to wonder, do I, the observer, fit into this picture?

Then the Shimadas emerge on stage, initially as little more than furniture inside a merchant's house. But they are the sole human beings in the unfolding scene—no other adults, certainly no children, enter the frame. The Shimadas come to dominate the scene; and Kenzō, who is a clever lad, can see these people for what they are. Moreover, he understands his indentured situation—first, as the Shimadas' prized possession, indulged and cosseted, then as a pawn in their sorry excuse for a marriage. By and by, the womanizing father leaves, and the boy is left in the charge of the obsessive, hysterical mother.

In the process, though, he becomes aware of having been infected by the virus of family dysfunction to which he'd been exposed. The once-innocent boy, now thoroughly warped, has armored himself with cynicism, smugness, and self-importance—at which point he merges with the man, "forcing his way back into Kenzō's consciousness."

Kenzō managed to get free of the adoptive mother. But the adoptive father would return, like an *onryō*—a ghostly apparition who stalks the living, burdened with unrequited longings and attachments. Shimada's demands are ultimately about money, but he will remain for Kenzō a constant and haunting reminder of the quicksand that is one's past, and of one's uncertain and unhappy grasp of the present.

In a final attempt to make sense of his past and its relation to the troubled present, Kenzō turns once again to his childhood memories, drawing a comparison between his two fathers:

> Again he remembered his childhood, for a while forgotten. With the sharp, pitiless vision of a man who is suddenly made to see what he had never seen before, he cast his eyes on that point in the distant past when he was sent back to his parents.
>
> To his father he was simply a nuisance. He would look sometimes at the boy as though he could not quite understand how such a mistake had been made. Kenzō was hardly a child to him; rather, he was some animate object that had forced its way into his household. And the love that was in Kenzō's expectant heart was brutally pulled out by the roots and left to wither in the cold. . . .
>
> With too many children to take care of already, Kenzō's father was very reluctant to assume any responsibility for him. He had taken the boy back only because he was his son; he would feed him, but he was not going to spend a penny on him if he could help it. After all, he had thought that the boy was off his hands for good.
>
> Besides, Shimada saw to it that Kenzō remained legally his adopted son. From his father's point of view, then, Kenzō was a bad risk, for what

was the point of spending money on the lad when Shimada could come and take him away any time he wished? I'll feed him if I must, was his attitude, but let Shimada take care of the rest—it's his business.

Kenzō had no home, either in the seas or in the mountains. A wandering creature that belonged nowhere, he found his food sometimes in the water and sometimes on land. To his father and to Shimada both, he was not a person. To the former he was no more than an unwanted piece of furniture; to the latter, he was some kind of investment that might prove profitable at a later date.[33] (*Michikusa* 91)

An extension, in effect, of the earlier recollection, this account begins as a "screening" of the projected scene, set in Kenzō's natal home upon his return from the Shimadas'. And the scene is arid and bleak. He reflects on the two fathers responsible for raising him—one more despicable than the other. Basking in self-pity, Kenzō proclaims himself, almost willfully, to be utterly alone and unloved—"a wandering creature that belonged nowhere." His self-pitying melancholy has come full circle, as he stands alone, tormented by questions that cannot be answered—but that he cannot help asking, again and again. Confusion and doubt will remain; the one certainty—scant consolation, to be sure—is decay and death.

Mother

With Sōseki's biological father relegated to the margins and his adoptive father resurrected as a living ghost whose relentless entreaties must somehow be appeased, one might expect the mother's portrayal to be rather more sympathetic. The mother-son bond has earned a privileged place, after all, in Japanese literature and lore, and it has become enshrined as well in certain nativist conceptions of the Japanese psyche.[34] Yet compared to Tanizaki Jun'ichirō, whose literature is deeply inscribed with mother longing, Sōseki provides, at best, only tantalizing glimpses of the mother. With his *shōhin*, the picture is further obscured—as the following episode will bear out—by the narrator's intense self-scrutiny.

SEARCHING FOR MOTHER

I wish to write something in remembrance of my mother. Unfortunately, she has left me with precious little material to work with. Mother's name was Chie—a name that even now evokes strong feelings of nostalgia. I've wanted to think of this name as belonging exclusively to my mother, and that no one else must be allowed to use it. Happily, I've yet to meet another woman who bore the name Chie.

Mother passed away when I was around thirteen years old. As I trace the strands of memory in search of her distant, wraithlike image, I envision an older lady. You see, Mother gave birth to me later in life, which meant that I would forever be deprived of any vision of her as a vibrant, young woman. In my mind's eye I see a woman wearing large eyeglasses—the old-style wire-rimmed glasses—at work on her sewing.

I remember Mother with those glasses on, staring at me with her chin tucked close to her neck. Since at the time I couldn't understand this characteristic posture as being connected with poor vision, I merely regarded it as one of her idiosyncrasies. I also remember the *fusuma* screen in front of which Mother worked. The screen was covered with a hodgepodge of old, pasted-on fragments and images. One that vividly comes to mind is a print of a Buddhist saying—something about life, death, and the evanescence of all things.

In the summer, Mother would always wear a dark blue silk kimono with a thin black satin obi. Strange as it may seem, I can only envision her in this one summer outfit. If I strip away the kimono and the obi, all that remains in my mind is her face. My sole recollection of Mother together with my older brother is an image I have of the two of them playing Go out on the veranda. As always, she has on the blue kimono and the black obi.

I don't recall ever having been taken to Mother's childhood home, and for a long time I knew virtually nothing of the family she came from. Nor did I have any great curiosity in this regard. Here, once again, my memory is hazy and indistinct....

I vaguely recall having heard that before getting married, Mother served in one of the daimyo residences in Edo. Alas, I have no knowledge of which residence this might have been, what her duties were, how long she served. Nor is there any way of ascertaining the facts in this regard. All that remain are the faintest of traces, like the fleeting fragrance left in the wake of dying incense.... (*Garasudo* 37, 1915)

How I'd wish to see Mother again, and to speak with her about these things.

Being stubborn and mischievous, I was not cosseted by my mother, as would normally be the case with the youngest child. Nonetheless, I've cherished a memory of her as having lavished affection upon me, more so than anyone else in my family.

Such personal feelings aside, there is no question but that Mother was a refined and charming woman. Everyone thought her rather more clever than my father. Even my peevish, fault-finding older brother held her in high regard. Indeed, there was no one he respected more.

"It's not anything she says, but there's a frightening side to Mother." These words of my brother, buried deep in some remote region of the past, remain etched in my mind. But like writing that bleeds and blurs when immersed in water, only to return to its original shape, this is little more than a fugitive shard of a perilously flawed memory. Aside from such fragments, my mother is nothing more than a phantasm, a dream. No matter how painstakingly I glean the disparate bits and pieces, they will not yield a coherent whole. Indeed, the past itself, composed entirely of such fragments, has grown so faint and obscure that it is no longer within my grasp.

As a child, I would go upstairs alone to take a nap. Strange visions would torment me during these naps. My thumb would suddenly start to grow bigger and bigger. The ceiling would gradually descend until it pinned me down on the bed. My eyes would be taking in a familiar scene—except I'd be in a trance, unable to move my limbs. Even afterwards, I couldn't tell if I'd been conscious or dreaming.

It was just such a bizarre incident that I experienced on one particular day.

It seems that I'd spent a large sum of money that didn't belong to me. When and where this happened, why I took the money and what I did with it—none of this is clear. All I know is that the sum was more than a child could ever begin to repay. Anxious and fretful, I was beset by terrible distress. I awoke, screaming for my mother, who was downstairs.

The stairway was directly behind the *fusuma* screen. And so no sooner did Mother hear my cries than she ran upstairs to my side. As she stood there looking at me, I told her why I was so upset.

"Please do something!"

"There's no need to worry," Mother assured me with a smile on her face. "I'll give you whatever money you need."

How happy this made me! Relieved of my fears, I had no trouble falling back to sleep.

I cannot tell whether this little episode has any basis in truth or is merely a figment of my imagination. Nonetheless, I remain certain that I actually did cry out for my mother, and that she did in fact come to me and utter those soothing words.

One more thing—she had on the dark blue kimono with the black satin obi.[35] (*Garasudo* 38, 1915)

Memory yields little of the mother—a face, a pair of eyeglasses, a certain kimono, a brother's impressions ruefully related. As a counterpoint to these disembodied fragments is the *fusuma* screen, the literal and figurative backdrop to the remembered scene, with its own assorted scraps. And one of these scraps is inscribed with a Buddhist verse concerning evanescence—*mujō*. Such details form an integral part of the "re-membered" mother, as a pastiche figure in a tableau.

The narrator, keenly aware of our unsure claim to knowledge of the past, laments the paucity of concrete detail, the haziness of his recollection. Yet at the same time he lyricizes this very quality of haziness, through its association with *mujō* and the lingering fragrance of dying incense. And the mother, the memory of whose love the son has constructed, is tied to notions of dream, obscurity, phantasm. Storytelling abhors a vacuum, and so the very absence of a past built upon a scaffolding of concrete evidence will be compensated for by imagination, in the service here of the utterly basic need for a mother's love. It is a truism that we ultimately—and inevitably—construct the desired image of those we want to love, and whose love we crave.

Hence, the above episode appropriately culminates in a dream, retold in a fittingly sentimental voice, of the mother comforting the fearful son. The dream has about it the flavor of a Freudian primal scene, and it naturally begs interpretation. But what strikes one is the episode's guileless, straightforward quality and the bond that the narrator establishes with a mother who has in effect challenged him to create something out of nothing.

The autobiographical signature of this *Garasudo* episode contrasts with an earlier mother fantasy, included in the *Eijitsu* collection:

THE VOICE

When Toyosaburō moved into his new lodgings, he diligently set to work putting his belongings in order, arranging his books, and moving about the place like a restless shadow in the fading light of day. He then went to the local bathhouse, and as soon as he returned he fell asleep.

The next day, when he got back from school, Toyosaburō sat at his desk to study.

But he was not at all in the mood, perhaps because of the new surroundings. He heard the sound of someone sawing outside the window. Reaching over to open the shoji, Toyosaburō saw, right before his eyes, a gardener energetically pruning a parasol tree.... The cut-away branches revealed a broad expanse of sky, as though converging upon his window. He propped his chin upon his hand and dreamily gazed off into the distance. With eyes fixed upon the clear autumn sky, Toyosaburō was overcome by a powerful emotion. The feeling gradually resolved itself, like a tiny image emerging somewhere in his mind, into a recollection of his home, which was so dear to him. The image was far off in the distance, but it looked as sharp and clear as if it were right there on his desk.

The path leading up from the village at the foot of the mountain ends at the gateway to his home.... "Toyo! Toyo!" His mother is calling out to him. The voice comes from far, far away, yet it sounds so clear that one could reach out and touch it. His mother had died five years earlier.

Toyosaburō suddenly emerged from his reverie.... He felt as though something was holding him down. Looking out beyond the tree and over the fence, he saw a row of squalid *nagaya* houses. The autumn sun beat down on the shabby, torn futon mats left out unceremoniously for an airing. A woman in her fifties was standing nearby. She wore an old striped kimono, faded with age and bound with a cheap obi. Her thinning hair was coiled around a large comb. With a vacant expression she looked up at the top of the parasol tree, through the branches below. Toyosaburō could see the woman's face—pale and bloated, her swollen eyelids blinking in the bright sunlight. She was staring at him. Toyosaburō immediately looked down at his desk.

On the third day, Toyosaburō stopped at the florist's to buy chrysanthemums. He had hoped to find the variety that grew in his garden back home. But failing to come across any, he made do with what was available. He had the three blossoms bundled in straw and returned to his lodgings, placing them in a vase shaped like a sake bottle. He then took out a small scroll from his wicker trunk—the work of Hoashi Banri[36]—and hung it on the wall. He'd brought the scroll back from a visit home some years earlier, specifically for this purpose.

Toyosaburō sat for a while, contemplating the flower arrangement and hanging scroll. Then he heard the sound of a voice, coming from the *nagaya* across the way. "Toyo, Toyo," the voice called out his name. It was his mother calling him.

Toyosaburō threw open the shoji and looked outside. There stood the bedraggled old woman from the day before, her forehead bathed in the waning autumn sunlight, beckoning to a snot-nosed urchin. Attracted by the clattering sound of the shōji, the woman quickly turned and fixed those pale, swollen eyes upon Toyosaburō.[37] (*Eijitsu* 21, 1909)

Seated at his desk, Toyosaburō is precisely in the position of the *Gara-sudo* narrator ensconced in his study, musing on the world seen through glass doors. From his fixed vantage point, Toyosaburō gazes off at two worlds—one, the "real" world outside his window, which yields the figure of an aging woman, shabbily dressed, who vacantly returns his gaze; the other, an inner world of the imagination that yields an archetypal dreamscape of home and mother—his "real" mother, no longer alive, beckoning to him. He then *hears* his mother calling, but *sees* the old lady, who again looks up at him.

Those who endorse the notion of the "mother quest" as a cornerstone of Japanese literary thematics might wish to claim this as a key to Sōseki's *shōhin* project. His mother fantasies—*Ten Nights of Dream,* in particular—all but demand a psychological reading. I prefer to see them in the context of the author's early experiments with fictional narrative.[38] With *Garasudo,* written toward the end of Sōseki's life, fantasy gives way to more sober reflection on one's marginal status within his own family. The following episode is frequently cited as an especially revealing childhood memory:

THE MAID

I was born the last child of aging parents. To this day I hear how my mother, around the time of my birth, made it clear that she was not at all pleased with a pregnancy this late in life.[39] For this among other reasons, I was placed in foster care as a newborn. I have no direct recollection, of course, but as an adult I learned that the foster family had been a poor couple who made a living in the secondhand trade. They evidently had me in a little basket that would be set out, every evening, together with the assorted bric-a-brac in their stall along the main road in Yotsuya.

One evening, as I've heard the story told, my sister happened to be walking along that very stretch of road when she recognized me, lying in that little basket, and thought it so pitiable that she took me back home, nestled in the sleeve of her kimono. Unable to settle down, though, I cried the whole night through, which led to my father's giving my sister quite a scolding.

I have no idea exactly when I was taken back from the foster family. But it was not long thereafter—I was around two at the time—when I was sent out for adoption. I grew up in the home of my adoptive parents, but certain problems arose in the family when I was around eight years old, on account of which I was returned to my original home. As I moved from Asakusa back to the house in Ushigome, though, I was convinced that these people were my grandparents, not my actual parents. And I proceeded to address them accordingly, thinking it perfectly natural and correct. For their part, "Grandma" and "Grandpa" appeared content with this arrangement, evidently disinclined to make a sudden break with established practice.

Unlike the typical youngest child of the family, I was not at all doted upon by my parents. This only stood to reason, given that I was not obedient or docile by nature and had lived away from them for years. What is more, I remembered just how harshly I'd been treated by my father. Yet despite all of this, I was positively bursting with joy once I'd moved back with them, and my happiness was there for one and all to observe.

Who knows how long I persisted in this idiotic conviction that my parents were actually my grandparents. Then one night, as I slept alone in my room, I heard a voice, near my pillow, whispering my name again and again. I awoke with a start. Staring into the pitch darkness, I was unable to tell who was crouching beside me. Remaining perfectly still, I simply listened to what was being said. It then came to me that this was the voice of our maid.

"Your grandma and grandpa," she whispered to me in the dark, "well, they're actually your mom and dad. I heard them talking—about how strange it is that you seem to like it here so much, and that it must be because you think of them as your parents. I thought you should know this. But you mustn't tell anyone. Do you understand?"

"I won't tell anyone." This was my only response. But at that moment I felt deeply grateful—not for having learned the truth, but simply because the maid had been kind to me.

Strangely enough, I've forgotten the name of this maid and what she looks like. All that remains in my memory is the kindness she showed me and the happiness it brought.[40] (*Garasudo* 29, 1915)

A companion to Kenzō's far more elaborate reminiscence in *Michikusa,* the *shōhin* narrator here encapsulates the pathos of his childhood experience. Unwanted and unloved by his parents (especially the father), the infant spends a brief period in foster care, until the sister happens upon her baby brother lying in a basket out on the street and returns him home—much to the father's displeasure.[41] By and by, the child is put up for adoption, and he would grow up in the Shiohara household. Many years spent with the adoptive family came to an end when unspecified circumstances (ugly marital spats, in fact, which culminated in divorce) led to his being restored to the natal home. But there has been deception, and it is the maid who reveals the truth to him. Of the woman herself there is no trace—only the grateful memory of that single act of kindness.

The gist of this episode is foreshadowed in the figure of Kiyo, the beloved maid in Sōseki's enduringly popular novel, *Botchan.* She alone understands the young man, who has a decidedly wild streak, and she loves him unconditionally. All the others are schemers and posers. Honesty and integrity—the quality of *shōjiki*—emerge as cardinal virtues. These qualities, as much as the individuals who embody them, are part of the legacy of Sōseki's past, and strongly orient his moral compass. Yet duplicity, self-centeredness, and outright betrayal persist, much like the disease that would continue to ravage his body, and they would indelibly mark some of his best-known literary creations.

Reconstituting Sōseki's Pasts

As these episodes suggest, Natsume Sōseki explored the tensions and travail that complicate our attempts to reach out to others—especially those closest to us—and to lay claim to them through our recollection. *Kokoro* and *Michikusa*, two emblematic works, are tours de force of self-delusion, alienation, and betrayal. A son abandons a dying father. Friends turn on one another, deceive one another. Husbands and wives live together in splendid isolation and smug indifference. Yet the simple need for connection remains—even (or, rather, especially) for those enclosed within walls of vanity, pettiness, and insensitivity.

The great Sōseki themes are amply represented in his *shōhin*. What is more, I would point to a sacramental quality that marks these small acts of memorializing the past and those who went before. Memory does not always cooperate; it can never offer up the unmediated past. Understanding this, one can either abandon the effort or wrest from one's imagination that which will fit the story we wish to tell. Sōseki's psychological acuity—his awareness of the complementarity of memory and imagination—is surely part of what makes the *shōhin* narratives so compelling, and so convincingly modern. We live lives confined within our small, private spaces. We struggle to look out, and our view is obscured; we try to look within, and we see faint glimmers, and a looming fog. What persists is the awareness that this is how we must live—seeking to capture that which is beyond our vision, beyond our grasp. Fully cognizant of our limitations, our fragile hold on who we are, we are equally attuned to the unexpected turn, the casual encounter, that promises something new. But mainly we sit and think, and wish to be left alone.

The past cannot be weighed on a scale of accuracy, of fidelity to experiences actually—and measurably—lived. Rather, experience disappears upon contact, so to speak, and our notion of "the past" must be created, and forever re-created, in our minds. As a quintessentially modern writer and thinker, Natsume Sōseki understood the embracing solitude that defined his world, the contingency of memory, the corrosive self-centeredness that keeps others at bay and poisons the spirit. His *shōhin*—together with the novels that complement them—lay bare the process of this ongoing reflection.

This and the preceding chapter have presented episodes, written over a quarter-century span, that recount events and scenes from the past. Some are firsthand accounts; others, second- or thirdhand retellings. Sōseki's narrator, and his relationship with the events recounted, shifts, often perceptibly, with each episode—just as the author himself changes over time and recalls his past in different ways, and for different reasons. Here, the sequentiality of episodes within a collection, and the sequence of the collections themselves, is of obvious import. The older narrator reflecting on his childhood occupies a different position from that of the younger narrator reflecting on the more recent past. Both, however, are equally engaged in constructing these narrative versions of the past and in reflecting on the process of their construction.

At times painfully aware of the need to supplement the inevitably flawed and imperfect mental residue, Sōseki's narrator invents, fantasizes, reflects on being here, now, engaged in this frustrating—yet endlessly creative—act of retrospection. Frequent reference to haze, obscured vision, and liminality suggests the narrator's sense of isolation and helplessness. The anxiety—however it may have been experienced by the author—is a convincing and artfully crafted literary effect. And the lyrical moods evoked by one's very isolation are not to be overlooked. There is a poetry to be gleaned here—a lyrical melancholy of one's lonely place in the universe, which is to be both pondered and savored.

In chapter 4, we will revisit these matters in the context of Sōseki's ruminations on the here and now of family and domestic circumstance.

Burdens of Domesticity

The Writer and His Family

A s noted in the Introduction, the Meiji modernization project hinged in part on the creation of a new family institution symbolized by the term *katei* (household, domicile).[1] This radical departure from Tokugawa norms and practices would eventuate in sweeping social changes. But the process of breaking with the entrenched shogunal system and adopting Western legal and political institutions was a tortuous one. It was not until the 1890s that the Meiji Constitution was promulgated and a code of civil law enacted. It took this long, as well, for the revamped educational system, conceived as the bedrock of modern nationhood, to become fully operational.

On *Katei* and Meiji Domesticity

Western models and practices were a necessary but not sufficient condition for the new nation as envisioned by the Meiji oligarchs. Their vision was of a modern Japan *with a difference*—a difference conceived in terms of *kazoku kokka*, a "familial state" under the patriarchal authority of the emperor. Its citizens—notwithstanding new legal institutions and a discourse of individualism that invoked Western notions of liberty, freedom, and personal autonomy—were defined by the state as loyal imperial subjects, subsumed under a pervasive neo-Confucianist family system.[2] Herein lies the incongruity that can be said to characterize the period and that would color the literary and intellectual climate of the age. The new Meiji domicile—the *katei*—would be a microcosm of intersecting conservative, neotraditionalist doctrine and individualist ideology.

By the beginning of the twentieth century, the Japanese household, long a bastion of patriarchal authority, had undergone a major shift in lifestyle and living arrangements, changes that would in turn affect the quality of social interaction. For one thing, as an integral part of a growing economy and an expanding consumer marketplace, the new *katei* was burdened with money management. Sōseki's Tokyo witnessed the rise of a middle class of salaried officials, professionals, and businessmen. As living standards rose, so did a concomitant bourgeois concern for property and possessions. Money mattered, and criteria of wealth and achievement gradually displaced the old order of ascribed status based on family pedigree. Living a comfortable life became an achievable goal. But in the meantime, the children had to be clothed and fed, and bills had to be paid. In a society driven by ambition and material aspiration, a breadwinner's income—in tandem with a wife's home economy and frugality—was an empirical index of one's social standing, irrespective of what one did to earn it.[3]

What concerned Meiji writers, especially those who found themselves on a lower rung of the socioeconomic ladder, were problems they faced every day—keeping one's family together, paying the bills, making a living, and trying to achieve, against all odds, a sense of self-worth. As participant-observers of the new *katei* paradigm, these writers had no shortage of material for a literature centering on domestic circumstance. In fact, a genre of *katei shōsetsu* (family-based fiction) enjoyed widespread popularity in the 1890s, predominantly among a burgeoning readership of housewives and young women.[4] Works in this genre helped pave the way for Sōseki's *katei*-oriented dramas, which would unfold within the physical spaces of a home and its environs.

Virtually synonymous with its resident family, the notion of "house" is also a metonym for modern society as a whole.[5] Indeed, the Japanese term *ie* conflates meanings related to the physical house, the family that occupies it, the extended family—even the nation itself. But as physical structure, *ie*—house—stood as a tangible symbol of Meiji aspirations and material culture. The house was a repository of people, their possessions, and the complex "terms of engagement" forged, privately, therein.

One interesting aspect of Meiji history concerns the changing face of the family as a function of the physical spaces it inhabited. Recent research on consumer and media culture has enhanced our understanding of the material circumstances of Japanese in the early twentieth century. Jordan Sand, for example, has studied the history of the domicile as centerpiece of modern Japanese bourgeois society and culture and the physical locus for the harmonious interaction that the modern family was to epitomize.[6] As Sand notes, the sense of privacy that the Meiji home would ostensibly afford was that of the family unit as an entity independent of the public sphere. This contrasts, however, with individual privacy—the desire of those under the same roof to be free of one another. Here, again, lies the fundamental incongruity of Meiji society—the conflicting claims of a Western-inspired individualism and a state-sponsored ethos of familism and collectivism under an authoritarian regime.[7]

Analogously, research into what can be termed literary topology has addressed questions of how characters function in the narrative spaces they occupy and how their interaction is mediated by these spaces and their social ecology. Sōseki's novels, together with the *shōhin,* are illuminating in this regard, insofar as they portray the physical interiors—the rooms, furnishings, and the like—within which the characters' psychological interiority plays out.[8]

Keeping in mind the interior spaces that characters inhabit, let us examine a series of *shōhin* episodes that allow us inside the home of a middle-aged professional man who lived with his family in a pleasant Tokyo neighborhood early in the last century.

Nichijō: The Writer as Family Man

The daily routine—one's being in, and responding to, the flow of everyday events—is a recurrent motif in Sōseki's *shōhin,* his fiction, and the larger sphere of *kindai* literature as well. This is the domain of *nichijō.* Notwithstanding the crafted persona of *shosai ningen*—the study-bound recluse—Natsume Sōseki lived under the same roof as his family, and it was a large and growing family at that.[9] His desire for privacy is understandable, given that he worked out of his home office, but this desire did not go unchallenged. The household, in short, was contested space. The Natsume brood had competing claims, and an undercurrent of tension marks the domestic situation as depicted in the personal writing—a circumstance that will strike one, of course, as utterly familiar. Sōseki's *nichijō* persona of reluctant and recalcitrant domesticity appears in his earliest *shōhin,* and it would remain a fixture of his personal writings.

The following *Eijitsu* episode details a day in the life of the workaday writer:

HIBACHI

By the time I woke up, the small heater that I'd placed in my bed had grown cold. Gazing out through the glass doors and beyond the eaves, I saw a dull, gray sky that looked like an unbroken expanse of lead. The pain in my stomach had eased quite a bit. Finally working up the energy to get out of bed, I found it colder than I'd anticipated. Beneath the window, yesterday's snow remained. The bath glistened with its coating of ice; the water line had frozen and the spigot would not budge.

FIGURE 2. Sōseki (*fourth from left, rear row*), his family, literary protégés, and friends, in the garden of his residence in Waseda. Photograph taken on April 12, 1911, following his convalesce in the wake of the Shuzenji episode of August 1910. (Iwanami shoten)

I managed to rub myself down with some hot water and went into the sitting room for a cup of tea. Then the baby started crying.[10] He'd been at it constantly for several days.

"Is something wrong with him?" I asked my wife.

"No, it's just the cold."

That couldn't be helped. But his cries didn't seem to indicate any serious pain. Then again, the mere fact of crying must indicate some sort of discomfort. And so I listened anxiously for any telltale signs, and in the end *I* was the one in distress—with a measure of aggravation mixed in. I felt like giving the little one a good scolding, but he was just a baby, after all, and so I restrained myself. My mood soured, though, as the realization dawned that I would likely have to endure yet another day of relentless bawling.

Having made it a rule not to eat breakfast—on account of my bad stomach—I took my morning cup of tea with me into the study. As I warmed my hands by the hibachi, the crying continued unabated. My palms, directly exposed to the heat, were all but scorched, but the rest of me was ice cold—my toes painfully so. I remained perfectly still, fearing that if I touched any spot that was cold, it would feel as though I'd be stabbed by thorns. Even just turning my head would be unbearable, what with my neck having to rub against the cold shirt collar. Entirely hemmed in by the cold, I cowered in the middle of my study...staring helplessly at the bare wooden floor, as the baby cried on and on. I could not bring myself to do any work.

At that point, my wife came in, needing to borrow my watch. "It's snowing again," she mentioned. I looked up, and indeed a light snow had started falling—silently, unhurriedly, indifferently—from the perfectly still, overcast sky.

"Remember last year when one of the children was sick and we had to use the heater—how much did we spend for the charcoal?"

"It came to twenty-eight yen at the end of the month."

Hearing this, I gave up on the idea of warming the study with the portable heater, which had been put away somewhere in the storage shed out back.

"Look, can't you do something to quiet him down?"

My wife responded with a look that conveyed her resignation to the baby's crying.

"Omasa says her stomach hurts," she mentioned. "She really seems to be in pain. Shouldn't we have her seen by Doctor Hayashi?"

"Yes, you should call him right away." I'd known that Omasa had been in bed for several days, but I hadn't realized that her condition might be serious. Having gotten the sought-for approval, my wife left the study, taking my watch with her, and went to call the doctor.

"This room is freezing," she remarked, shutting the *fusuma*.

Numb with cold, I had no desire to work. But there was so much to do. There's the manuscript due in to the newspaper. I'm supposed to have a look at some stories by a young writer I don't even know. I've agreed to send off a letter of endorsement to a journal regarding someone's work. A great pile of books has been accumulating on my desk over the past several months— when am I supposed to get to them? This past week, whenever I've been at the point of getting started on my work, someone comes by to see me with some proposal or scheme. And to top it off, my stomach is troubling me. In that sense, at least, I have a reprieve today. But the cold has rendered me inert. I simply cannot remove my hands from the *hibachi*'s warmth.

Just then, a rickshaw pulled up to the house, and the maid came in.

"Mr. Nagazawa is here to see you."

Huddling up close to the hibachi, I look up as Nagazawa enters the study. I tell him that it's too cold for me to budge. He takes out a letter and starts reading it. No doubt another request for money, I thought. I was right. I'm being urged to manage something by the fifteenth of the month—the lunar New Year.

It was past noon before Nagazawa finally left. But the cold was still unbearable. Concluding that I'd best go to the bathhouse and try to revive my spirits, I was just about to leave the house, with towel in hand, when Yoshida showed up to see me. We repair to the sitting room and I listen to *his* tale of woe. He breaks down and the tears start flowing. In the meantime the doctor has arrived, and there is much commotion going on. No sooner does Yoshida leave than the baby starts crying again. At long last I make it to the public bath, which warms and refreshes me.

Returning home, I entered my study and found the lamp turned on, the blinds drawn, and fresh charcoal kindled in the hibachi. I plopped down onto the cushion to begin working when my wife came in with some hot broth. When I asked about Omasa's condition, she replied that the doctor thinks it might be appendicitis.

"If it appears serious, we should have her hospitalized," I said, taking the bowl of broth. Expressing her agreement, my wife went back into the parlor.

Now that I was alone, everything was suddenly quiet—the still silence of a snowy night. The baby had evidently fallen asleep. For this I was grateful. Sipping the broth, I found myself drawn to the crackling sound of the charcoal burning in the hibachi. Amidst the encircling ash, a reddish glow faintly flickered. Here and there, tiny jets of blue flame would shoot out from between the burning pieces. In the glow of that little fire, I felt warmth and peace of mind for the first time that day. And for a short while I stared at the gradually spreading surface of ash.[11] (*Eijitsu* 5, 1909)

A winter's day, with its litany of domestic travail. A day not unlike other days, marked by the numbing cold, the crying baby, visitors coming by to ask for money. The maid is sick, and one can't get any work done. Charcoal expenses are exorbitant, and one has to economize. And so the cold persists. Yet this day, with its many aggravations, gives way to a healing night, with its gift of silence, warmth, and peace of mind.

Praised by postwar novelist Shōno Junzō for its "unfettered view" of Sōseki's *katei* persona, this *Eijitsu* episode captures the intersection of the writer—the *shosai* denizen—and the family, whose demands must be addressed, however reluctantly.[12] The householder, whose voice dominates the account, is aware of his responsibilities, and his peevish self-pity appears both understandable and slightly perverse. By way of recompense, there is the hibachi, the source of warmth. But it is the solicitous wife who'd entered the study, in his absence, and seen to replenishing the charcoal and, later on, to providing the warming broth. Yet one suspects that her thoughtfulness will, at some later date, draw the ire of the penny-pinching husband. In the larger context of Sōseki's literature, this domestic vignette stands as a preliminary sketch for the fully elaborated novelistic portrayal of marital relationships.[13]

Another *Eijitsu* episode presents a different domestic scene from the perspective of the *shosai*-bound narrator as he takes note of a small spectacle that enters his field of vision:

THE PROCESSION

I chanced to look up from my desk and noticed that the door to the study was ajar, revealing a two-foot expanse of corridor. At the end of the corridor stands a Chinese-style balustrade, and beyond it the glass door that encloses the space. The sunlight shines down under the eaves, slanting through the glass, and brightens the veranda, managing also to bathe the entrance to my study in its warm glow. As I stared for a while at the spot being illuminated by sunlight, thoughts of spring come welling forth, like the dazzling filaments of light that dance upon my eyes.

It was just at this moment, as I happened to glance up and notice the open door, that a figure materialized in the two-foot expanse of corridor—a figure about the same height as the balustrade, appearing to tread on air. Encircling the forehead and hairline was a red and white braided ribbon, in figured arabesques, decorated all around with what seemed to be crab-apple blossoms and leaves, the pale crimson flowers like large droplets, in sharp relief against the field of black hair. A single length of purple kimono, trailing from just beneath the bunched-up chin all the way back to the veranda, swept airily by, revealing no sleeves, hands, or legs. The shadow passed, as though eager to escape the sunlight cast upon the corridor.

And then a somewhat smaller one, sporting a thick scarlet garment from head to shoulders, the lower back adorned with a diagonal bamboo-leaf design. The torso revealed the green of one single leaf, set against a charcoal black ground. So bold that bamboo leaf design—larger even than the feet traversing the corridor, feet that seemed to waft across the study doorway in a mere two or three steps, passing by in silence.

The third has on a hood with a blue and white checkered pattern, and beneath its peak a full, round face with plump red cheeks. The space beneath the brown eyebrows, only an extremity of which was visible, appears suddenly hollow, so that out of nowhere, it seemed, the little round nose protrudes just enough beyond the cheeks for its tip to come into view. Aside from the face, the entire body is swathed in yellow stripes, with the trailing end of long sleeves dragging behind. This one has a bamboo walking stick, considerably taller than its owner. To one end is attached a little cluster of bird feathers, luminescent in the sun's rays. The underside of the yellow-striped sleeves shines with a silvery glint—just barely noticed as it passes from view.

Following behind, a pure white face appears, as though daubed with paint from the forehead down to the flat cheeks, then down to the jaw and back to the ears—a white surface still and silent as a wall. Only the eyes are alive. The lips, thickly rouged, look pale in the reflected sunlight. The front of the garment is the color of pigeon plumage, but my view down to the hem is obstructed. This one is carrying a small violin and solemnly shouldering its long bow. A pair of feet march along, and in their wake a square patch of black satin cloth at the back, the gold-embroidered figure in the middle buoyant in the sunlight.

The final one is tiny, just on the verge, it seemed, of tumbling down under the railing. But the face is prominent, and the head, quite large in proportion to the body, is adorned with a many-colored tiara, which towers above the head. The figure has on a tight-sleeved garment with a cross-hatch design. A cape of some sort, with mauve-colored velvet tassels, hangs down the back in a triangular expanse reaching well below the waist. For footwear, this one has on red *tabi* slippers. A hand grasps a large Korean fan, fully half the size of the one holding it, decorated with a comma-shaped swirl in red, blue, and yellow lacquer.

The procession moves by in silence. And as I bask in the stillness and solitude of the moment—the study door open to that square patch of veranda before me, ushering in the vacant, empty sunlight—I could make out, from the far side of the house, the sound of a violin. Then a sudden chorus of high-pitched laughter.

This is how the children amuse themselves, taking out Mommy's things and making merry.[14] (*Eijitsu* 19, 1909)

Five figures enter the writer's field of view, and each is depicted, in the manner of a *shasei* sketch, as a moving tableau of light, color, and shape—picture-scrolled *objets* fashioned of garments and facial parts.[15] These, then, are Sōseki's daughters, as rendered by their "observant" father. The text, with its introversive figures—*shizukasa, munashisa, sabishisa* (tranquility, void, aloneness)—identifies the narrator in his *shosai* persona as a detached, lone observer. One is struck by the incongruity of elaborate physical detail and the studied avoidance of "human" reference. Yet this is by no means an unsympathetic view. On the contrary, the underlying pathos of the moment inclines one to read the parade of decorative mannequins as a metonymic displacement of the children, these apples of the fatherly eye affectionately refashioned in this clever (and notably modernist) manner.[16]

In his diary, Sōseki remarks on his children when they take sick or on the occasion of some family outing. By and large, he expresses concern and affection. But the larger picture is not always of a loving father surrounded by adoring children. Consider, for instance, the grim cast of a father's attitude toward his daughters in *Neko*. The scene is set at the breakfast table presided over by Kushami and related by our ever-observant and all-knowing feline informant:

> My master looked around impartially at his three daughters. . . . He knows that there will come a time when he must see to it that they get married. But he's at a loss what to do about this. Since he can never hope to take care of them properly, he should not have had children in the first place. But this is a common failing in humans, who continually accumulate what they don't need and then pity themselves for the burden. . . . His was a strictly laissez-faire policy, as far as the children were concerned. While still only schoolgirls in their sailor outfits, all three could end up running off with common-law husbands, and my master would probably not have much to say one way or another.[17] (*Neko* 10, 1906)

During his convalescence in Shuzenji, following the nearly fatal hemorrhaging of August 24, 1910, Sōseki's children paid a visit to their ailing father. The episode is recounted as follows in *Omoidasu:*

THE CHILDREN'S VISIT

"The children are here," my wife whispered in my ear. "Do have a look at them." Lacking the strength to move any part of my body, the best I could do was catch a glimpse of them through the corner of an eye. And there they were, sitting some six feet from my bed. . . .

The children appeared strangely remote—perhaps on account of my awkward position. So much so that it would be a misnomer to claim that we'd actually gotten together. Rather, I was merely observing them—and clumsily, at that. In any event, this would be the only time I'd see the children during my Shuzenji convalescence.

Despite having had little more than a moment's glance in their direction, I was able to take in the entire scene. Three of our children had come to visit—the eldest girls, ages twelve, ten, and eight. They were seated in a neat row, in order of age. Up until the day before, they'd been happily scampering around the beach at Chigasaki, where they'd been sent, together with two other siblings, to spend summer holiday. When word of their father's critical condition reached the family there, one of the relatives took our daughters and immediately set out for Shuzenji, leaving behind the sandy beaches and pine groves.

The girls were surely too young to understand the meaning of the term *kitoku* [critical condition]. They obviously knew the word "death." But their little minds had yet to be touched by a hint of its awesome reality. Nor would they have any conception of how death would transform their father's body, or what sort of fate would befall them in its wake. All they knew was that they'd been taken by train to see their sick father in some town where he was staying. Their expression contained no trace of concern that this might be the last time they'd see their father alive. Theirs was a look of perfect innocence. Yet how constrained they must have felt, being forced to sit perfectly still and obediently in a tight little row, amidst the solemnity and sobriety of it all.

My own expenditure of effort on this occasion had amounted to the single glance at the three of them. I could only think it cruel to have subjected these darling children, who understood so little, to such treatment. And so I called my wife over and insisted that she allow them to sightsee in the area and enjoy themselves. I would probably have displayed more interest in them had I harbored any fears that this might be our final farewell. But I did not share the sense of urgency regarding my condition that the doctors and those around me had adopted.

The children returned to Tokyo, and about a week later I received get-well cards from each of them, enclosed in the same envelope. . . . I tore a page out of my diary and wrote back, telling them to be sure to listen to Grandma and that I'd been sending them souvenirs of Shuzenji.[18] I had my wife mail it immediately. When I later returned home to Tokyo, the children were happily amusing themselves. I suspect that the Shuzenji souvenirs had already been broken by then.

As for this little episode written by their father—what might they think of it, as adults, if they were to happen upon it?

KANSHI

> Autumn's sorrows have already arrived
> Blood was lost, spurted out, but bones live on
> How long before I depart my sickbed?
> The village revisited by the evening sun[19] (*Omoidasu* 25, 1911)

The children arrived in Shuzenji on August 25—the day after their father's attack, when his condition was still critical. They would leave on the twenty-seventh. Immobilized, the father can do little more than look at them—adding, in retrospect, a gesture of affection and solicitude. Whereas the children in the "Procession" episode are marching by in a straight line, here they've been formally placed on display, lined up for the cursory inspection of their sick father.

Sōseki's narrator regrets having been unable to interact with his children, and he empathizes with the unpleasant situation into which they'd been placed. Hence, this episode serves as a belated expression of gratitude for their visit—a "gift" that one hopes will prove more enduring than the souvenir toys, which will surely not last.

Death is in the air, though, and the *Omoidasu* narrator turns to a reflection on mortality from the perspective of his innocent daughters, who would be incapable of comprehending the gravity of their father's situation. Yet theirs is a welcome intrusion. These, after all, are his "darling children," whom he takes up in a silent yet warm embrace.

The Author as Father

Sōseki's Kushami surrogate, tied up in his own emotional and intellectual knots, had no time to concern himself with household affairs. Children, evidently, were to be neither seen nor heard. How, then, did they fare elsewhere in the personal writings? Several diary entries, for example, cast the children as a collective nuisance. On July 18, 1909, the author notes, "Oppressive heat. Daughters running all over the house, totally naked. Not a normal thing to do, the heat notwithstanding. The master of the house goes about writing his fiction, surrounded by barbarians."[20] And consider the scene toward the end of *Michikusa,* following the birth of Kenzō's third child:

> "It was a safe delivery," the midwife said to Kenzō. "Congratulations."
> "Well—is it a boy or a girl?"
> "A girl," said the midwife, looking at him sympathetically.
> Kenzō did not hide his disappointment. "So it's another girl."
> He was now the father of three girls. What did his wife think she was doing, he thought bitterly, ignoring the fact that she hadn't exactly made them herself.... That his third daughter might grow up to be a decent-

looking person was somehow beyond hope. "One ugly child after another, and to what end?" Often such a thought, not very proper in a father, entered his mind. And of course it expressed his hopelessness not only as a father but as a husband too.[21] (*Michikusa* 81, 1915)

Sōseki's children would appear in other *shōhin* as well—in connection with the family pets, for example, to which they were attached. But they play at best a marginal role. While this may bespeak an indifferent and remote attitude, the Natsume paterfamilias was evidently a dutiful father in certain respects—as a breadwinner, for instance. And in several *katei*-related interviews, he extols the virtues of family life, although this may reflect a predetermined journalistic agenda.[22]

In any event, the memoirs of his wife and children tell a different story— that of a harsh and difficult man who on occasion became a tyrannical presence in the home. Further evidence can be gleaned from remarks attributed to Sōseki by those who knew him. For instance, Nakamura Murao wrote in his 1949 *bundan* memoir of the many interviews he conducted with the author, in his early role as professional reporter *(hōmon kisha)*. In one memorable interview, Sōseki held forth on his theory of marital spats, which he traced to women's being impervious to logical reasoning. When asked how he dealt with his wife, the author remarked, "What's there to do but go ahead and smash a cheap pot or something? You can't reason with the woman; and I'm not strong enough to physically overpower her. But the sound of a smashed pot usually shuts her up."[23]

For those who hold Natsume Sōseki in reverential esteem, this sort of account may prove disturbing, or simply irrelevant. On the one hand, we recognize that the man, beset by physical and emotional distress for most of his adult life, and the literature, which acknowledges the misunderstanding and pettiness that poison our relations with others, must not be equated. Nonetheless, these two exist in a complementarity that cannot be ignored or denied.

Some insight into Sōseki's complex and conflicted temperament—at once caring and curiously disengaged—can be gleaned from his writings in connection with the tragic death, on November 30, 1911, of his year-old daughter Hinako. While not touched upon in the *shōhin,* the events surrounding Hinako's death are recorded in detailed diary accounts, and an extensive fictionalization appears in the novel *Higan sugi made* (To the Spring Equinox and Beyond), which began its serial run on January 2, 1912.[24]

Hinako

Chapter 4 of *Higan sugi made,* entitled "Rainy Day," concerns the death of Yoiko, the infant daughter of Matsumoto and his wife, Osen, who are modeled upon Sōseki and his wife. Interestingly, the sad course of events is related not from the parental vantage point, but chiefly from the point of view of their niece Chiyoko, who adores the little girl.

Sōseki's fictionalization of Hinako's death owes a good deal to his diary account. Let us examine several episodes that take place toward the end of the "Rainy Day" chapter, following Yoiko's cremation. These will be compared first with the corresponding diary source, then with Kyōko's memoir account.

> Four persons went to gather Yoiko's ashes: Osen, Sunaga, Chiyoko, and the maid Kiyo, the one who had actually looked after the infant.... It was Chiyoko's first experience at a crematory. The suburban sights, which she had not seen for a long while, provided her with the kind of pleasure that one has in being reminded of something long forgotten. Green wheat fields came into view as did radish gardens and forests of evergreen in which were mingled various reds, yellows, and browns.... As the rickshaws went down a gentle shadowy slope, Sunaga pointed out a tall, lean pagoda standing amidst a clump of high cedars.... Down the slope at the foot of a bridge was a tea stall, behind which was an artesian well surrounded by a thick growth of bamboo, all lending picturesqueness to the country lane. Small leaves of various colors fell occasionally from the nearly bare branches of tall trees.... The crematory, its front facing south, stood on sunny, level ground.[25] (*Higan* 1912)

Diary source: The above passage draws heavily upon Sōseki's detailed entry for December 3, with its rich, *shaseibun*-style description of the locale. Chiyoko's delight in the passing scene strikes one as somewhat jarring, given the purpose of this particular "outing."

> When Osen gave her family name at the reception window of the crematorium, which looked like a counter at a post office, the man sitting there asked if she had the furnace key with her. She looked puzzled and began groping for it in her kimono bosom and the folds of her old sash. "Now I've done it! I've left the key on the cabinet in the living room and..." Sunaga, who had been listening apathetically behind them, said,

"If it's the key you're worried about, I have it." He took from his kimono sleeve the cold, heavy object and handed it to his aunt."[26] (*Higan* 1912)

Diary source: Sōseki notes in the December 3 diary entry that he had gone to the crematorium with his wife and maid Fuji to fetch Hinako's remains and that he'd been upset with his wife for having forgotten the key to the furnace. He proceeds to send the maid back home to retrieve the key, then wanders around the premises, noting the comings and goings of the crematorium clientele.

While they waited, drinking tea, a few people arrived to gather the ashes of their deceased relatives. The first of these was a rustic-looking woman who spoke little.... Next came a father and son who both had their kimono hems tucked up into their waistbands. In a lively voice one of them asked for an urn, bought the cheapest for sixteen sen, and then went off. The third party consisted of a girl in a violet *hakama* leading a blind person.[27] (*Higan* 1912)

Diary source: This is a nearly verbatim transcription of the corresponding diary account, which sketches the scene as the narrator awaits the maid's return. Of interest, too, is the running account of expenses incurred with the funeral, the crematorium, and the like. Everything is duly itemized.

Since Yoiko was cremated in the top-grade furnace, a violet curtain hung over its folding doors. On a table in front of those doors was the garland of flowers brought the previous day, lying quietly, slightly withered. To Chiyoko, these seemed a memento of the heat that had burned Yoiko's flesh the previous evening. She suddenly felt as though she were suffocating....

The black iron doors opened on both sides, and at the dim farther end of the cavity something gray and round was visible, something black and white, all in an amorphous mass. The cremator said they would have it out shortly and, attaching two rails, put what looked like two iron rings at the ends of the coffin rack. Then, with a sudden rattle, out under the very noses of the four bystanders came the shapeless mass of what remained of the burned corpse. Chiyoko recognized in the remains Yoiko's skull, all puffed out and round, just as it had been in life with its resemblance to a rice-cake offering. She immediately bit down hard on her handkerchief. The cremators left the skull and cheekbones and a few of the other larger bones on the rack, saying they would sift the rest neatly and bring them soon.

Each of the four gatherers had a pair of chopsticks, one of wood, the other of bamboo, and all picked up whatever white bones each thought fit to place into the white urn. And they wept as if invited to by each other's tears, all except Sunaga, who, pale-faced, neither spoke nor sniffled. The cremator asked if they wanted any of the teeth set apart from the other bones and deftly picked a few from the jaws, which he had begun to crush. Seeing this action, Sunaga said almost to himself, "Handled this way, it no longer resembles anything human. It's like picking small pebbles out of sand." Tears fell from the maid's eyes to the concrete floor. Osen and Chiyoko laid their chopsticks aside, their handkerchiefs pressed to their faces.[28] (*Higan* 1912)

Diary source: Chiyoko's point of view is privileged here, insofar as hers is presented as the deepest affection for the dead child. Note the interesting (if morbid) details regarding the evident status hierarchy vis-à-vis crematorium furnaces, which are based on the December 2 diary entry: "Placed the coffin in one of the first-class furnaces. It would normally cost ten yen, but we managed to get it for six, since this was a child. We were then given the key for opening the oven and retrieving the bones the next day." Again, Sōseki's attention to money details is noteworthy, as is the sense here of a small victory earned through getting a bargain rate for his daughter's incinerator. The chilling emotional "disconnect" here is only reinforced in the next day's diary entry (December 3):

The cremator proceeds to extract the contents of the oven—first, the head and several larger bones; the rest he sifts through, and brings everything to the entrance area. Then, with bamboo and wooden chopsticks that we're provided with, we place the contents in a white urn. We were about to place the skull inside, but the man said that this should go in last. He gathers the teeth together for us. Then pieces of the jawbone. The man shows us a blackened mass that he says were the contents of her stomach. Perhaps he meant the intestines. I'm not sure. Finally, he stirs around the contents of the urn, to make more room, then inserts the skull, which serves as a lid of sorts. But in sealing the urn, the skull breaks into pieces. The urn is now sealed shut, full to the brim. He presents the urn to us, tied with a wire and wrapped in a cloth (*furoshiki*) with wooden chopsticks placed inside. I had the urn on my lap on the ride home.[29]

On their arrival home, Chiyoko placed the ashes in front of the Buddhist family altar. The children immediately gathered around and asked her to take off the lid to let them see what was inside, but she absolutely refused.

Soon the entire family sat down to lunch in the same room. It was Sunaga who started the conversation. "I guess it still looks like you have lots of children, but one is missing now, isn't she?"

"I don't think I made so much of the child while she was alive, but now that she's gone," Matsumoto said, "it seems I've lost the most precious thing. So much so that I almost wish one of these here could take her place."[30] (*Higan* 1912)

Diary source: The long December 3 entry, upon which the above excerpt is based, concludes as follows:

> When she was alive, I hadn't thought of Hinako as any more important than the other children. But in death, she assumed a very different significance. She was now the darling, and the other children were insignificant (*shinde miru to, are ga ichiban kawaii yō ni omou. Sō shite, nokotta ko wa iranai yō ni mieru*). I'd see children playing outside and wonder why it was that they could enjoy life in good health, while our child had her life cut short.... All the effort that had gone into the funeral, the cremation, the other rituals. And for what? It's all for naught. The dead can't be brought back to life. There's a fissure in my stomach; now it felt as though there was a fissure in my heart (*jibun no seishin ni mo, hibi ga haitta yō na ki ga suru*). Some would say that having another child would replace the one that died. But even were another Hinako to be born, the rancor would be the same. Love, after all, is a personal matter (*pāsonaru na mono*).[31]

Sōseki as Father: Kyōko's Account

Nearly a week elapses following the death of the author's daughter before he finally betrays a personal emotion in his diary. In like fashion, Sōseki's Matsumoto surrogate is allowed only the single expression of grief. Again, it is the niece Chiyoko who assumes the role of designated mourner for the dead girl. As for the diarist, as though announcing an end to the Hinako episode, he turns to an entirely different concern in his next entry, on December 4—namely, a troubling rectal disorder for which he is being treated.[32]

By contrast, Hinako's death is an event recalled in her mother's memoir some seventeen years after the fact.[33] Kyōko notes, in the first place, that their daughter was born in March, at the time of the Doll Festival (*hina matsuri*)—

hence her name, "Doll-child." Hinako was a precocious little girl, and feisty, too. She would toddle out back with the older children and go over to offer water at the cat's grave, but ended up drinking the water herself.

Kyōko's subsequent account of Hinako's seizure and sudden death is more detailed than that of her husband, who at the time was occupied with a visiting friend and all but refused, as she relates, to come out, despite the household's being in an uproar.[34] The girl was unconscious and unresponsive by the time the doctor arrived, and despite all efforts to revive her, she passed away. The funeral arrangements were a source of considerable anxiety, owing to Kyōko's inexperience in this regard. The question arose as to which Buddhist temple should officiate, and it was decided to opt for her husband's family temple, the Honpōji, a Jōdo shinshū (Pure Land) temple in Koishikawa. Sōseki let it be known, though, that he wanted no part in the observance of *tsuya*—the wake—a formality he detested. Kyōko mentions having had to talk him out of his opposition, which would be most unseemly. Her husband relented, but hastened to add that he wanted no such ceremonial nonsense when he died.[35]

Kyōko goes on to remark on the wake, noting that the priest sent by the temple was boorish and unrefined, actually trying to cadge donations to his temple. Then there were problems with transporting Hinako's remains. And since the cause of death had not been determined, Kyōko considered an autopsy, but abandoned the idea. "I later regretted not having had one done. It was guilty conscience, I think, that led me to request the autopsy for my husband."

Reflecting on those sad events, Kyōko observes that despite her husband's failure to express any emotion, or to say much at all, he was at the time deeply pained. She makes a point of emphasizing how devoted he was to the children—as long as he was not subject to one of his depressive states *(atama sae waruku nai toki)*. He'd often play with the children, she notes, and managed quite well even with the kids running riot all around him—which they most emphatically did. For instance, the eldest daughter, Fudeko, would lead the younger ones around, wielding a broom and giving marching orders, and they'd tramp up and down the hallway outside his study—and he'd be just fine.

Kyōko then calls attention to the "Rainy Day" account in *Higan,* which she considers a fitting memorial to their daughter. Here she can't help but attribute some karmic significance to her husband's having begun his draft of this chapter precisely on the little girl's second birthday.[36] Turning to his subsequent relationship with the children, Kyōko remarks on the recurrence, early in 1913, of his mental disorder, notwithstanding which he was able to show interest in the children and plan outings with them.[37]

Different insights can be gleaned from her thoughts on the 1915 *Michi-kusa* serialization.[38] Reminding her readers that the novel was based on the family situation following Sōseki's return from London, Kyōko recalls, in a somewhat peevish tone, that her husband had just finished involving certain members of her family in the *Garasudo* serialization, so they weren't keen on the idea of yet another exposé. Moreover, she herself had been liberally "exposed" in *Neko,* and wished to be spared further embarrassment. But in response to her request for restraint as he embarked on the new novel, he responded, dismissively, "Look, this is what I do for a living. How do you think we manage to pay our bills?" And that was that. Even little Aiko—the ten-year-old—approached her father and asked him to spare the family gossip and try to be more creative. He got a good laugh out of this. "Keep it up, little girl, and I'll write about *you!*"

Kyōko goes on to relate another amusing episode regarding Aiko. Her husband had a real sweet tooth; in particular, he loved *yōkan* (sweet bean-jelly, a popular confection). He had a stash in his study and would regularly indulge. Concerned that sweets weren't good for him, Kyōko went into his study one day and hid them. Shortly thereafter, Sōseki started turning the study upside down, looking for his stash. Aiko felt sorry for her father in his predicament. A clever little girl, she combed through the study and retrieved his sweets. "Ah, such a fine, dutiful daughter *(omae wa nakanaka no kōkōsha)!*" he exclaimed, then proceeded to gorge himself.

Evidence does point to Aiko as her father's favorite.[39] This is borne out by Kyōko's subsequent remarks on her husband's approach to the children's schooling. On the one hand, he was generally indifferent toward the girls' education, espousing a policy of benign neglect *(hōnin shugi)*. Chiefly, he wanted them to play a musical instrument. The boys, though, were another story. Their father had a hand in choosing schools and assessing the curriculum. He was especially desirous of their learning foreign languages. He had it all planned out. First they'd study French, in primary school. Then English in middle school—he would teach them himself, or so he said. Then German in higher school. Thus, by the time the boys entered college, they'd have all three languages under their belt.

This, at any rate, was the plan. But things took a wrong turn early on, when he set about checking his son's progress in French.[40] According to the memoir account, he called the boy into his study, wanting to drill him on what he'd learned. Eavesdropping from the next room, all that Kyōko hears is her husband screaming "You idiot! You idiot!" *(baka yarō! baka yarō!)*, followed by the boy's tearful flight from the study. Very troubled by this, Kyōko

FIGURE 3. Sōseki and his two sons, Jun'ichi (*right*, age 7) and Shinroku (*left*, age 6). Photograph taken in December 1912, in the garden of their Waseda home. (Iwanami shoten)

roundly admonished her husband: "Don't browbeat the boy, for heaven's sake. Try actually *teaching* him something, instead of humiliating him!"

And to the man's credit, he did relent. In the end, Kyōko defends her husband as someone who would try to mend his ways once made to realize that he'd been in the wrong.[41]

Judging the Evidence

Such episodes surely beg judgment of the evidence at hand—be it on ethical or psychological grounds. We may demur, questioning the ultimate value of learning that a man screamed at his wife or broke his daughter's toy. Will such knowledge enhance our appreciation or understanding of his work? Yet personal writings by definition open up private rooms—in their occasionally sordid disarray—to public scrutiny. Many of us positively savor the voyeuristic delight in peeking in on the nasty underside of famous lives and relish the schadenfreude pleasures gained at the expense of others' misfortunes. On the other hand, some would prefer a higher purpose to the study of literature and a more judicious assessment of private lives gained through the window of personal narrative. Are we not warranted in using such texts as cultural or historical documents? Or do we want simply to be entertained? Our readerly predispositions and biases will incline us in this or that direction. And our choices, be they conscious or merely habitual, principled or frivolous, define us in some small measure.

Kyōko's memoir, representing her position as wife and mother, recreates events of a relatively distant past and voices attitudes and opinions that had evolved over the years. Sōseki's diary speaks of present circumstances in several distinct registers—by turns impromptu and elegantly crafted. His *shōhin* narrator recalls the past in different ways. In turn, the fictional protagonists may be said to represent the author in a definable manner, but they can also be granted autonomy as literary creations. There is no simple summation of parts that yield a whole, no single authoritative reading of the evidence at hand.

Yet patterns do remain. As I've noted, the theme of *kodokusei*—isolation and insulation—strongly marks Sōseki's work. The notion of being alone with others, of looking out upon one's world "through a glass, darkly"—if one seeks a quintessential Sōseki voice, perhaps it can be found here, in this master trope of modernity.

Having reflected upon the Natsume father, let us turn to the Natsume husband, through the author's portrayal of his wife and their relationship.

The Natsume Husband and His Wife

Evidence pointing to a troubled relationship, marked by an ebb and flow of crises and periods of relative calm, is tempered by an understanding (in Kyōko's case, the wisdom of hindsight) that, despite personal differences and the occasional crisis, the marriage would survive. There were separations, and divorce loomed as a possibility in 1903. But the couple managed to weather the storms.[42] For his part, Sōseki did not use the *shōhin* as a vehicle for attacking his wife or airing the family's dirty laundry, despite the personal demons and physical ailments gnawing at his body and spirit. The diary, however, would occasionally serve this purpose. Rather, it was the novel *Michikusa* that enabled the author to probe the tensions and dissonances of his marriage with remarkable restraint and equanimity. The following excerpts depict the marital tête-à-tête and the shifting emotional terrain upon which this relationship was built.[43]

FIGURE 4. Photographs of Nakane Kyōko and Natsume Kinnosuke, taken in March 1894. These were exchanged with one another as part of the *miai* (arranged marriage) protocol. (Iwanami shoten)

Kenzō doubted her sincerity. She thinks she's being clever, he told himself; she's not going to fool me with her phony charm. Chilled by his attitude, she quickly left the room. As he watched her leave, he thought unhappily: I have been forced somehow or other to behave like this to my wife.... They were getting nowhere. Each thought the other pigheaded and unsympathetic, not worth talking to seriously, and each thought that it was up to the other to make amends.[44] (*Michikusa* 21, 1915)

Kenzō too was subject to sudden changes of mood, and he was not always so ready to pacify his wife, even in that abstracted, mechanical way of his. At times he would be irritated beyond endurance by the sight of her lying cheerlessly on the floor, and from spite would command her to get up and immediately attend to his needs. She would remain where she was, resting her bulging belly ponderously on the floor, and look quite unconcerned. Kick me if you like, she seemed to be saying, see if I care. And in smug silence—she said little at the best of times—she would watch her husband being consumed by rage.[45] (*Michikusa* 54)

Her thinking was not complicated, but her ideas were her own, and she adhered to them with primitive tenacity. Her attitude toward Kenzō was typical: "No one is going to force me to respect this man simply because he is my husband. If he wants my respect, he has to show me that he deserves it. His being my husband says nothing about him as a man." Kenzō, for all his superior education, tended to be more old-fashioned in this respect. He believed sincerely in personal independence and strove hard to realize his ideal; yet shamelessly he assumed that wives existed only to please their husbands: "In all matters, the wife is subordinate to the husband." Herein lay the cause of most of their trouble.[46] (*Michikusa* 71)

"Hardly anything in this life is settled," Kenzō said. "Things that happen once will go on happening. But they come back in different guises, and that's what fools us." He spoke bitterly, almost with venom. His wife gave no answer. She picked up the baby and kissed its red cheeks many times. "Nice baby, nice baby, we don't know what daddy is talking about, do we?"[47] (*Michikusa* 102)

For Sōseki, marriage may have seemed too important a subject, and too delicate a personal matter, to consign to the *shōhin*. Instead, this would be the grist for his later novels. As Sōseki's only explicitly autobiographical novel, *Michikusa* begs to be read as a displaced case history of the author, via his Kenzō proxy. For his part, Kenzō can be seen as a recapitulation of the foibles and failings of Sōseki's first novelistic protagonist, Kushami—a triumph of self-parody who embodies the cardinal vices of pride, pique, pettiness, and self-absorption. Kenzō, though, is endowed with an introspective depth that Kushami lacks, emerging as the very model of the brooding loner—chronically anxious, melancholic, fatalistic. His wife knows him only too well, as the above excerpts make clear, and cannot be gulled or beaten down. In turn, Kenzō, notwithstanding the blinders that restrict his understanding, ultimately knows her and, in his own maddening way, cares for her.

Yet the husband and wife live together in their separate spheres. They both wish that things were different, but they accept, with a mix of fatalism and pride, the modus vivendi of shared isolation. The wife has resigned herself to this uncaring and insensitive husband and a marriage that leaves much to be desired. But she has evidently succeeded in winning over the children—by default, owing to his indifference. Outflanked by his wife and outnumbered by her strategic alliance with the children, Kenzō is the loser in the marital skirmish that drives the plot—a point underscored at the very end of the novel: "Nice baby, nice baby, we don't know what daddy is talking about, do we?"

Sōseki's alter ego appears incapable of remedying his situation. As for his own marriage at the time he wrote *Michikusa*—twelve years following the events depicted in the novel—nothing much had changed in terms of his relationship with Kyōko. Under the sway of chronic mood swings, bouts of depression, and generally bad health, Sōseki cast himself, at times, as a virtual stranger in his own home, a self-righteous cad who positively chafed against his familial role. Despite having lived through periods of serious marital discord—or perhaps precisely on that account—here was an author who brought an exquisite sensitivity to his portrayal of the posturing and jousting that had become the marital routine. With his last complete novel, in other words, Natsume Sōseki constructed an arena for a contest of wills, played out through accusations, counteraccusations, and reservoirs of hurt feelings, spite, and rancor. Yet there is the occasional truce, the healing moments when defenses are relaxed and the couple express conciliatory words and signs of affection.[48]

In sum, Sōseki has created an utterly convincing psychological portrayal, one that privileges Kenzō's point of view (more to the point, his pained interiority) but at the same time allows his wife a strong and confident voice and an unhindered view of her husband's peccadilloes. Whether this is an "unhappy marriage" or a "dysfunctional marriage" and precisely how it accords with the author's "real" marriage—I will not pretend that there is a definitive answer. But my understanding of the contemporary society—its institutions, its norms, and the wealth of literary evidence produced by Sōseki's contemporaries—leads me to believe that it was not at all aberrant. Meiji marriage was not expected to be a romantic idyll; rather, husbands and wives (with the latter bearing the primary responsibility) were expected to make a home and raise their children. Divorce occurred, to be sure. But one was expected to make the best of things. Sōseki and his wife would remain together, in spite of all the nastiness. As for Kenzō and his wife—we cannot know how their story ends. But with it, the author had brilliantly succeeded in constructing a Meiji household as a microcosm of Japanese modernity, where self-absorption and pride intersected, day in and day out, with the need to live together in some semblance of harmony.

CHAPTER 5

Inside Glass Doors

The Writer at His Desk

Natsume Sōseki made a living writing about unexceptional individuals and their social relationships. Reminiscent of European novelistic depictions of bourgeois society and circumstance, Sōseki's fictional works—specifically, the novels beginning with *Sorekara* (1909)—both mirrored and challenged the *katei* paradigm of family-centered domesticity that developed late in the nineteenth century. With his very first novel, *Neko,* the author erects an elaborate edifice of domestic routine, centering on the master of the Kushami household, who is subject to the relentless send-ups of the omniscient (yet contentedly housebroken) feline narrator.[1]

As literary representations of this tangled intersection of self and other, personal needs and social obligation, Sōseki's characters reflect late-Meiji social norms and gender relations and the new *katei*-centered morality associated with family harmony and the promotion of virtuous conduct.[2] For their part, the *shōhin* writings present a more eclectic mix of personal musing and reminiscence. In these literary intermezzi that punctuate the line of serialized novels, the ironic spirit of *Neko* would be only one voice in the author's narrative repertoire.[3] As evidenced by the episodes in chapter 4, the Natsume household provides a backdrop for the ebb and flow of confrontation and accommodation, drama and drudgery. The quizzical head of the house has established a modus vivendi with his family, whose comings and goings he observes with a mix of bemusement, pique, and sympathetic concern.

The Writer, the Desk, the World

Natsume Sōseki was in a sense a typical *yamanote* householder—a relatively well-heeled breadwinner, husband, and father to his children.[4] As a literary journalist employed by a daily newspaper, he spent much of his time at home, working in his study—the *shosai,* one's private enclave within the Meiji domicile. Among the family spaces that might offer a measure of privacy, the study was both a workplace—containing desk, books, and writing implements—and a sanctuary for its occupant. The tools of one's trade, the material appurtenances of the writer's life—these would occasionally appear as *shōhin* subjects.[5] As for the wife and children—together with the family pets, they are a potential nuisance for the busy writer and are largely ignored in the personal writings. Their cameo appearances, though, would remind the reader that the author did in fact share his home with others. But the dominant *shōhin* persona is that of the slightly peevish intellectual seated in his study, giving free rein to his musings, misgivings, and memories.[6] This voice is established at the very outset of *Garasudo no uchi:*

INSIDE MY GLASS DOORS

As I look out from inside my glass doors, certain things catch my eye—the banana plant sheltered from the frost, the holly branch with its red berries, the brazenly perpendicular utility poles. Little else enters my field of vision. The world that I see from my study is remarkably monotonous and confined.

What is more, I've had a severe cold since the end of the year and have hardly gone out. I spend my days inside these glass doors, seated at this desk, and so I have no idea what is going on in the world. Since I haven't been feeling well, I've done very little reading. I spend my time sitting and sleeping. This is all I do.

From time to time, though, my mind is active and my mood changes as well. Events occur—small events, to be sure, in keeping with the narrow confines of my world. And on occasion, someone enters through these glass doors, which mark the border separating the great world outside from my own small self—some unexpected visitor, who will have unexpected things to say and do. I've actually been known to express interest in the comings and goings of such individuals.

I'd like to continue writing in this vein. But I'm painfully aware how trifling this will appear in the eyes of those occupied with weightier affairs. It embarrasses me to take up valuable space with my idle jottings and attempt to foist these upon busy readers heading to work on the city's trolleys, entirely absorbed by the headline news. For such people, a newspaper must either cover the momentous events of the day or else provide material with sufficient shock value to jolt the nervous system—crime, murder, and mayhem. Why purchase a newspaper otherwise? . . .

Last year a great war broke out in Europe, and there is no end in sight. This nation has become involved in the war, a decision that led to the dissolution of the Diet. The upcoming general elections present major problems for our politicians. Rice has fallen dramatically in the marketplace, and the rice growers are feeling the pinch. Everyone is talking about the current economic slump. And in the midst of all this, the New Year's Grand Sumo tournament is about to begin.

There is so much going on these days. Why in the world should someone like me, who spends his time sitting at a desk inside glass doors, presume to take up valuable space in the newspaper? Should I really wish to compete with our politicians, military people, businessmen, and sumo fans? This is not exactly my forte. But the fact remains that I've been asked to come up with something new for the New Year. And so here it is—a series of trivial accounts of no interest to anyone but myself. How long this will go on is anyone's guess.[7] (*Garasudo* 1, 1915)

Embarking on this new *shōhin* serialization following completion of *Kokoro,* Sōseki situates the narrator within his private space, looking out through glass doors. The world is at war; political and economic developments are front-page news. In the midst of great and momentous events, the author will sit at his desk and reflect upon whatever happens to come to mind. Affairs of state, public events and institutions—these will not be allowed to intrude, however trivial and inconsequential the substance of one's reflections may prove to be. Of course, these literary ephemera, having been commissioned by the *Asahi,* would indeed be intended to rival the "great events" reportage for the reader's attention.

What is established at the outset—and the connection with the *Eijitsu* series is evident—is the ironic, self-deprecatory persona. The world is large, and I am small. I will purvey my "small talk," but why should anyone want to read it? Yet it is precisely one's position inside this private space (and within the *Asahi* inner circle) that engenders the free-ranging excursions and their universe of possibility. The ironic self-deprecation notwithstanding, Sōseki's *shōhin* (especially *Garasudo*) amount to a *shosai monogatari*—tales told from one's study, where the line separating the writer and the site of writing is all but erased. In other words, the *shosai*—this "room of one's own"—is a physical correlative to the interiority that would be a criterion of modern literary discourse in the Meiji and beyond.

Yet this is only a single room in a house with many rooms. And the glass doors, which invite both outward gaze and inner reflection, function as a semipermeable membrane of sorts, a symbol of the literary osmosis that the *shōhin* manifest.

The Lifestyle of a Professional Writer

It was in April of 1907 when Natsume Sōseki abandoned his academic career to become a *bunshi*—a professional writer. He joined the staff of the *Tokyo Asahi shinbun* and was under contract to write a novel a year in daily serialization.[8] Working at home, he would turn out his daily installments for nearly a decade, virtually until the day he died. The novels made him famous, if not wealthy, and the media, which had a vested interest in showcasing name writers, provided outlets for their remarks on one another and on themselves as well. As noted in the Introduction, the public would get to know—after a fashion—how famous writers lived and what sort of people they were.

The following transcribed interview, part of a 1914 newspaper series on *bunshi no seikatsu* (writers' lifestyles), was intended both to satisfy readers' curiosity and to promote it:

FIGURE 5. Sōseki in his study. Photograph taken in December 1914, shortly before he embarked on his *Garasudo* serialization. (Iwanami shoten)

A WRITER'S LIFE

There are rumors circulating to the effect that I've amassed a great fortune, built a luxurious home, and that I'm getting rich on real estate transactions. Well, they're all totally groundless! If I were rolling in money, how could I stand living in such a rundown house? As for real estate dealings—I haven't the faintest idea how property is bought and sold. I don't even own this place—it's rented. All this gossip is just irresponsible. . . .

Frankly, I'd rather be in a position not to have to write books for a living. When one's aim is to sell things, greed inevitably emerges as a motive—you crave popularity and notoriety. One's personal integrity is tarnished, and the quality of one's work tends to suffer as a result. The ideal situation would be to publish at one's own expense and then give the books away to those who really wanted them. Unfortunately, I can't afford to do this.

As for creature comforts—it's not as though I have no desire to live well. I'm not against nice clothes, fine dining, and having a lovely home. It's simply beyond my reach, you see. And so I make do with accommodations such as these.

I will admit to having a taste for fine clothing. That said, I have no interest in pursuing the current fashions. The stylish look wouldn't quite do for someone my age, and so I consent to wear whatever my wife chooses. Then again, I do enjoy seeing women dressed in elegant kimono.

As for food, I prefer rich and robust dishes to the lighter, plainer fare. Japanese food doesn't particularly appeal to me. I do enjoy Chinese and Western cuisine, although my palate isn't so refined that I have to insist, like a finicky gourmet, on such and such a dish at this or that restaurant. I have rather crude tastes in food, actually—something thick and heavy will often suit me just fine.

I'm not much of a drinker. One cup of sake is about all I can handle. On the other hand, I have a taste for sweets. If some happen to be around, I'll indulge myself. But I don't make a point of having them always available.

I'm a smoker.[9] I did give it up once, but not having felt any particular pride in kicking the habit, I started up again. When my tongue feels irritated or my stomach troubles me from excess smoking, I'll stop—but only until the symptoms go away. I'll only smoke Asahi brand cigarettes at home. I'm not sure how much they cost. I think they're on the inexpensive side, but my wife buys them for me, so these are what I smoke. . . .

I'm as interested in houses as anyone else, I suppose. The other day, in fact, on my way back from browsing in the Azabu curio shops, I compared the various properties along the way. For each one that caught my eye, I assigned a score. It's not my ultimate purpose in life to own the house of my dreams. If money were no object, I'd be happy to indulge myself. But since there's no hope of this happening in the near future, I've made no plans of any sort.

Our house has seven rooms.[10] Two of these are for my own use—which makes it quite small, given that we have six children. The monthly rental is thirty-five yen. My landlord would want me to say forty yen, to bring it more in line with the going market rate. But I see no need to misrepresent the facts, and so I've given you the true figure. I'm afraid this won't sit well with him.

The property is relatively spacious—three hundred *tsubo*—large enough for a fair-sized garden.[11] And since I've put in all the plants myself, a rental of thirty-five or forty yen for a house with such a garden is quite a bargain. Then again, gardeners have a mind of their own. Once you set them to work, they do things their own way. They'll bring in extra help without consulting you, then endlessly monkey around with this and that. I keep my mouth shut, though, not being one to put a halt to this sort of thing. But it ends up costing me plenty.

I'd actually prefer a house with more light. Again, I wouldn't mind living in a nicer place. The walls in my study are falling apart. The roof leaks, and the ceilings are water-stained and filthy. Since this doesn't particularly bother us, though, we leave things as they are. But the fact remains that the wind comes in through the bare wooden flooring of my study. Winters can be quite unbearable. Exposure to sunlight is poor. It's not easy to sit here and do my work. But if I let such things bother me, there's no end to it. So I put up with it. Someone came by the other day offering to repaper the ceiling, but I begged off. It's not that I prefer living in such a dark and dingy environment. Rather, I'm a victim of circumstances.

I have no particular penchant for leisurely pursuits. I don't play billiards; I know next to nothing about Go or *shōgi*.[12] As for theater—I take in the occasional play, but not a single one has inspired much admiration. I'm afraid it's the same with music. I've yet to hear any Western music that arouses the pleasure I derive from a fine work of art. As for Japanese music—it bores me terribly. But I do practice Noh chanting *(yōkyoku, utai)*. I've studied with Hōshō Shin for six or seven years. Recently, though, I've slacked off and haven't been making much progress. I don't approach *yōkyoku* as high art. My moaning and groaning are as much a form of calisthenics as anything else.

Actually, it's only in the area of painting and calligraphy that I've developed any sense of confidence. My accomplishments are quite modest, but I'm discerning enough to respond to a fine work with the respect it deserves. I produce calligraphy for people who request it. Having had no special training, though, I don't adhere to any conventional style or school. I do things my own way, even if it means making a fool of myself.

I enjoy curios and antiques, but my financial situation doesn't allow me to get carried away. I collect only things that fit within my budget. Questions of provenance—who produced the object, where it's from, what the market value might be—I'm absolutely indifferent to such concerns. If it's something I didn't like, I wouldn't touch it, no matter *how* valuable it might be.[13]

There is the old saying about the "well-lit study and spotless desk."[14] This expresses my taste. I treasure serenity and tranquility. My wish is to live the simple, carefree life. Brightness and warmth—these are good things. By nature, you see, I tend to be hypersensitive. It troubles me that I can get carried away in almost any situation. Yet I can be terribly insensitive as well. I doubt that this stems from any strong-willed self control on my part. Rather, it would appear that there's been a serious deadening of the nerves.

I have strong likes and dislikes. There are things in my possession that I'm fond of and things I'm repulsed by. As for people, I'll decide whether to like or dislike someone depending on one's speech mannerisms, attitudes, habits, and opinions....

I get up at seven in the morning and normally get to bed around eleven at night. After lunch, I take an hour's nap, which refreshes the mind. By nature I'm a homebody. I don't go out very much. But I do take the occasional stroll. There are times when I'm needed to run an errand. This of course can't be helped. And I do call on people if the need arises, but never on formal occasions such as New Year's or the Bon Festival. I see absolutely no need for this sort of thing.[15]

I have no set time for writing. Any time of day will suffice. I produce one installment of my serial fiction every day. Writing any more than this simply won't do. Sitting for long stretches and producing a greater volume of work is not my style. When I finish the daily quota, I put down my pen and give my head a rest until the next day. This practice has served me well over the years.

The typical installment takes me about three or four hours to complete. But there are times when I work all day on a given episode and can't finish it. If I don't feel particularly pressed for time, I'll work longer hours; if I'm under some constraint, I'll complete the installment in the time available to me.

I'd prefer to write in a room with *shōji* screens that receive ample sunlight. Unfortunately, there's no such room in this house. So what I do is bring my desk out onto the veranda and set to work, while basking in the sun.[16] If it gets too hot, I'll put on a straw hat. By and large I work much better in bright surroundings.[17]

Sōseki is responding here to questions posed by the interviewer, who adheres to a set format for the *bunshi no seikatsu* interview series. This comprised six separate categories—income, food-shelter-clothing, hobbies and interests, likes and dislikes, domestic routine, and writing habits. The writers interviewed for this series, published in the Osaka edition of the *Asahi,* complied with the journalistic aim of situating the *bundan* elite firmly within the domestic sphere.[18] The focus is upon the writer himself; marriage and family matters are not broached. Be that as it may, Sōseki's remarks are rather perfunctory—an artifact, perhaps, of the questionnaire format that sought concise answers to straightforward questions.

Interestingly, the interviewer for the *bunshi no seikatsu* piece paid another visit, in October 1915, for an article dealing with current happenings in the *bundan.* With a nice flair for irony, he prefaces the published *danwa* by setting the scene: It was a rainy morning, he notes. As always, the Natsume entry gate was locked. But he managed to get in through the side gate and went over to the doorway. It's entirely covered with ivy. He tries to open it, but to no avail. He then looks for the doorbell, but this, too, is concealed in the ivy thicket—purposely, perhaps, as though the master of the house might fear its discovery. Everything points to someone who wishes to keep visitors at bay. This is the same person, he observes wryly, who in the *bunshi no seikatsu* interview had proudly proclaimed his minimalist credo. He continues:

Finally the maid appeared, as I watched the rainwater rush through the corroded gutter spout. She took my calling card without opening the door. I was at long last permitted to enter the house, and proceeded to remove my coat next to a washtub filled with rags—could it be that rain had been leaking onto the tatami? Finally, I was shown into the study.[19]

An earlier interview, which likewise points to the *danwa* interviewer as comic sideman in what seems a variant of the popular *yose* entertainments, appeared in April 1910, in connection with a book project on prominent figures and their connection with Zen. The *danwa* begins as follows:

Whatever one reads by Mr. Natsume—it all possesses a certain Zen flavor. This was the reason for my visit to the esteemed writer of fiction and scholar of English literature at his home in Waseda, Minami-chō.

Upon my arrival, I'm ushered into the living room and told to wait. By and by, in comes the author. "Sorry, but you woke me up. I'm still tired. What do you want with me?" Rustling rain-speckled fronds of the banana plants—Mr. Natsume's eyelids are indeed tinged with slumber.

"I do apologize. Actually, I'd like your thoughts on Zen and literature." "What in the world do I know about Zen?! You must be mistaken. Look, would you let me at least wash my face. I'll be back in a minute."

So I waited. Thirty minutes. An hour. Is this going to take him all day? Exasperated, I crossed my legs and continued to wait. The sun felt good, and I myself started to feel drowsy. I tried to stay awake but ended up dozing off. Then I hear a shouting voice: "What's that smell? Hey, what's going on here?!" Mr. Natsume had returned at long last, and he was greeted by the spectacle of yours truly, slumped over, my hair having caught on fire by the *hibachi!*[20]

Studies and the Still Life

Through this journalistic dialogue—by turns facetious and serious—the reader is afforded a variety of personal glimpses. Amidst the litany of domestic detail in *A Writer's Life,* one may detect a note of irony in the remark "I treasure serenity and tranquility. My wish is to live the simple, carefree life"— which is revisited to comic effect in the subsequent interview. Yet the notion of a spiritual corrective to the hectic pace of life and the relentless materialism and commercialism was a prevalent sentiment during this period. In fact it would be echoed by Nagai Kafū, in his own *bunshi no seikatsu* remarks.[21]

Kafū, clearly a kindred spirit, comments that "like Sōseki, I believe in cultivating one's enclosed, private universe. I don't like going out in the world, loaded with ambition, running all over in a dither. I want nothing to do with formal meetings. In particular, I have no interest in taking charge of things. Living quietly in a small space—that's for me." Both espoused an ethic that challenged the rampant careerism and routinization of their age. And both remained on guard against the predatory inroads of literary journalism. Of the two, Sōseki was the more measured in his attitude—understandably so, given that he himself was a professional journalist on the company payroll.[22]

The photograph of Natsume Sōseki seated alone in his book-strewn *shosai* is an iconic representation of the man and, by extension, the entire *bunshi* class. This and similar images—together with endless references to the *shosai,* the writerly life, the world of books and manuscripts and solitary endeavor— suggest a reclusive existence and a miserly, misanthropic spirit. But the figure of writer encamped among books is at once iconic and cleverly ironic—a still life of the still life, whose very stillness belies the invisible dynamism of the writer's mind.

As for Sōseki—here was a recluse who would prove to be, in his own way, a surprisingly social animal. Just as he had written of Thomas Carlyle's private lair, on the top floor of the London flat-turned-museum, those in Sōseki's own circle would write about Sensei encamped in his *shosai,* and how centrally this space figured in their memory of the man.[23]

From an economic perspective, the private study in a home of one's own was a desideratum of those who made a living—be it as writers or bankers. Affordability was an issue. While the *shosai* serves as a metonym for the writer and the larger *bundan* collectivity, it is also an index of social class and a status symbol, embodying Bourdieu's notion of cultural capital. One would naturally want to collect books (among other material objects), and the well-stocked library would enhance one's stature, in a crudely materialist sense. And impressive collections were indeed amassed. In Sōseki's case, however, acquisitiveness did not reach any grotesque proportion. It may be that the credo of minimalism—if we are to take the author at his word—curbed his appetite. But one suspects that money was the chief constraint.

One object of curiosity, if not obsession, was the humble pen, the worka-day tool of the writer's trade. It is featured in the following essay, a stylishly droll study in literary personification:

ON FOUNTAIN PENS

I was speaking with Uchida Roan the other day on the subject of fountain pens.[24] Roan mentioned, in the course of our discussion, that Maruzen sells around a hundred of them on a good day.... In view of the fact that so many of these remarkably durable items are selling at Maruzen, one could conclude that the demand for fountain pens must be witnessing a robust expansion. One noteworthy segment of the expanding market consists of hobbyists and collectors. They will purchase a pen, use it for a while, then feel compelled to have a different one, which in turn they'll tire of and crave some new brand or style. Consider the pipe fancier, a common breed in the West, who will proudly display his collection—pipes large and small, in all sizes and shapes—neatly arranged on one's mantelpiece. He is driven by the same mania for collecting that afflicts those with a passion, say, for sake cups, decorative gourds, or —fountain pens.[25] They all place great store in the special power, lost upon the uninitiated, to detect and appreciate fine gradations of difference among objects that appear virtually identical to the casual observer....

It was only several years ago, however, that I made up my mind to try out a fountain pen—never having actually *used* one before. The reason for my decision escapes me, but I suspect that the motive had to do with ease of use and practicality. Be that as it may, I went to the Maruzen store and returned with two Pelican pens.[26] I've used them since then, despite the regrettable fact that their performance has left much to be desired. My Pelicans have in fact behaved very badly. They would stubbornly refuse to release the ink when this was what I required of them, and then they'd leak all over my manuscript paper at the most inopportune times.

Perhaps their owner should shoulder some of the blame, however, for failing to provide sufficient care and maintenance. I'm a slothful type, by nature, and when a fresh ink supply is needed, I'll think nothing of filling the Pelican's belly with any ink that happens to be within arm's reach. Then there's my instinctive dislike of blue-black ink, which requires that I go out and purchase the sepia-tone ink that I've come to favor.

Truth be told, I never did understand how properly to care for fountain pens. Even when the mechanism would clog and the ink flow would be especially bad, I never once cleaned or washed the pen. Eventually we reached a standoff—the Pelicans gave up on me, and I gave up on them. And so it was that when I embarked, at New Year's time, on my new serialized novel,[27] I opted to turn back the clock and revert to my old habit of dipping pen nibs into inkwells. But like the divorcé who ultimately longs for his estranged wife, I felt a lingering attachment to the abandoned Pelicans. The older pens seemed such a nuisance—how could I bear having to dip the pen in ink, again and again and again? For various reasons, though, I set out to complete my novel using the old pen. My resolve seems to have been rooted in a certain unwillingness to admit defeat....

As a matter of fact, I am writing this very essay with a new fountain pen—an Onoto, which Roan was kind enough to give me.[28] I must say that it's a pleasure to use, in every respect. And so it is that I have gone from renouncing the Pelicans to taking in a close relative, so to speak—a gesture of penance, I should add, toward the larger family of fountain pens.[29]

This essay, requested by Sōseki's friend and *bundan* confrere Uchida Roan, was published by Maruzen in a catalogue produced in conjunction with an exhibit of fountain pens at their Nihonbashi store.[30] Although easily dismissed as little more than a stylish publicity piece for Maruzen's wares, the essay bears the signature of Sōseki's *shōhin* style. Note the ironic self-deprecation, which harkens back to its roots in *Bicycle Diary*—the narrator as creature of habit, out of touch with the times, and challenged by even the simplest of mechanical devices; and the comic pose of indolence and negligence, which results in the nasty clogging of the pen's chief artery. Yet Sōseki does conclude his essay with an undisguised plug for the Onoto pen *and* a strategic mention of his recent book—both of which would be available for purchase at the Maruzen store.

The Writer Besieged: Schemers, Crooks, and Supplicants

Sōseki's home was by no means a monastic retreat. People visited, regularly. Some were familiar faces—colleagues, protégés, and acquaintances. Others were strangers. Some sought out the author's advice on matters both literary and personal; others, representing this or that periodical, came by to solicit a manuscript, an interview—even a casual remark that could find its way into print. As the *shōhin* record attests, several were crackpots, who would appear at his doorstep or—in one memorable instance—by epistolary proxy, in his mailbox. And there were those who, lacking *bundan* credentials and with no literary pretense whatsoever, came to rob the place. Hence it is only natural that an indignant sense of one's victimization by an uncaring, unfeeling world should emerge as a refrain in Sōseki's writing—the personal narratives as well as the novels.[31]

Shōhin accounts of the comings and goings of visitors—from friend to foe—provide a useful perspective on the intersecting social circles of this *bundan* notable, while revealing how he tried to negotiate the many demands made upon him.

Unwanted Solicitations

Sōseki's cloistered persona gave rise to contrasting narratives of serenity and repose, at one extreme, and paranoid anxiety, at the other. The *Garasudo* collection includes several noteworthy examples, each with a wry comic touch, of the workaday author as hapless victim of predatory journalists and intrusive, impertinent readers.

THE EXTORTED SMILE
I received a telephone call the other day from the office of a certain magazine.[32] They wanted to come by and take some photographs of me. I told the caller that I wasn't interested in being photographed. I'd never

had any dealings with this particular periodical, but I did recall having thumbed through an issue or two in recent years. What struck me was the sheer quantity of photographs of people with smiling faces. The forced quality of these smiles was truly repulsive. Hence my refusal of the telephone solicitation.

The caller persisted, though, explaining that the magazine was planning a special feature for its upcoming New Year's issue.[33] Nineteen-fifteen being the Year of the Rabbit, they wanted to run a photo-montage of individuals who were born under this sign. This was indeed my sign.

"Isn't it the case that the individuals you feature are made to smile when they're photographed?"

"No, not at all!"

It was as though my earlier impression had simply been mistaken.

"Well, then, I'll agree to being photographed—but only on the condition that you will be satisfied with a normal, unsmiling pose."

"Yes, that will be fine."

With that understanding we arranged an appointment, and the conversation ended.

Several days later, the person arrived at the appointed hour, dressed in a handsome suit and carrying his camera equipment. He was shown into the study, and we spoke for a while about his magazine. He then proceeded to take two photographs. For one, I was seated at my desk. For the other, I was standing outside in the cold, frost-covered garden.

The poor lighting inside the study necessitated the use of a magnesium flash device. Just before setting off the flash, the fellow emerged from behind his camera.

"I realize our agreement," he said, "but mightn't I prevail upon you to smile—just slightly?" There was a comic aspect to all of this, together with a sense that the man was behaving like a fool.

"No, this is the way I'd like it," I responded, ignoring his request.

We then went out to the garden, where the fellow had me pose in front of the small stand of trees. Adjusting the camera lens, he repeated the same request, in the same deferential tone of voice: "I realize our agreement, but..."

If anything, I was even less inclined than before to break into a smile.

Several days later, the two photographs arrived by mail. Lo and behold—there I was wearing the very smile that had been requested of me! I stared at the smiling faces, like someone whose expectations had been foiled. No doubt they'd managed to manipulate them in order to produce the desired effect. Just to make sure, I showed the photos to four or five people who called at the house. They were unanimous in concluding that the smiles appeared artificially contrived.

There have been numerous occasions when I've conjured up a smile for people despite my reluctance to do so. I have the magazine photographer to thank for repaying me for my pretense. Then again, while he did send me the photos with those ghastly, repulsive smiles, I've yet to receive a copy of the magazine that featured them![34] (*Garasudo* 2, 1915)

Pointing to the unseemly realities of *kindai* literary journalism, Sōseki's "victim" accounts carry a distinctive ironic signature that harks back to the comic universe of Kushami sensei in *I Am a Cat*.[35] No stranger to deception and dissimulation, the passively acquiescent *shōhin* narrator, wishing only to be left alone, is an easy target for the little schemes perpetrated by unscrupulous journalists who come calling. And the calls, as the first line attests, could come via the telephone—a relatively recent vehicle of intrusion into one's private domicile.[36]

Seen from the larger perspective of *kindai* media culture, this episode calls attention to the manner in which writers could be drawn into the popular media, only to be subject to the editorial agenda of the periodical in question and to bait-and-switch methods of achieving the desired end.[37]

In another *Garasudo* episode, the easily gulled author confesses to a similar incidence of "extortion" in the context of his remarks on patronizing kabuki theater.[38] Claiming ignorance of its arcane conventions and styles (and evidently not a great patron of the art), the narrator lets on that he is easily brought to tears in scenes involving a child actor who exudes pathos in the requisite high-pitched voice. "It's so exasperating when I find myself fooled into crying." And when an acquaintance more knowledgeable about kabuki than he attempts to change his thinking on this score, he will hear nothing of it. One's sensitivity to being taken advantage of remains unassailable.

One final *Garasudo* episode is a rather more elaborate account of victimization—in this instance, instigated by a total stranger.

IWASAKI

People ask me to write poems for them. Some will go so far as to send me the *tanzaku* paper on which I'm to inscribe the verse, without first taking the trouble of getting my consent. I used to think it rather callous of me to disregard a legitimate request, and so I'd dutifully write out something appropriate, notwithstanding my mediocre skills. One's goodwill, however, can last only so long. I now find myself routinely refusing most solicitations of this sort.

I've often thought that humans are put on this earth in order to experience humiliation on a daily basis. Why, then, should I shrink from the prospect of sending off a mere scrap of poor calligraphy? However, if one happens to be ill, or occupied with work, or simply in no mood to engage in such foolishness, a succession of poem requests is simply too much to take. After all, these typically come from people I don't know—people, moreover, who appear indifferent to the trouble it takes to send off the inscribed *tanzaku* strips.

My most unpleasant encounter in this regard was with a fellow named Iwasaki, from Hyōgo Prefecture. Several years ago, he started sending me postcards requesting haiku poems on this or that theme. I complied with each request. Some time passed, and I received a parcel in the mail—a thin, squarish package from Iwasaki. Not wanting even to bother opening it up, I tossed the package into my study, where it ended up sandwiched between some books when the maid came in to clean. I was thus spared having to deal with the nuisance.

About this time, a canister of tea arrived in the mail from Nagoya. No indication of who sent it, or why—just a canister of tea from an anonymous donor, which I proceeded to consume without any further scruples. Shortly thereafter, I received a note from Iwasaki, asking me to return the picture of Mt. Fuji. *What* picture of Mt. Fuji? I hadn't received any picture from him, and so I paid no heed to his bizarre request.

Then three or four letters from Iwasaki arrived in quick succession, insisting that I return the Fuji picture. I found myself questioning the man's sanity. Concluding that he was indeed out of his mind, I decided simply to ignore his repeated demands.

Several months passed. As I recall, it was early summer. I was in my study one day, feeling depressed at having to sit amidst the clutter and disarray. And so I set about putting some of my things in order. Going through a random pile of reference works, I chanced upon the forgotten package from Iwasaki. I opened it and was even more surprised to find inside a neatly folded picture of Mt. Fuji! The package also contained a letter requesting that I produce a suitable inscription for the picture. It further mentioned that a canister of tea was being sent as a token of appreciation.

My frame of mind was not at all conducive to inscribing a picture of Mt. Fuji. I was preoccupied with other things, and it would take too much trouble to come up with an appropriate haiku. However, I did regret my clumsy handling of the situation, and so I wrote a letter apologizing for my negligence and expressing thanks for the tea. This I enclosed in a small package together with the uninscribed picture.[39]

Figuring that this would put an end to the Iwasaki affair, I promptly put him out of my mind. And then lo and behold! Another *tanzaku* arrives from the man. This time he wants a poem concerning the Loyal Retainers.[40] I sent word that he could expect something in the near future, but the opportunity failed to present itself and so the haiku never got written.

I should have realized that this fellow was not about to let the matter remain unresolved. He went to absurd lengths to demand his poem. Every week or so, a postcard would arrive—it was invariably a postcard. And each one bore the same prefatory phrasing: "Dear sir, I regret having to bring this to your attention, but..."

I became increasingly upset as the Iwasaki postcards kept arriving, one after another. What is more, they began to take on a nasty tone. At first he reminds me that he *did* send the tea canister. Then, when I fail to respond, he sends a card insisting that I send back the tea. I was tempted to write back and suggest that if he wanted the tea so badly, he could come to Tokyo and get it himself! But I abandoned the idea, out of concern for how this might reflect upon me. And so having received no response from me, Iwasaki becomes even more insistent. "It makes no difference to me if you refuse to return the tea," he writes, "but I must ask you to pay me one yen by way of recompense."

I was quickly growing to despise the man. In the end, I simply lost control of myself and sent him the following note: "Sir: I drank your tea and I lost your *tanzaku* paper. Kindly stop sending me any more postcards!" I felt disgusted at the turn that this affair had taken. Here I am being forced into a position of resorting to very unbecoming behavior. How terribly degrading. And it's all on account of this Iwasaki.

But the man remained entirely unfazed. He sends yet another postcard: "Dear sir: I regret having to bring this to your attention," it begins, followed by an expression of displeasure over my letter. I resolved then and there to have nothing more to do with Iwasaki, although such a decision would have no bearing on his behavior. And in due course, more postcards arrived. "How about this," he proposed. "If you'll compose a poem—say, on the Loyal Retainers—I'll send you another tea canister." The postcards stopped coming. And then he started sending letters. For these he would use only the cheapest available envelope—the greyish sort they use in the local government offices—and he would purposely not attach a stamp.

That's not all. He would post the letters without a return address, which meant that I ended up having to pay *twice* the postage. Finally, I gave the mailman Iwasaki's name and address and asked that all subsequent mail be returned to the sender unopened. This appears to have had the desired effect, possibly because of the extra postal charge that *he* would now be incurring.

But the story does not end here. About two months later, toward year's end, I received a greeting card from Iwasaki. A standard season's greeting, with no threats or demands. Impressed with the turn he had evidently taken, I was moved to compose a haiku and send it to him inscribed on a *tanzaku*. Unfortunately, this was not quite enough to satisfy the man, who sent a letter complaining that the poem card had arrived in an unacceptable condition—bent, or soiled, or something of the sort—and that I should kindly send a replacement. And then, to top it off, about a week into the New Year another letter arrives: "Dear sir," it began, true to form, "I regret having to bring this to your attention, but…"

Never in my life have I had to deal with anyone like this.[41] (*Garasudo* 12–13, 1915)

This comedy of epistolary victimization plays on the figure of Iwasaki as stock oddball—a true *kijin,* who remains impervious to reason and good sense.[42] To this is added the comic self-portrayal of the cloistered writer, living absentmindedly amidst the clutter and confusion of his study, who endures, and ultimately complies with, the bizarre importunings of some crackpot from the provinces.

His pride having been wounded by this little encounter, the writer vents his righteous indignation—a victim's entitlement, after all. But compared to the source account for this episode—a *danwa* interview published in April 1914—the portrayal of Iwasaki is decidedly toned down. In his remarks to Morita Sōhei, who conducted the interview, Sōseki made a point of castigating the man for being outrageously stingy, observing that "only an *eta* or a Jew could be so cheap."[43]

That Sōseki would vent his spleen in this manner is more a reflection of prevailing stereotypes, I would argue, than any sinister anti-Semitic impulse on the author's part. Shakespeare's Shylock, after all, served as a familiar caricature, during the Meiji and beyond, for the stock skinflint figure.[44] In this connection, we should also keep in mind the frequency with which the author, beginning with *Neko* and in a number of the subsequent *shōhin,* pokes fun at his own miserliness.[45]

Thieves

Burglary played as much a role in the Japan of Sōseki's day as in any society where individuals live in private homes and accumulate wealth and property. Breaking and entering in Meiji-era Tokyo was evidently quite common, although data are not easy to come by. Within the framework of the modernizing nation-state, Meiji criminal codes went through a series of changes, an index of the increasing sophistication of Japanese legal institutions. And as Meiji society evolved, so did the very notion of crime and the treatment of offenders. Yet studies of crime in Japan have tended to focus on the more notorious criminals, ghoulish murder cases, and the exploits of the famous *yakuza* crime syndicate. Petty theft has not garnered much attention.[46]

Be that as it may, Sōseki incorporates burglary episodes, and encounters with detectives and police, in a number of his works. For instance, *Koto no sorane* (Hearing Things, 1905), an early fictional work, mentions the local neighborhood as "crawling with burglars," a situation that has the police on their toes. And *Mon* (The Gate, 1910) features an extensive account of a robbery at the home of Sōsuke's neighbor, the Sakais.[47]

Setting aside the question of fictionalized episodes as reliable indicators of prevailing social conditions, let us turn to several *shōhin* accounts of robberies and their aftermath. The first is from the *Eijitsu* collection:

THE BURGLAR

It was late one night—past eleven o'clock. On my way back from the toilet before going to sleep, I detected a strong odor coming from the *kotatsu* heater in the adjoining room. I mentioned this to my wife, cautioning her not to use so much fuel, and returned to my room. I fell sound asleep, lapsing into peaceful dreams....

All of a sudden, I was awoken by a woman's cries. It was our maid, who has been known to burst into tears whenever surprised or flustered.... I was sure that the hysterics were coming from the room adjacent to my wife's. Just then, a reddish light shone through the paper-covered *fusuma* into my dark study. No sooner did the light strike my eyes than I assumed the house was on fire. I jumped out of bed and threw open the *fusuma* partition, fully expecting to see the *kotatsu* heater overturned and a futon on fire. I'd imagined billowing smoke, burning *tatami*. But what greeted my eyes instead was the room lamp, glowing normally, and my sleeping wife and children. The heater was exactly where it belonged. Everything was as it was when I'd gone to sleep—the only difference being that our maid was crying.

The maid had gone over to my sleeping wife and was pressing down on her futon and talking excitedly. My wife awoke and started batting her eyes, but she showed no signs of getting up. I was standing bolt upright at the threshold, absentmindedly surveying the scene, and at a loss to understand what was going on. From the maid's frantic account, one word stood out—burglar (*dorobō*). As soon as I heard the word, I strode through my wife's room, as though the mystery had been solved, and rushed into the adjoining room.

"What's all this about?" I hollered.

The room was pitch dark, but something was wrong here. Lovely shafts of moonlight were shining onto the floor. I noticed that one of the shutters in the adjacent kitchen had gotten out of place, allowing the moonlight to penetrate through to the interior of the house. The scene sent a chill through my body. In my bare feet I went out onto the wooden floor of the kitchen and over to the sink. Not a sound could be heard. I looked out the window. Only the moon was visible. I was not about to set foot outside.

I returned to my wife's room and reassured her that the burglar had gotten away and that nothing was likely to have been stolen. At long last she got up. Without saying a word, she went into the darkened room, carrying the lamp, and shone it onto the dresser. Its hinged doors had been removed, and the drawers were pulled out.

"We *have* been robbed!" she exclaimed, looking me full in the face. Indeed, it did appear that the burglar had made off with some of her clothing. It was all quite absurd. The room belonging to the maid contained a second dresser, next to her futon, on top of which was a small chest of drawers. One of those drawers happened to contain a good deal of money, to be used for paying the year-end doctor's bills and such. I asked my wife to check, and the money was still there. It may be that the maid's running in from the veranda had caused the burglar to make a premature getaway.

In the meantime, the children, who had slept through much of the hullabaloo, were now up and about, chattering away. Several of them regretted having missed all the excitement. One said she had to go pee just a little earlier; one said she couldn't get to sleep and was actually wide awake until two in the morning. Then our eldest daughter, Fudeko, who is going on ten, chimed in: "Well, *I* knew all along that a burglar had broken in. I heard him walking along the veranda, making creaking sounds on the floorboards."

"You *what!* Are you serious?" exclaimed my niece Ofusa, who was sharing the room with Fudeko.

I got back into my bed and went to sleep.

Because of that night's commotion, I woke up somewhat later than usual. I washed up and went in to have breakfast. But the maid was making so much fuss in the kitchen, trying to locate the burglar's footprints, that

I retreated into my study. Some ten minutes later I heard someone at the entranceway, asking to be allowed inside. The voice was strong and assertive. But the maid appeared not to hear it, so I went out myself to greet the caller. It was a policeman.

"I hear you've had a burglary," he said, smiling. "Was everything locked?"

"No, I'm afraid not," I replied.

"Well, there you have it. If things aren't properly locked and secured, someone can get in with little trouble. You've got to be sure to fasten all the shutters."

"Yes sir, I understand." I felt duly chastened. It was as though the guilty party was not the burglar at all, but rather the negligent householder.

The policeman went around to the kitchen, where he took my wife aside and had her enumerate each missing item, which he carefully entered in his notebook.

"Now let's see. One *maru-obi* sash—satin—with decorative filigree. Is that right? One thing—what exactly *is* a *maru-obi?* Will they understand if I write it down like that? Maybe if I just put down "one satin obi." Fine. Now for the other items..."

The maid grinned in amusement as it became clear that the policeman knew nothing whatsoever about women's clothing. There were ten missing items in all. For each, the policeman wrote down the estimated value, then tallied the numbers.

"It comes to a total of a hundred fifty yen," he informed us, then went on his way. It was then that I realized that every single stolen item was an obi sash. We'd been robbed by an obi thief!

My wife, concerned about the impending New Year's season, looked upset. She feared that the burglary would mean the children wouldn't have enough outfits for the three-day round of festivities. This would be a pity.

That afternoon a detective stopped by the house to look for evidence. Thinking that the burglar might operate at night with the help of a candle placed inside some receptacle, he examined the various pails and buckets in the kitchen. When he was done with the inspection, I suggested that we sit down and have a cup of tea in the parlor, where it would be warm and sunny.

According to the detective, our burglar had likely come by trolley from one of the working-class areas—Shitaya or Asakusa, perhaps—and he'd have returned there early the next morning.

"I seriously doubt that they'll catch him," he added. "If they do, though, *I'll* be the one on the losing end, since I'll have to pay the trolley fare to bring him back to headquarters. And when the case goes to court, I'm the one who has to pay for meals..."

I'd always been one to believe that the police could handle anything, if it was at all within their power. Our little chat left me disheartened, and the detective himself appeared to feel the same way.

We got in touch with our handyman, wanting him to repair the locks and shutters. But as luck would have it, he had his hands full with various end-of-the-year jobs and could not oblige us. Night fell, and we had no choice but to secure the house as best we could. None of us slept very well that night. I, for one, was not in a good frame of mind, thanks to the police having insisted that the responsibility for preventing burglary rested with us.

Still, as I lay down to sleep I tried to adopt a more positive outlook. Things will be fine; after all, tomorrow is a new day. Then, in the middle of the night, my wife woke me up. She'd been hearing strange sounds coming from the kitchen. She's nervous, convinced that the burglar is back in the house, and wants me to look around. Sure enough, I heard a sort of clattering noise.

Trying not to make a sound, I got out of bed and tiptoed across my wife's room, where I heard the maid snoring in the room beyond. I opened the *fusuma* as quietly as possible and entered the pitch-dark room. I could hear something moving around. The sound is definitely coming from the kitchen. I take several steps, moving stealthily in the direction of the sound. I come to the *shōji* screen at the far side of the dark room. Beyond is the wood flooring of the corridor.

I put my ear to the *shōji* and listen intently for the sound. There it is! Something is moving around. It stops, and in a moment I hear it again. Then it stops, and again I hear it. This pattern repeated itself several more times before I ascertained that the sound was coming from inside the kitchen cupboard.

I headed back to my wife's room, assuming a more normal gait.

"It's just a mouse gnawing on something. Nothing to worry about."

"So *that's* what it was," my wife responded, in a grateful tone of voice. Our anxieties allayed, we went back to sleep.

I awoke the next morning and went into the parlor for breakfast. My wife greeted me with a seriously gnawed-upon slab of dried bonito *(katsuo bushi)*.

"*This* is what was going on last night!"

"Just as I suspected," I said, examining the mutilated slab of dried fish.

"And by the way," my wife added in a slightly peevish tone, "while you were at it, you might have thought about chasing the mouse away and putting the *katsuo bushi* in a safe place."

She's right, I thought to myself. That's definitely what I should have done.[48] (*Eijitsu* 3, 1909)

What begins as a house robbery—an obi theft, to be exact—turns into a nicely wrought comic vignette in which the hapless victim himself becomes the guilty party, accused by the police—and the wife—of negligence, the cardinal sin of the Meiji householder. But the satire extends to the police officer as well, as he carefully notes each stolen obi, despite not having a clue about women's clothing. The account of petty thievery becomes a domestic drama in one act—a small stage upon which the Natsume family players enact their respective roles. The anonymous thief, in other words, sets the family in different directions, each with a different view of the event.[49]

I have already noted that many of the *shōhin*'s domestic scenarios are anticipated in *Neko*. Burglary is no exception. The novel contains a detailed account of a robbery that cost the Kushami household most of its clothing. The subsequent police investigation occasions yet more lampooning of the professor and his proneness to kowtow before authority.[50]

Supplicants

As noted above, Natsume Sōseki's reclusive, ineffectual persona belies the fact of his stature as a public figure, one who made himself available to those requesting an audience—whether male or female, literary or otherwise. Several of the *Garasudo* episodes concern women who came to him for advice and counsel. One tells of a woman with literary aspirations who wished to be mentored by the author, which inspired the following acerbic reflection on such solicitations:

The woman's request put me in mind of the many people who've approached me, asking that I read their work. The manuscripts would occasionally be quite massive. Whenever time permitted, though, I'd do my best to accommodate them. I would naively assume, though, that having duly read the material, I would have fulfilled my obligation in the matter. But that was rarely the end of it. The person in question would want me to get the thing published in some newspaper or magazine. In no small number of such cases, it appeared as though I was being used as a means of achieving the goal of turning manuscripts into money. And so I became less and less willing to wade through indecipherable texts submitted by strangers....

Notwithstanding these misgivings, Sōseki meets with the woman, whereupon he holds forth on the sort of relationship he will agree to:

"As your mentor, I will be entirely honest with you. This is the sort of reciprocity that our relationship must be based on. This means that I may have some very harsh things to say about your writing. I won't hesitate to tell you exactly what I think, but you mustn't be angry with me. You mustn't take my criticism personally, since it's not intended as such. By the same token, if you find any of my remarks dubious or wrongheaded, by all means press me for an explanation. Press hard.... In short, what I have in mind is the antithesis of a run-of-the-mill relationship, which would amount to little more than a round of empty socializing and conventional pleasantry. Do you understand what I'm saying?"

"Yes, I understand."

And with that, she left.[51] (*Garasudo* 11, 1915)

Thus the episode ends. Of the woman herself, and the fate of the proposed literary mentorship, we learn nothing. Rather, Sōseki's narrator assumes the high ground, holding on to his vision of an idealized tutorial relationship. One can interpret this as a kind of verbal foreplay—a gambit aimed at having the woman unburden herself and strip bare for him, as it were. But there remains only the tantalizing foretaste; the story—if there ever was one—is left to the imagination. The point is to conceal, through this demonstration of circumspection and professional scruples. After all, having been taken advantage of in similar circumstances, one must remain on one's guard.

A second encounter, retold in several consecutive *Garasudo* episodes, concerns a woman who approaches her neighbor, the renowned writer, with a deeply troubling tale:

Satisfied by my reassurances, the woman began relating the events in her life over the past eight or so years. I sat in silence, my eyes upon her face as she spoke. For the most part, however, she avoided my gaze and simply stared down at the hibachi, continuing to poke at the ashes with the brass fire tongs she grasped in her lovely hand....

The woman's cheeks gradually reddened as she continued her account. I was particularly struck by their flushed condition—perhaps she hadn't applied any face powder. Her eyes were cast down, and I found myself naturally drawn to her luxuriant black hair.

The woman's confession was unbearably touching.... I'd learned that she was indeed alone in the world, caught in circumstances that allowed no movement whatsoever. I'd come to realize that hers was a truly desperate situation, and that nothing I could do would be of any avail. And so I'd become a mere bystander, observing the agonies of an individual to whom I could not extend a helping hand. . . .

The woman's disturbing account of suicidal despair yields a solemn reflection on the human condition, and an apologia for one's response to her entreaties:

As I continue to plod along this cheerless, forlorn road of life, thoughts of death—our inevitable destination—are constantly with me. I've become convinced that death brings with it a peace denied to the living. There are times when I consider it the most sublime state attainable by human beings.

"Death is more precious than life itself"—the thought has been reverberating inside my head constantly these days. Yet I inhabit the here and now. I am alive. The legacy of countless generations, transmitted from remote ancestors over thousands of years down to the present—one cannot easily gain deliverance from these deeply ingrained ways. And so I cling to life, as always. . . .

Yes, we must cling to life. And so I was unable to tell the woman who'd visited me that death would be preferable to life. She had suffered emotional wounds from which she might never recover. But these same wounds had become the source of beautiful memories, quite unimaginable to ordinary individuals, memories that made her radiant. The woman sought to embrace this beautiful thing, to lock it inside her heart and treasure it forever, like some precious jewel. To her great misfortune, this treasure is precisely the source of her merciless torment. Like opposite sides of a sheet of paper, the two are inextricably bound together.

"Time heals all wounds," I'd counseled the woman, encouraging her to persevere, to endure the pain. She feared, however, that with the passage of time the precious memories would fade away. Time, indifferent to all things, might well wrest away her treasure, but at the same time it would gradually heal her. . . . And so I'd counseled "time" as the means of stanching the blood that dripped from her wound, albeit at the cost of depriving her of passionate memories rooted in a serious love affair. For this woman, in my judgment, remaining alive, however commonplace a life it might be, would be preferable to dying.[52] (*Garasudo* 6–7, 1915)

Not much is known regarding Yoshinaga Hide (1887?–1916), the woman who came to visit Sōseki late in the autumn of 1914. It appears that she had moved to Tokyo from her native Shikoku, graduated from a woman's teaching college, and married a well-to-do businessman. A subsequent affair with a young man ended in his suicide, a divorce, and the desperate resolve to take her own life. This, then, is the matter that she entrusted to her confessor, Natsume Sōseki.[53]

Setting aside the philosophical turn of the *Garasudo* episode, it bears noting that tales of personal misfortune had a certain currency within the *bundan*—a reflection, perhaps, of the angst-based confessionalism favored by the naturalists. It was not uncommon for troubled souls to seek out name writers in order to have their tale of woe transformed into a literary work. In fact, Sōseki had been approached earlier—in November 1907—by a young man who had worked in the hellish Ashio copper mines and who wanted to sell his story. What resulted was the 1908 novel *Kōfu* (The Miner), a work that, whatever else can be said of it, ended up incorporating precious little of the actual drama as related by the young man.[54]

In Yoshinaga Hide's case, too, there is nothing of the actual circumstances that precipitated the visit. The reader can only surmise her story. As for Sōseki's narrator—he fixes his gaze upon the lovely woman as she pokes the embers in the hibachi, listens in silence to her agonizing tale, and finally bids her farewell—as though putting down a novel one has just finished. The encounter, notwithstanding certain erotic overtones, inspires a soliloquy on life and death that turns upon a melancholy assessment of the human condition. Of the woman and her fate we learn nothing.

The world-weary skepticism with which the narrator concludes the Yoshinaga account would be revisited in a later *Garasudo* episode:

ON BEING DUPED

As a functioning member of society, I cannot very well live in isolation from others. Inevitably, we must deal with one another. Even for someone like me, who leads such a spare, uncluttered life, how difficult it is to avoid human contact—be it the casual greeting, the routine exchange, or some more involved transaction.

Must I always take people at their word and insist on interpreting everything they say and do quite literally? If I entrust myself to this inborn naivete of mine, I will inevitably fall victim to the schemes of outrageous individuals and become the object of derision and ridicule. In the extreme case, I will be made to endure unspeakable insults personally directed at me. Why not, then, simply conclude that people are shameless liars, that their words are false, masking some sinister ulterior motive? Mightn't I be justified in thinking how clever I am in having come to this realization, which at least promises to bring some peace of mind?

In fact, such thinking would only lead to misunderstanding. I would need to resign myself to committing terrible blunders in my dealings with others. I would have to conjure up sufficient impudence to disparage entirely innocent individuals. It would be agonizing to have to choose the more suitable of these two postures. I do not want to put my faith in bad people, nor do I wish to bring any harm to good people. Those with whom I come into contact are neither entirely good nor entirely bad. Consequently, I must somehow deal with each one fairly and without prejudice. We must all make such judgments, but how accurately do we judge the unique character that every individual possesses? How well do we walk this precarious tightrope of subjectivity? I have long harbored doubts in this regard.

My own peccadilloes aside, I possess bitter memories of having been duped any number of times in the past. But at the same time, I've also had the experience of deliberately misreading people's words and deeds, as if to tacitly impugn their character.

How I judge people ultimately stems from my prior experience and is further conditioned by social context and environment. Moreover—and I recognize how vague a notion this is—my own native intuition comes into play as well.... But insofar as my own range of experience is remarkably narrow, while the social milieu is broad and complex, when it comes to judging people, I end up relying on this hopelessly abstract entity called intuition. Who knows if it even exists! Indeed, the very absence of any objective means of ascertaining its reliability further compounds my anxiety, suspending me in a miasma of doubt and uncertainty.

If there existed an omniscient, omnipotent god, I would kneel down before that god and pray for absolute clarity of vision and deliverance from my fears and torments. Failing that, I would pray that all who come into contact with this poor, benighted soul be transformed into paragons of honesty and decency, with whom I might enjoy an abiding harmony of spirit. As things stand, though, it appears that I can only play the fool who is duped by others or the cynic incapable of trusting anyone. I am miserable and cheerless, with no peace of mind. I lack both insight and wisdom. If this is all that life has to offer, then the human condition is truly a sorry state of affairs.[55] (*Garasudo* 33, 1915)

This bitter reflection, a legacy of self-doubt and cynicism traceable to Sōseki's early years, also recapitulates the underlying theme of *Kokoro* and *Michikusa,* the works that flank the *Garasudo* essays. We live alone with others, and the pain of this sadly paradoxical condition runs deep.[56] Acutely aware of the pitfalls that mark our relationships, and at the same time yearning for connection with others, the soliloquist points to bitter memories of the past that linger on, poisoning one's sense of belonging to the human community. There is no escape from dealing with others, yet the obstacles are many, and wisdom is not at hand.

Broken in Body, Broken in Spirit

The episodes recounted above lament the unhappy circumstance of *fuyukai ni michita jinsei*—the cheerless, forlorn quality of human existence. Such world-weary pessimism strongly colors Sōseki's fiction, which abounds in lost souls. And his *shōhin* narrator, as well, regularly pauses to reflect upon his world in equal measures of skepticism, exasperation, and hope. It was some years earlier, during the prolonged convalescence that followed his brush with death in late August 1910, that the author had occasion to write even more extensively in the meditative vein. Freed from the constraints of novelistic serialization, Sōseki approached his *Omoidasu* project in a heightened philosophical and spiritual frame of mind. Confined to his sickbed, the narrator of these reflections had many things to say about our imperfections and failings—and the light that can penetrate even the darker corners of the soul.

ON LIVING INSIDE A BROKEN BODY

I was taken aback by what had happened to my body. On the morning following the fateful episode, I went to move my hands, which rested on my chest, up to my face. Try as I might, though, my arms would not budge—it was as though they were no longer attached to me. Reluctant to disturb anyone, I tried forcing them up at the elbows—a major expense of time and effort that yielded only a modest upward movement.

Having exhausted myself in the futile attempt, I then tried to bring my slightly uplifted arms back to their original position. Yet even this proved no easy matter. Of course I could have simply let go and allowed the force of gravity to intercede, but I was concerned about the physical impact of the falling arms and how this might affect my body. Rendered helpless by indecision, I could figure no way out of my predicament. Here I was, painfully conscious of these two arms, caught in midair, incapable of being moved up, or down, or kept in place.

By and by, one of the nurses took notice of my plight. She placed my hands in hers and brought them up to my face, simply and naturally, then placed them back upon the bed. I found myself struggling to comprehend how I'd been reduced to such a hollow state of existence, so totally emptied of substance. . . .

Yet at the same time, I'd never before had such a keen awareness of the hardness of my bones. What I recall most vividly about waking up that morning was the searing pain that seemed to emanate from every bone in my body. By that evening, the pain had beaten me down and rendered me senseless, like a drunk who, in his stupor, takes on a mob and is thrashed within an inch of his life. So this is what cloth goes through, I thought at the time, when it's being thrashed about on the fulling block. . . .[57]

Those who saw to my care understood that my condition the night before was critical, and that I was not expected to survive. Even I, who knew so little, could appreciate the pity of it all. Yet I equally sensed that life for me had reduced to the precise juncture of my body and this bed, and insofar as these points of contact did not change, my world was simple in the extreme—and, consequently, safe and secure.

It struck me at the time that this attitude could be likened to the frame of mind of a corpse—if a corpse can be said to possess such a thing— resting in its padded coffin, never leaving its confines, undisturbed by those outside. Some time passed, and I started sensing a numbness in my head. It felt as though my body had been stripped of everything but bones, laid on top of a wooden plank. My legs felt deadened and heavy. And so my small, private realm of existence, safely indemnified against the perils of the larger society, was not immune from suffering after all. Yet I had no means of making even the slightest move to escape. I had no idea who was sitting beside me, or what they might be doing there. My nurses, observing me from some point outside my field of vision, might as well have been spirits from the Great Beyond.

Alone in this miniature world of tranquility and torment, lying flat on my back, I would rest my gaze on things beyond my body's reach. I would stare, for instance, at the long cord of the ice pack that hung from the ceiling. The cord, together with the cold bag attached to it, pulsed sharply upon my stomach.

> Morning chill—
> No moving these bones
> These living bones[58] (*Omoidasu* 18, 1911)

Safe and secure within his enclosed space, the *Omoidasu* narrator fore-shadows the circumstance of the *Garasudo* episodes, told "from within one's glass doors." But from these confines there would be no access to the world beyond. As though to compensate for this physical helplessness, the mind springs into action, making a detailed "damage assessment" of the newly immobilized body. Pain is the chief sensation, and its intensity beggars description. The body's moving parts will not respond to the patient's mental commands, and so endurance is the only option. This is terra incognita—an unexplored realm of experience—and one's inability, in this retrospective recounting, to properly chart its features proves frustrating. Hence, the haiku serves as an appropriate and effective coda.

Having become a living corpse, one can only observe whatever falls within the narrow field of vision. One sees and is seen, by whoever enters the room. But those beyond the visual field are in effect nonexistent.

Sōseki's narrative sketching of his sickroom environs calls to mind Masa-oka Shiki, who famously recorded his own sickbed observations in the form of haiku and *shaseibun* sketches.[59] In an important sense, the *Omoidasu* collection, especially its emblematic poetic codas, stands as an homage to his friend and mentor—arguably, Japan's greatest literary invalid.

What ails Sōseki's *Omoidasu* narrator, however, is not merely physical. Perhaps stimulated by the pain and discomfiture, his reflections move him to a dim assessment of the larger world in which he lives.

ON LIVING INSIDE A BROKEN SOCIETY

I feel terribly ill at ease about living in a world bereft of kindness. While I am naturally thankful when someone fulfills an obligation, the very notion implies a concern for doing one's duty, rather than a concern for others per se. Consequently, despite my willingness to acknowledge having benefited from duties performed on my behalf, I'm disinclined to feel a debt of gratitude toward the person who was merely being dutiful.

The exercise of kindness, on the other hand, presupposes an intrinsic connection with me *as a human being.* And for that reason, everything about such actions is deeply meaningful to me on a personal level. This implies a bond of mutuality—which might incline one to regard our cold, machinelike society in a hopeful light. How much more genuinely human it is, I would argue, to be forded across a stream on someone's back than to be sped across town on a trolley....

In everything they say or do, young people today are caught up in a display of self-assertiveness. This is unfortunately what our society has been reduced to, and it constitutes a positive abuse of our young people. When understood for what it really is, self-assertiveness is repugnant on many accounts. Yet we have foisted this pernicious notion upon the young, beyond their capacity to resist or reflect....

145

Adults, unlike children, have the capacity to grasp the complexity of things, their intricate weave and pattern. It is sadly ironic that this very capacity deprives them of something utterly basic to human life—the experience of pure, untainted emotion. As adults, can we ever claim to have felt sheer happiness, sheer gratitude, sheer admiration? Such occasions, I suspect, are few and far between. For my part, I've wished to preserve within me, as faithfully as possible, the feelings that so moved me at that time, be they "pure" or not. Yet I'm desperately afraid that in due course they will gradually, inevitably be reduced to mere scraps of memory. And why? Because I feel terribly ill at ease about living in a world bereft of kindness.

KANSHI

So many things in our world
All subject to the winds of change
Deepening autumn—saddened by this white hair
Deepening illness—dreaming of the blush of youth
I watch endless flocks of birds traversing the heavens
And clouds, unending, like the inexhaustible Way
Left to live on, I shall honor these bones
And not heedlessly grind them into dust[60] (*Omoidasu* 23, 1911)

Earlier episodes of *Omoidasu* include generous expressions of gratitude to those many individuals—among them, total strangers—who had provided care, come to visit, and sent wishes for a speedy recovery.[61] Here, though, the grateful sense of connection with a caring community gives way to a bitter indictment of modern society and its degeneracy.

Two expressions dominate this dark assessment of one's world: *kōi no hikarabita shakai* (society devoid of good will) and *jiga no shuchō* (ego-assertion). Indeed, the first of these expressions is a repeated refrain—a mantra-like incantation of the episode's theme. Sōseki's disdain toward modernization and egocentrism was shared by many of his contemporaries, who in the period following the Russo-Japanese War (1904–1905) saw clear signs of moral decline and social decay—especially among young people—in the fast-paced, alienating environs of modern Japan.[62] An even deeper concern is for the loss of something within—the experience of pure, untainted emotion (*junketsu na kanjō*). This, however, is not so much a disease of the modern age as a function of the aging process itself; and even the memory of these treasured experiences, like all else, will gradually decay.

The Healing Muse

Natsume Sōseki understood only too well that his body was a damaged vessel that would eventually succumb to its many imperfections. Yet the *Omoidasu* narrator has occasion to reflect on his convalescent state as something other than a prolonged rehearsal for his funeral. He came to regard it as a welcome opportunity for spiritual healing and repose.

ON ILLNESS, MEMORY, AND MEDITATION

When my illness was most serious, I lived only from day to day. And from day to day things changed. I understood the manner in which my spirit flowed on, like water. I was equally aware, though, that my mental faculties, disappearing and reappearing like clouds, were entirely unexceptional. It crossed my mind, then, that it might be worth keeping an account of the small episodes and incidents, so lacking the gravity and moment of the illness from which I suffered, that accumulated with each passing day. Such a record, I thought, might be instructive.[63]

At the time, though, I was unable to write. The days came and went, effortlessly. And in like manner, the thoughts and feelings that had grazed my mind, sending forth their ripples of awareness, were gone before I knew it. I'd gaze at the phantom traces of memory as they gradually faded into some distant oblivion, wishing that I could somehow retrieve them.

The story is told that Hugo Münsterberg[64] was once called to testify in court regarding details of a robbery in his home, whereupon his testimony was found to be at odds with the facts of the case. Even this famously methodical scholar, for whom accuracy and precision were bywords, suffered memory lapses. And so it's only to be expected that the memories recorded here lose their vibrancy with each passing day. A great deal has been lost during the time I was unable to write, and more will slip away even now that I've regained sufficient strength to use my pen. Such is the rationale for my choosing to keep an ongoing account—albeit random and fragmentary—of my illness, and the thoughts and feelings that it has engendered.

Certain of my friends have been delighted to see me well enough to be writing again. Others have expressed concern that I might be overdoing things. The one who made the greatest fuss was my colleague at the *Asahi*, Ikebe Sanzan. No sooner did he hear that I'd written something than he took me to task—in a decidedly brusque tone of voice, I might add. I defended myself by noting that I'd gotten the doctor's permission, and that I was merely doing what anyone would do to alleviate one's boredom.

"Doctor's permission or not, what really matters is having your friends say it's all right!" he retorted.

Thankfully, Dr. Miyamoto came to the rescue several days later.[65] When I broached the subject, he pointed out that prolonged inactivity could indeed cause a buildup of gastric acidity, which might aggravate my condition.

I sent the following *kanshi* verse to Sanzan:

Putting aside the new poetry, going nowhere,
Casting a vacant gaze through the window at distant woods:
A monk on a path made golden by the setting sun
Heads toward a village in shadow, its temple hidden by autumn leaves
Hanging a scroll in the alcove, burning the Buddha
Seeing clouds in the sky and taking up the koto
Sheer bliss: growing old by the river
Together with barking dogs and crowing cocks[66]

The question of aesthetic quality aside, I should note that insofar as there is no temple to be seen outside my hospital window, nor do I happen to have a koto in my room, this poem bears little relation to my actual circumstances. But I regard it as a perfectly faithful expression of my state of mind at the time. . . .

A life divorced from the meditative spirit and the tranquility of solitude is an unhappy life. The joy that I derive from indulging, if only briefly, my need for solitude has taken the form of this poem comprising fifty-six kanji. Such a meditative sentiment has ancient roots; there is nothing new here, nothing out of the ordinary. And nothing, what's more, of Gorky or Andreev, Ibsen or Shaw. The mood of which I speak belongs to a sphere as yet unknown to such writers, a state of mind they've not explored.

The sad and incontrovertible fact remains that insofar as our lives are beset by harsh and bitter realities, our literature is equally harsh and bitter. Caught up in the so-called modern temper, which governs our every thought and deed, how confining and bleak is our existence. Yet the occasion may arise when some archaic notion brings a fresh spirit into our lives. As for myself, I have my illness to thank for this very ordinary happiness, this modest, unhurried state of mind—which may be likened to savoring a bowl of plain rice upon returning from travels in some exotic land.

I've set out to record these memories lest they be forgotten. Having recovered from my ordeal and returned to Tokyo, I am already in the process of losing the wonderful tranquility that my illness made possible. I've even feared that my poem for Sanzan, composed while I was still unable to move about on my own, might end up being the final written expression of that peace of mind.

In the final analysis, these recollections are little more than the sickbed musings of a quite ordinary soul, related in a quite ordinary manner. But notwithstanding the commonplace sentiment, they harbor much that is sadly lacking in our world. And so I strive to remember, and to record that which I remember, and thus savor the precious fragrance of a bygone age. This I would share with my readers—the up-to-date people of our day, the tormented people of our day.

While bedridden in Shuzenji, I composed a number of haiku, which I recorded in my diary. And from time to time I tried my hand at the more challenging Chinese verse form, *kanshi,* with its complex tonalities....

I am normally unable to give myself over to the sheer enjoyment of writing poetry. This may in part reflect a certain diabolical quality of modern existence itself, a kind of jealousy whose shadow coils itself around the very spirit of poetic pursuit. Then again, it may speak to my own exasperation with composing verse, and the sense that the very poems I've slaved over have come back to haunt me....

But the situation is entirely different when I've taken ill. I feel myself one step removed, as it were, from the everyday world. People seem more indulgent, looking upon me as one who has withdrawn from society. I gain peace of mind, knowing that I am freed from my normal work routine, and people understand my situation and do not make untoward demands.

At such times, a restorative balm of tranquility and quietude wells forth in me—something utterly unattainable when I am well. It is precisely this spirit that imbues these poems. And as their creator, having set aside all concern for their literary merit, I've come to treasure them as mementos of a tranquil mind.[67] (*Omoidasu* 4–5, 1911)

It is with the episodes that precede those quoted above that the rationale for the *Omoidasu* series is fully established. The author, confined to his sickroom, will proceed to reconstruct the past several months of his life—the aftermath of the near-death experience. And in so doing, he will reflect on the quotidian routine, on poetry and the spirit of solitude, and on the meandering course of his ongoing recollection.

Mortality, however, underlies these reflections, and death is Sōseki's interlocutor. In this sense, the preceding episodes had actually set the stage for the *Omoidasu* project, insofar as they speak of two individuals whose demise he learned about from his sickbed. Both, as fate would have it, passed away at the very point when Sōseki's own life was in deepest peril. First, and with no small hint of irony, there was Dr. Nagayo Shōkichi, director of the Tokyo clinic where he was being treated (notice of whose death was purposely withheld from the doctor's gravely ill patient); second, William James, whose philosophical and psychological writings had so deeply resonated with Sōseki.[68] Indeed, the very formulation of *Omoidasu* as an "introspectionist" exercise—an inventory of his percepts, his awareness of things—owes much to a Jamesian approach.

But death will have no dominion in Sōseki's quiet room, as the convalescent comes to treasure the meditative space that his illness has afforded him.[69] Poetry would be a balm, a gateway to tranquility. Invoking a traditionalist aura of transcendence, Sōseki constructs, within the confines of his small room, a bulwark against both death and the depredations of modern civilization. The gravitas to his rhetoric here invokes the spirit of Kamo no Chōmei's early-thirteenth-century *Hōjōki* (An Account of My Hut), the locus classicus of Japanese spiritual minimalism. Chōmei's reclusion in the mountains outside Kyoto is coterminous with the spare dwelling that helped inspire his Buddhistic meditations on the human condition.

The lyrical raison d'être for the *Omoidasu* project is given a powerful impetus in the above episode, as the narrator sets out to extol the unique virtues of explicitly *Japanese* poetic and aesthetic forms. Revisiting his haiku muse—and with a bow to Shiki—he records a series of autumnal verses, which he then attempts to explicate. But the poet is tongue-tied, and he can only observe that the poems were the product of a dreamlike state of ecstasy.[70]

"At the time," he continues, "I was enthralled by the spirit of *fūryū*—this quality for which there is no corresponding term in the languages of the West. Above all, I was deeply drawn to that particular aspect of *fūryū* expressed in these haiku of mine."[71]

The episode concludes with the following observations on the poetry of Japan:

> It is only at such times, when I'm able to gain sufficient distance from the everyday world, and when my spirit is not troubled, that poetry—haiku and *kanshi*—springs forth, spontaneously, in all its variety. Looking back on things, it dawns on me that this was the happiest time of my life. I cannot imagine there being any other poetic vessel, here in Japan, for containing the spirit of *fūryū* than those fugitive syllables of the haiku and those lines of crabbed Chinese characters that form a *kanshi*. I will

gladly endure the challenges that these forms present, in exchange for the deep aesthetic pleasures they afford. It troubles me not in the least that there are no suitable alternatives for the Japanese poet.[72] (*Omoidasu* 5, 1911)

For the most part, *Omoidasu* consists of prosaic reflections. Its soul, however, is to be found in the verse—and the uniquely Japanese sensibility that it purportedly expresses. For Natsume Sōseki, poetic composition was a healing act in every sense—physical, psychological, spiritual. *Kanshi* would be an especially congenial vessel for his poetic genius, and he achieved an unparalleled stature in this genre. In fact, during the very difficult last year of his life, Sōseki established a daily routine of *kanshi* composition as a means of calming his troubled mind.

Let us examine yet another *Omoidasu* episode that dwells on the quietist moment and its essential goodness. Here the narrator is attempting to convey his state of mind following the brush with death:

THE SICKBED SANCTUARY

A peaceful night gradually gave way to the dawn. As the enveloping shadows receded into the distance, I was, as usual, able to make out the faces of those gathered around my bed. And these were the usual faces. And I was my usual self. Lying at ease, with no pain or agitation, I wondered what had become of my illness. No forebodings about death hovered about. The confusion and commotion of the night before—or what I remembered of it—seemed like a dream of long ago, viewed from afar. I greeted the morning sun that shone through the shoji screens with a fresh spirit, reinvigorated by the notion that death had departed with the dawn's first light. Yet I would learn soon enough that death had merely deceived me. It had entered my veins, where it flows even now, dominating the weakened blood that it has encountered.

My wife's diary entry for that morning reads as follows: "When I asked about [my husband's] condition, the doctor said it was critical, but might improve with complete rest."[73] It was only later when I learned that my condition had been thought to be hopeless, that no one expected me to survive that first night....

Dr. Sugimoto, having returned to Tokyo, requested that two nurses be dispatched immediately to provide care. He conveyed such a sense of urgency on the phone that the nurses spent much of their time on the train wondering whether I'd still be alive by the time they reached Shuzenji. This I heard from the nurses themselves who, among other things, shared their misgivings at the time—what a waste, they'd thought, to have to travel all that way only to learn that their patient had died before they got there!

And so I lay in bed, unaware of anything, forsaken by the world at large, like a babe abandoned in the wilderness. Yet at the same time, my life was remarkably free of worry or anxiety. All that mattered was this—I am here, in my room, in my bed, with not a care in the world. Thanks to an unforeseen illness, I was the beneficiary of the care and solicitude of many individuals. I'd been transported to a safe haven, a place unaffected by the vicissitudes of the life I would lead were I in good health. My wife and I lived in peace, here at the foot of the mountain, where the ill winds of life's struggle could not reach us.

> In this village
> Heavy with dew—
> My peaceful disease[74] (*Omoidasu* 16, 1911)

The author's ravaged body—and the immobility and dependency that followed in its wake—has become an agent of healing, through the heightened state of consciousness that his circumstances have made possible. This spirit of serenity and transcendence is reinforced by the measured, elevated language of his reflections. Its echoes are palpable in several episodes that call to mind the example of Dostoyevsky and his own crises. The first relates to that author's lifelong experience with epilepsy—a "sacred disease" *(shinsei naru yamai)* marked by a trancelike, ecstatic state that Sōseki likens to his own state of mind in the wake of the Shuzenji crisis. The second concerns Dostoyevsky's famous brush with death—in the form of a firing squad, following imprisonment on trumped-up charges of fomenting rebellion. The *Omoidasu* narrator muses on the state of mind of the writer, exiled to Siberia, who literally faced his executioners—only to be given a last-minute reprieve. Struggling to make sense of the scene he reconstructs in his mind, in light of Dostoyevsky's claim that the experience had helped rescue him from madness, the narrator concludes that it lies beyond his powers of comprehension.[75]

Stepping Outside

Sōseki's *shōhin* narrator, in keeping with the protean quality of the genre, speaks in many voices. Just as the *Omoidasu* narrator moves between extremes of despair and regeneration, bewilderment and inspired awareness, the *Gara-*

sudo series is brought to a deeply satisfying close as its narrator, finally exiting his glass-door enclosure, reverses the negative pole of self-reflection.

A SUNDAY AFTERNOON IN SPRING

Today being Sunday, the children have no school. On this account, the maid appears to have relaxed her vigilance by sleeping in later than usual. Even so, I was out of bed at a quarter past seven. I washed up, had my usual breakfast of toast, milk, and soft-boiled egg, and went to the toilet. As luck would have it, though, the night-soil man was busily cleaning it out,[76] and so I walked out to the garden in the back, which I hadn't been to in a while. The gardener was puttering around in the storage shed. And there were three of my daughters, gathered around a burning pile of used charcoal sacks, cheerfully warming themselves by the gathering flames....

I stared off in the distance, above the stone fence, at the wet roof tiles, their coating of frost having melted away, as they glistened in the morning sun. And then I went back inside. Having to wait until our niece, who'd come by to help with the chores, finished straightening up my study, I brought a desk out onto the veranda, which was bathed in sunlight, and leaned up against the railing. I just sat there, with chin resting in my hand, lost in thought. I remained perfectly still and gave free rein to my spirit. A light breeze would occasionally stir the long leaves of the potted orchid. From somewhere in the garden, a nightingale gave forth its clumsy chirping. Having spent my days inside the glass doors, I'd imagined that winter would never end. But without even realizing it, spring had begun to revive my spirits.

For as long as I sat there, I remained lost in reverie. I reflected on the devil-may-care attitude that recognizes the inexhaustible supply of things to write about, then gets confused by all the choices—Should I write about this? No, perhaps I should write about that? And in the end one concludes that it's all a waste of time.

As my mind lingered on in this vein, I reflected upon these episodes and how pointless they are. What could have possessed me to write them? Thankfully, I was sensible enough not to be undone by the self-mockery. In fact, I derived exquisite pleasure from harnessing the derisive voice and rising to the heights of contemplation. There, far above the clouds, I could look down upon myself and enjoy laughing at my own folly. Cosseted by my self-mockery, all the while I am little more than a child asleep in his cradle.

I've written randomly here about people I know and about myself. When writing about others, I've sought to minimize any possible

153

embarrassment. When writing about myself, on the other hand, I've taken considerable liberty. Still, I've yet to succeed at eliminating all nuance and shading in dealing with myself. While I may not have been guilty of egregious arrogance, it's also the case that I haven't truly divulged my shortcomings—the baser, meaner aspects of my character.

Someone has remarked that however thoroughly we read the classics of confessional literature—Augustine, Rousseau, de Quincy—in the final analysis, ultimate truth is beyond the capacity of human expression. Far be it from me to regard my own work as "confession." My sin—if it's proper to speak of it as such—is in having cast my shortcomings in an excessively positive light. Some may not be pleased with this. But I've risen above this. Looking out upon the great expanse of humanity, I can only smile. And as I cast the same gaze upon myself, the author of these trifling accounts, it's as though someone else had written them all. And I can only smile.

The nightingale continues to chirp in the bushes. The spring breeze occasionally stirs the leaves of the orchid, as though remembering to do so. The cat sleeps peacefully, exposing the wound on its head to the healing rays of the sun. The children, who had been playing around in the garden with their balloons, have all gone off to the movie theater. The house is still and hushed, as is my spirit. And so I open wide the glass doors, and bathed in the quiet light of spring, and in a mood of quiet rapture, I bring this work to a close. And when it's done, I will lie down here on the veranda and take a nap.[77] (*Garasudo* 39, 1915)

This moving coda to Sōseki's *Garasudo* reflections, whose meandering course has traced the narrator's moods and fancies, marks a return to the narrative frame established at the outset. It is Sunday. One's work is done. The work is flawed, insubstantial, unsatisfying. But it is done. This is an ordinary day. People are doing ordinary things. The house is still. The spring day beckons. It is time to rest.

A far cry from earlier expressions of tedium and disquiet, here the quality of domesticity *(nichijōsei)* borders on the transcendent. Angela Yiu, in her remarks on *Garasudo,* interprets the sense of serenity evoked in the final passage as deriving from a specific Confucian literary allusion.[78] Seen more broadly, the episode points to a recentering of the narrator's spirit, which has endured much in the course of these reflections, and a healing sense of resignation and indulgence. Solitude, in this instance, is rendered as a state of grace, recalling the *Omoidasu* narrator in his sickroom sanctuary. Here it is drawn in primal figures of sleep and calm, and the narrator as a child in his cradle. For some, this final resolution of the travails of the *Garasudo*

narrator—whose shape-shifting forays into dyspepsia, philosophical speculation, jeremiads, and comic asides have brought him to this beatific Sunday
afternoon—may appear contrived. For others inclined to attribute a higher
wisdom to the author, the episode bespeaks an enlightened state of mind.

Neither view of the author squares with the *Michikusa* serialization,
which began, following a hiatus of several months, on June 3, 1915.[79] In the
view of Angela Yiu, this work represents the author's return to "chaos and
fear, nightmares and decay."[80] In short, there would be no easy transcendence
of ego and anxiety, of one's ingrained habits, prejudices, and fantasies.

On the Domestic and Transcendent in Sōseki's *Shōhin*

We possess a natural, perhaps inevitable, curiosity regarding the private lives
of famous people—the "frenzy of renown," to cite the title of Leo Braudy's
illuminating study of fame and its cultural history.[81] In our own day, the
market for sensationalism, scandalmongering, and paparazzi journalism is,
to say the least, thriving. Meiji literary journalism exhibited no less a passion
for celebrity gossip, and Natsume Sōseki, in his own way, helped meet the
demand.

What is revealed in the above episodes? To my mind, the self-absorption
of Sōseki's narrator is as evident as the artful concealment that it entailed.
Sōseki created voices, in his *shōhin* and novels alike, for individuals who lived
unspectacular lives, relished solitude, and remained immersed in self-doubt
and uncertainty. House and home became contested sites, a stage for quotidian encounters and endless stock taking. As we have seen, his *Garasudo* narrator is peevish and depressive, his glass-door enclosure providing an imperfect
barrier between self-obsession and engagement with the world.

Yet this is not the man in full. It is but one of several figurations. Natsume
Sōseki cultivated many relationships with those in the literary, academic, and
journalistic fields, and he recalls these in a number of his personal writings.
The following chapter will examine how this *bundan* doyen crafted sketches
of colleagues and mentors, literary protégés and those on the margins.

Literary Portraits

Mentors, Protégés, and Eccentrics

O ver the years, many of Natsume Sōseki's acquaintances in the literary, academic, and journalistic spheres would become the subject of reminiscence. Working within prevailing styles of anecdotal portrayal, Sōseki fashioned an amiable and solicitous voice quite distinct from, yet complementary to, the figure of the study-bound recluse.

As I have written in connection with Mori Ōgai and his *shiden* biographies, the literary anecdote has stood as a time-honored mode of biographical portrayal, revealing traits of character through the telling detail and episode.[1] Of course biographers have no monopoly on anecdotal characterization. It is equally available to novelists and poets, filmmakers and playwrights. Moreover, even the most seemingly faithful portrait of another is at the same time a mirror of the artist, whose point of view is inevitably represented. Biography and memoir, in other words, amount to veiled autobiography. And the veil may be quite thin.

Such is the case with Sōseki's literary portraits, whose subjects include young protégés whose careers he fostered, writers and editors with whom he had close ties, and foreign scholars who served as mentors. Some of these accounts are contemporaneous with the narrated events; others relate remembered incidents. The aim of this chapter is to explore Sōseki's anecdotal portrayal in order to assess both the contours of his literary and intellectual affiliations and the personal voice that would be the medium for commemorating the lives of others.

London Revisited

Little is known of Natsume Kinnosuke's literary researches in London aside from the fact that in the early months of his stay, he took to working in virtual isolation. Evidently intending to pursue a formal course of study upon his arrival in London, Natsume elected not to study at Oxford or Cambridge, where living expenses would evidently be exorbitant, but chose instead to remain in London. He opted for University College, where he would audit courses taught by William Paton Ker (1855–1923), a scholar of medieval literature who enjoyed a sterling reputation.[2] For several months, Natsume commuted to the college and sat in on Ker's lectures, but he found this too troublesome a schedule to maintain. Through Ker's introduction, though, he was able to arrange for a weekly tutorial with William James Craig (1843–1906), a noted Shakespearean scholar who had given up a university post to become an independent researcher. The two met on Tuesdays, from late November 1900 until October 1901.

It is hard to assess the intellectual fruits of this tutorial, which covered diverse materials in an evidently haphazard fashion. But their relationship generated an unusual *shōhin* sketch, years after the fact, with which the *Eijitsu* collection ends—one that casts the aging scholar, paradoxically, as both an insufferable eccentric and a kindred spirit.

PROFESSOR CRAIG

Like some swallow, Professor Craig built his nest high up on the fourth floor. From the pavement below, not so much as a window could be seen. By the time I'd complete the arduous climb up the stairs to his flat, my thighs would be aching. The entranceway was nothing more than a plain black door, less than three feet wide, with a brass knocker attached. Waiting a moment to catch my breath, I'd rap the knocker against the black door. When it opened, I'd be greeted by a middle-aged woman. She had on a pair of glasses, possibly for nearsightedness, and invariably seemed surprised to see me. . . . "Please do come in," she'd say, eyes wide open on account of that regrettable knock on the door.

No sooner did I enter than the woman would disappear. I made my way into the parlor—a room virtually devoid of decor, with its two windows and a mass of books. Initially it didn't appear the sort of room fit for entertaining guests. Here, though, is where Craig would encamp. . . .

We had agreed on a weekly tutorial fee of seven shillings and that I would pay the cumulative amount monthly. But there were occasions when the professor would unexpectedly press me for payment, claiming to be in need of money. I'd reach into my trouser pocket for a gold coin and politely hand it over to him. "Sorry to trouble you," he'd say, taking possession of his payment with that limp hand, which he would hold open just long enough to inspect the coin before putting it in his pocket. It galled me that Craig would never give me back any change. And whenever I'd try to adjust

157

the next month's tuition accordingly, he'd be at it again, mentioning some books that he just had to buy.

Professor Craig was Irish, which may account for the extreme difficulty I had in understanding him. The situation would truly get out of hand when he'd become agitated, at which point he'd become totally incomprehensible. . . . And given his propensity for confused and erratic displays, I had little recourse, when he'd get carried away, but to trust in providence and appear to be paying attention to him, training my eyes on his face.

Nor was this any run-of-the-mill face. . . . Craig had an unkempt, rusticated look about him. His beard was a sorry sight, a chaotic mess of white and black hairs. When I happened to run into him one day on Baker Street, I actually mistook him for a cabman who'd forgotten his whip. And I never once saw the professor wearing a white shirt and collar. He'd always have on a striped flannel shirt. And his feet, encased in great shaggy slippers, would be thrust into the fireplace. During our tutorial, he had the habit of tapping on his knees or rubbing his thighs as he conducted the lesson.

As for the lesson itself—one never knew *what* to expect. Craig would simply take me wherever he wished to go, and never back to where we'd started. He'd jump from subject to subject in wild disarray. . . . In a sense, the tutorial amounted to little more than gibberish. Looked at more charitably, the man was engaging in informal literary conversation, which is not without some redeeming value. In retrospect, I had no reason to expect a polished lecture in exchange for a mere seven shillings. . . .

The professor's forte was poetry. Whenever he recited verse, his upper body would gently sway, as though he were in a trance. It would actually sway—this is no exaggeration. But his was a private euphoria, the recited verse being meant not for my edification but for his own enjoyment. . . .

Craig would at times treat me like a child, asking if I happened to know the answer to some simpleminded question. Then, in a complete turnabout, he'd bring up a very difficult matter and engage me on an equal footing. On one such occasion he was reciting some verse by William Watson [1858–1935]. "There are those who liken his work to Shelley's," he observed, "and others who find it entirely different. What is your opinion?"

What was my opinion, indeed! I must confess that Western poetry was something that had first to appeal to the eye, and only then might it appeal to the ear; otherwise, I could make no sense of it. Having been put on the spot, however, I came up with some manner of response. It escapes me which position I took on the question of Watson versus Shelley. But I recall the keen embarrassment I felt when Craig proceeded to slap his knee and remark that he entirely agreed with me!

I also recall the time he went over to the window, where he took in the hustle and bustle of passersby on the streets below. "Look at all those people, will you. Not one in a hundred has any understanding of poetry. What a pity. The English, I'm afraid, are entirely incapable of comprehending poetry. Now the Irish are something else again. Far more receptive, more refined. People like you and me, who truly appreciate poetry—we must consider ourselves fortunate indeed."

I was grateful to have been included in this select company, but the fact remained that Professor Craig's treatment of me was remarkably distant. I never once witnessed any display of affection on his part and could only think of him as an old man behaving like some automaton....

Incorrigibly absentminded, Craig was always misplacing his books, and he'd fly into a fit of rage if the sought-for item failed to turn up. With an exaggerated tone of alarm, as though something had caught on fire, he'd scream for the housekeeper in the kitchen. Striking an equally histrionic pose, the woman would appear in the parlor.

"What's become of my Wordsworth?"

With her eyes pried open like saucers in that state of chronic astonishment, the housekeeper would scan the bookshelves, and with a sure eye that belied the disconcerted expression, she'd immediately home in on the missing volume.

"Here you are, sir," she would say, thrusting the wayward book at him in a slightly reproachful manner.

Snatching the book away from her, Craig would proceed to drum upon its filthy cover as he launched into a disquisition on Wordsworth. The housekeeper, appearing ever more astonished, would retire to the kitchen. For several minutes he'd continue drumming on the book, and in the end, despite all the fuss involved in locating the thing, he wouldn't even bother to open it up!

Professor Craig occasionally sent me a letter, but the handwriting would make it perfectly illegible.[3] And so I decided that whenever one arrived, I would spare myself the ordeal of decipherment by simply assuming that he'd written to cancel our next session....

The professor once asked me to read the preface he'd written for the *Hamlet* volume in the Arden series, of which he was editor. When I returned for our next session, I mentioned how much I'd enjoyed it. "Then would you do me the favor, when you return to Japan, of making this volume known among your colleagues?" Indeed, when I went on to assume the university professorship, the Arden *Hamlet* proved extremely valuable in my lectures. To my mind, there is no finer annotation available.

Speaking of Professor Craig's Shakespearean researches, there was a small study just off the parlor of the flat—a little nook in his fourth-floor cloister to which the man would betake himself. And in a corner of this hideaway could be found his private treasure—some ten enormous blue notebooks. In his every spare moment, Craig would take scraps of paper on which he'd made notes and carefully transcribe these into the blue notebooks. Bit by bit, word by word, like a miser hoarding his stash of small change, the collection grew.

This was none other than the manuscript for a great Shakespeare dictionary. Assembling it, gradually, piece by piece, was Professor Craig's consuming passion....

I happened to ask the professor when he had embarked on his Shakespeare research. He went over to the bookshelves and began frantically searching about for something. Then, in one of his petulant outbursts, he shouted for the housekeeper.

"Jane! Jane! What's become of the Dowden?"[4]

He was still looking for the book when the housekeeper appeared, the startled expression fixed upon her face, and handed him the missing volume. "Here you are, sir," she added, in her typically reproachful tone.

Craig grabbed the book, totally indifferent to the housekeeper's curt manner, and tore into it.

"Ah, here it is! Dowden mentions me here—'Craig, an exceptional Shakespearean critic.' This work was published in the 1870s, and my own research began long before then."

I was in awe of Professor Craig's sheer perseverance.

"When will your work be complete?"

"I'm afraid it's not a question of completing it," he responded, returning the Dowden volume to the shelf. "I'll be working on it until my dying day."

It was shortly thereafter that I stopped going to see Professor Craig. Just before our tutorial ended, he expressed some curiosity as to whether there might be a demand for foreign scholars in Japanese universities. "If I were younger I'd be interested in going," he added. I couldn't help sensing a certain vulnerability and resignation in his tone. This was the only time that Craig betrayed any private emotion in my presence.

"But you're still young," I said, in a gesture of consolation.

"No, I'm afraid it's too late for me," he remarked, strangely sullen and downcast. "I'm already fifty-six years old, you know."

It was some years after returning to Japan that I came across an article in one of the literary magazines noting that Craig had passed away. A mere two or three lines, mentioning the fact of his having been an authority on Shakespeare. Putting down the journal, I wondered whether his life's great labor, the Shakespeare dictionary, had ended up on the scrap heap after all.[5] (*Eijitsu* 25, 1909)

William James Craig died on December 12, 1906, and was buried, in Surrey, on December 15.[6] Several years before his erstwhile Japanese tutee composed the above reminiscence, the great British essayist E. V. Lucas (1868–1938) published a eulogy entitled "A Funeral." This is how Lucas remembered the man:

> He was an old scholar—not so very old, either—whom I had known for some five years, and had many a long walk with: a short and sturdy Irish gentleman, with a large, genial grey head stored with odd lore and the best literature; and the heart of a child. . . .
>
> His life was divided between his books, his friends, and long walks. A solitary man, he worked at all hours without much method, and probably courted his fatal illness in this way. To his own name there is not much to show; but such was his liberality that he was continually helping others, and the fruits of his erudition are widely scattered, and have gone to increase many a comparative stranger's reputation. His own *magnum opus* he left unfinished; he had worked at it for years, until to his friends it had come to be something of a joke. But though still shapeless, it was a great feat, as the world, I hope, will one day know. If, however, this treasure does not reach the world, it will not be because its worth was insufficient, but because no one can be found to decipher the manuscript; for I may say incidentally that our old friend wrote the worst hand in London. . . .
>
> Craig was abstemious in all things, save reading and writing and helping his friends and correspondents.[7]

Sōseki's *shōhin* was based on a much shorter acquaintanceship, and radically different circumstances, than Lucas's essay was. Nevertheless, the weekly tutorial, which had long since ended, yielded an amusing and curiously moving profile of his mentor. Sōseki's London diary makes numerous references to the Craig tutorials, even though the typical entry notes simply that the two had met and that he'd stopped off at the bookstores on his way home. Several are more substantial, generally casting Craig in a negative light. The diarist calls attention to the man's atrocious handwriting, his stinginess, the flights and tangents that he'd pursue during their time together.

The portrayal, which begins in a satirical mode, weaves together repulsion and attraction, exasperation and empathy. The absentminded professor, a prideful and querulous sort, must endure the indignities of having the housekeeper come to the rescue when something is misplaced—yet again. The man is portrayed as a bookish eccentric—socially awkward, on the verge of unseemly old age, miserly and unfeeling. He occasionally asks for an advance on his tuition so that he can buy books—ironic, in view of Sōseki's own financial straits (most of his own disposable funds went to the booksellers). The man inhabits a "swallow's nest" on the top floor of the building, where he lives in monastic reclusion surrounded by books and a mountain of half-digested Shakespeare notes.[8]

The Craig caricature recalls the comic spirit of *Neko,* with its gallery of satiric portrayals, and this in turn reflects Sōseki's earlier studies of Swift and Sterne, writers for whom he felt a strong affinity. But the very idiosyncrasies he attributes to the man, together with the skepticism regarding the ultimate worth of one's literary labors, he would in turn apply to himself through the voice of ironic self-deprecation that marks the *shōhin.*

Sōseki's Craig essay is, like Lucas's, a eulogy, insofar as the author had already learned of the man's death. By and by, caricature gives way to something approaching elegy. For Sōseki, Craig emerges as yet another *fugūsha*—the marginal figure, sympathetically portrayed, who is plagued by misfortune. His skepticism regarding the outcome of the Shakespeare project, which contrasts with Lucas's own sanguine assessment, reflects a strong ambivalence toward the obsessive research and note taking that had consumed him for years—in part through Craig's tutelage.

Notwithstanding the somewhat grudging affection he expresses toward the unkempt Irish scholar, Sōseki stops short of expressing either admiration or intellectual indebtedness. In a sense, the essay epitomizes the experience of that first year in London. Natsume Kinnosuke lived in bookish reclusion, much like Craig, but appeared to lack the man's passionate commitment to his research. Even the regular book-buying excursions seem more of a compulsion than a source of genuine satisfaction.

The Shakespeare dictionary, Craig's self-styled magnum opus, may have died stillborn. But the Craig portrait would see the light of day. In fact, it would inspire several literary parodies—poetic justice, one might say. Yamada Fūtarō (1922–2001), a writer of detective fiction among other popular genres, recast the Craig account in his novella "The Yellow Lodger," a Sherlock Holmes parody that plays on the Craig *shōhin.* The following is a brief excerpt: "The visitor did indeed appear Oriental—a small yellow-colored

man of thirty-four or thirty-five with a pointed moustache and slight pock-
marks on the end of his nose. He stood frowning at the spittle flying furiously
out of the professor's mouth."[9]

The Expatriate Scholar

Several years later, Sōseki produced another portrayal of a scholarly mentor.
His subject this time was Raphael von Koeber (1848–1923), with whom he
had studied philosophy at the Imperial University in the 1890s. Born and
raised in Russia and educated in Germany, Raphael von Koeber went to Japan
in 1893 to teach philosophy, and he remained on the university faculty for
twenty-one years.[10] Sōseki was a student in his classes on aesthetics, and the
Koeber portrait would attest to the bond that had developed between student
and mentor.

Strangely, though, the two failed to maintain contact despite their living
close to one another. Plans to dine together had been in the works for years.
Finally, on the evening of July 10, 1911, the author, together with his protégé
Abe Yoshishige (1883–1966), spent an evening at Koeber's home as his din-
ner guests. Sōseki's *shōhin,* an account of the visit, appeared a week later in the
Asahi.

PROFESSOR KOEBER

A tall window came into view through the trees, and there, in a corner, we
could see Professor Koeber, a thick plume of grayish smoke wafting by his
side. "He's smoking," I mentioned to Abe.

I forget exactly when it was that I'd last visited, but the area had
changed dramatically. Stately new homes had been built, each furnished
with an imposing gate—bold symbols of the power and wealth produced
in today's Japan. Professor Koeber's is the only remaining older residence
in the neighborhood. Once ensconced in the study of this rusticated
dwelling—itself a living memorial to the past—the professor rarely has
occasion to emerge.

Professor Koeber led the two of us up the long, uncarpeted wooden
staircase. It was dark and dreary, and each stair creaked with the advancing
footsteps. The study was just off to the right at the top of the stairs. I
sat down in the chair that the professor had occupied when we caught
a glimpse of him through the trees. Here the illumination was most
favorable. And with the evening sunlight bathing the room's interior, I was

able to have a good look at him. The man's features had changed little over his sixty-three years. . . .

In vivid contrast to Professor Koeber's abiding youthfulness and vitality, his study was cloaked in shades of unremitting gloom. I'd anticipated a display of gorgeous, leather-bound volumes, which might call to mind the pomp and circumstance of Western arts and learning— Chinese and Japanese books pale by comparison. But as I looked around, I saw not a single such volume. The study contained only a desk and four old chairs. . . .

When we were ushered into the dining room downstairs, I expected to see a white tablecloth, which I'd assumed was de rigueur among Europeans. But instead, the table was covered with a drab cotton print cloth. Seated at the dinner table, Professor Koeber had on an unassuming tan suit and pin-striped crêpe shirt with no necktie. In fact, we'd been advised not to dress formally, but fearing a possible breach of etiquette I opted for my dark blue kimono with white shirt and neckband.

The professor was first to speak. "You're so splendidly attired and here I am in this getup." It was an embarrassing compliment, but I suppose that if cloaking one's arms and neck in freshly laundered white garb can be considered "splendid attire," then I surely outdid him in this regard.

I asked the professor if he felt lonesome living by himself. "Not in the least." I then asked if he'd thought of returning to his native land.

"To my mind, there's nothing especially appealing about Europe. The only thing that troubles me about living in Japan is the lack of concerts, theater, libraries, or art museums. Otherwise, I'm perfectly comfortable here."[11]

"What if you were to take a year's leave and indulge yourself back in Europe?"

"That would certainly be a possibility," he remarked. "But I do not care to. You see, were I to leave Japan on such a trip, I'd likely never return."

Neither nostalgic toward his homeland nor altogether averse toward Japan, Professor Koeber has been witness to the gradual incursions of the so-called modern age, this great, seething void that is so inimical to his own temperament, whose force threatens to overwhelm everything it touches. Having managed to stand outside the chaos that is modern Japan and regard it with a sort of cosmic indifference, Professor Koeber has managed to live here for eighteen years with a remarkable sense of equanimity. He is like a Greek statue, discarded in some vast junkyard, that has come to life. Amid the hustle and bustle, he moves about ever so quietly. As he walks the pavements, his shoes move silently, no sound of hobnails clattering against stone. Like an ancient Greek wearing sandals of supple leather, he strolls soundlessly as the trolleys rumble by.

Professor Koeber used to have a pet crow—not a caged bird, but one that came by to be fed. He had a curious affinity for crows. I recall having seen him, long ago, taking out the collected works of Edgar Allan Poe from the University library. He'd mentioned being an avid reader of Poe and E. T. A. Hoffmann.

Over dinner that evening I thought of the crow and inquired about what had become of it.

"It froze to death. One winter's night it perched on a tree limb out in the garden, and the next morning it was dead."

And so we pursued our quiet chat in this incongruous setting—an old house, in the very heart of Japan's great metropolis, in the heat of mid-summer.... Having at long last gotten together, Abe and I departed the professor's house on that dark, dark summer's night. I could not help wondering how long he intended to remain in Japan. It had become clear that were it not for his students, he would surely have departed this bleak and dismal land long ago. "Were I to leave, I'd never again return"—these were his words. I recalled the famous line from Poe's *The Raven* which the professor had quoted—"Nevermore."[12]

Sōseki's account borrows from his July 10 diary entry, which lists some twenty topics discussed that evening.[13] In this sense, his narrator assumes the role of *danwa hikkisha*, the journalist-interviewer on assignment. Omitted in his *shōhin* account, though, is the mention made in the journal of a fourth person on hand that evening—Kubo Masaru (1883–1972). Kubo, who was one of Koeber's most promising students, was at the time living in the professor's flat as a *shosei*.[14]

This calls to mind the fact that Koeber, like Sōseki himself, was mentor to a circle of young protégés, some of whom—like Kubo—would go on to introduce sophisticated approaches to Western philosophy into the Japanese university curriculum. The essay points both to the personal bond uniting Sōseki and his old teacher over a nearly twenty-year span and the esteem in which the man had evidently been held by the student body overall.

The account begins with a view of the neighborhood—a disagreeably fashionable locale for the Meiji parvenu class, where the professor's home is alone in retaining something of the old flavor of the area. As with the Craig portrayal, then, Koeber is depicted as something of a throwback, a relic of a bygone era. And both are cast, not surprisingly, as prototypical *shosai nin-*

gen. But unlike Craig, Koeber commands unequivocal admiration. He is an intensely private and unassuming individual, whose needs are modest and whose values are unimpeachable. He has lived for his students.

Professor Koeber is cast, in other words, as a paragon of civility, integrity, and dedication to teaching and learning—a veritable Greek god, who has chosen, for reasons that one must respect if not entirely comprehend, to live in the "bleak and dismal land" of Japan. Sōseki's essay voices a powerful *bunmeiron* (civilizational) critique, contrasting the virtues that Koeber represents with the debased, depressing nullity of modern Japan—a variation on a recurrent *shōhin* theme.[15]

Finally, Professor Koeber is cast as a citizen of the world, whose contentment with long years as an expatriate in a faraway land stands in ironic contrast to Sōseki's own inability to adjust to life as a foreigner in England or fully to overcome the bitter aftertaste of the experience. But several years later, Koeber did in fact choose to leave Japan and return to Germany, and this occasioned a commemorative essay published on the day of the planned departure.

PROFESSOR KOEBER'S FAREWELL

Professor Koeber is to depart from Japan today, but I assume that he left Tokyo several days ago. The professor has a strong aversion to empty formalism and meaningless ritual. It's said that when he left Germany some twenty years ago to take up his post at the Imperial University, not a soul came to see him off at the train station. They all knew the man too well. Like a fleeting shadow he entered this country, and like a fleeting shadow he will depart.

During his stay in Tokyo, this quiet, gentle man lived in three locations. I would hazard to guess that his knowledge of the city was restricted to these three residences and the routes that got him to and from the university. . . . But when I asked the professor, at our recent dinner together, if he still had friends back in Germany, he said that with the exception of the North and South Poles, he had friends all over the world. The professor's joking manner only underlines the fact that here is a man who has transcended narrow boundaries and managed to achieve a truly global perspective. This also helps explain how he could remain for twenty years in a country that held no particular interest for him, without having to give vent to rancor or regret.

Professor Koeber's notion of time, too, sets him apart from the prevailing norm. I inquired as to why he'd chosen to return home on a slow freighter, which would prolong the voyage.

"Spending time at sea does not bother me in the least—the longer the better! What I can't fathom is this craving for efficiency and expedience, for arriving at one's destination as quickly as possible."

Morever, the professor has an indifference toward money that must be incomprehensible to the average Westerner.... What matters most is the love and compassion that bind us together as human beings. And there was the deep affection, in particular, for those many students he'd taught over the years.

When I was about to take my leave at the dinner party, the professor had a request to make. He wanted me to arrange for a simple message of "farewell and best wishes" to "his Japanese friends, colleagues, and—especially—his students," to be published in the *Asahi*.

Thus I've taken the liberty of offering these personal remarks as a means of conveying Professor Koeber's regards to those who've benefited from his tutelage over the years. On their behalf, allow me to wish the professor a safe journey, together with my heartfelt prayers for his future happiness and peace of mind.[16]

On August 13, the very next day, an addendum to the above article appeared in the *Asahi:*

THE VICISSITUDES OF WAR

Just after getting into bed on the night of August 11, I was called to the telephone and notified that Professor Koeber's departure had been postponed. Unfortunately, I'd already submitted my "Farewell" piece, and it was too late to print a retraction. For the time being, Professor Koeber is staying with the Russian consul-general in Yokohama. One might say that his being unable to leave Japan can be blamed on the current hostilities in Europe—which are equally responsible for my having to publish this correction. In other words, the war has ended up making liars out of two perfectly honest people.[17]

The 1914 essay is in effect a reprise of the earlier one. Both recount evenings spent conversing with the professor over dinner. Ostensibly written at Koeber's request as a proxy farewell note, the latter essay reinforces the man's exemplary character.

What elsewhere might appear in a satiric light—the indifference to material things, the strong aversion to formality and empty ceremony, the almost comical "cluelessness" regarding one's environs—are virtues here, wedded to the humanistic ideals that the man represents. Here indeed is a citizen of the world, in the finest sense of the term. Again, such a portrayal doubles as a critique of contemporary Japan and its sadly adulterated values.

But fate would intervene, in the form of the outbreak of war in Europe, to prevent Professor Koeber from leaving Japan. He would live out his remaining years in Japan, dying, in 1923, at the age of seventy-five. Having resided in Tokyo for thirty years, Raphael von Koeber was buried in the foreigners' graveyard in Zōshigaya, the temple where Sōseki himself had been interred seven years earlier.

Murdoch

Among Sōseki's instructors at the First Higher School was James Murdoch (1856–1921), a Scotsman who had come to Japan in 1889 as a *gaikokujin oyatoi kyōshi* (hired foreign instructor) to teach English and history. In the interim, Murdoch set about studying Japanese history, and he went on to publish the monumental three-volume *History of Japan* (1926).

Sōseki's relationship with James Murdoch is an interesting one, which only came to light in the wake of the so-called *gakui* incident in 1911. As the author relates in several essays, Murdoch, with whom there had been no contact whatsoever since his student days some twenty years earlier, sent a letter expressing his admiration for the "moral backbone" Sōseki had demonstrated in declining the official honor. The letter made a deep impression on Sōseki and occasioned a somewhat belated acknowledgment of the debt of gratitude to his old mentor. In the two essays, which appeared in quick succession, Sōseki expresses his own admiration for Murdoch's integrity as a man and his achievements as a scholar of Japanese history. And he fondly recalls his acquaintanceship with Sensei at the First Higher School. In addition to the five or six hours in class, there would be informal get-togethers at Sensei's lodgings, where he was in the habit of borrowing books on philosophy from his host's library.

Sōseki remarks with affection on Murdoch's open and welcoming nature and the interesting figure he cut in the classroom—invariably clad in a gray flannel shirt, sporting an odd scrap of a necktie. The man had an animated and histrionic lecturing style. He'd go and sit on the desk of some absent student and, thumping away on the desktop, hold forth on the topic at hand.[18]

Natsume Sōseki's Western mentors, with whom he associated in different capacities over several decades, do not represent a fixed type. They are not equally inspirational or praiseworthy, yet each is accorded a measure of respect. The mentors belong to different stages in the author's educational upbringing, and each is recalled from a different retrospective position. Having been in schools for most of his life, and himself a mentor to his circle of protégés, Sōseki fully understood the malleability of young minds and the potentially transformative quality of relationships—for good or ill—with one's sensei.[19]

Sōseki and His Circle

As a well-known writer with a secure reputation, Natsume Sōseki attracted a following of those who sought his advice, his patronage, or his autograph. As noted in the Introduction, the *bundan* milieu favored the formation of coteries and groupings that centered on a senior figure. Not all established writers made themselves available as mentors or patrons. Sōseki did. And as his career blossomed, so did his following.

The Waseda Minami-chō residence became the meeting place for a coterie that would include older acquaintances and younger writers. Beginning in October 1906, Sōseki's protégés—his so-called *monkasei,* to use the preferred term—would gather on Thursdays for their literary soirées, hence the name that attached itself to the group—the Mokuyōkai (Thursday Club). An inner circle of protégés were a regular presence in the home, and they would maintain their ties even after Sensei's death. The larger circle included some who had already achieved some note (or notoriety), others who regarded themselves as disciples, and others still who came by merely to rub elbows with the literary crowd.

In sociological terms, the Sōseki circle is best understood as an arrangement of concentric rings, reflecting the multiple relationships that the author formed over the course of his career.[20] The picture is further complicated by the fact that individuals came and went over the years. Some died. Others moved on. Most, however, remained in Tokyo, the locus of the Meiji *bundan* and the backdrop for much of its literature. And Sōseki would have occasion to write about them, fashioning a *shōhin* persona of social engagement that contrasts with the pensive loner voice. The group-centered episodes also serve to inscribe a human face upon the otherwise impersonal and abstract institution of the *bundan.*

Sōseki's broader literary affiliations cut across many lines and in effect recapitulate the various stages and segments of his career. Several groupings among the standard inventory deserve our attention. First, there is the so-called *shaseibun-ha*—those whom he met early on, through their mutual association with Masaoka Shiki (1867–1902). This affiliation is significant in several respects, not least of which concerns Sōseki's ties with *Hototogisu,* Shiki's literary journal. The key figures here are Takahama Kyoshi (1874–1959), who inherited the journal editorship, and Terada Torahiko (1878–1935)—both of whom enjoyed a long and intimate association with Sōseki.[21]

Monkasei: Sōseki Sensei and His Protégés

A larger grouping consists of those who regarded themselves—and were in turn regarded—as Sōseki *monkasei.*[22] Membership was not acknowledged in any official way, and the ranks changed over time. To put it in terms of kinship, there were those who belonged to the immediate family, and others more distantly related. In terms of age and length of affiliation, some had been Sōseki's students in the 1890s, while others—the younger ones—sought Sensei's patronage once he became established at the *Asahi* and instituted his Thursday literary soirées.

A standard listing of *monkasei* extends to nearly twenty names.[23] But the core group, in terms of the duration and intimacy of association, consists of three individuals—Suzuki Miekichi, Morita Sōhei, and Komiya Toyotaka. These three were fixtures in the Sōseki home from the outset of the Thursday get-togethers, and their relationship proved lasting.

Morita Sōhei (1881–1949), a graduate of the Imperial University, met Sōseki in 1905 and was among his earliest protégés. He is best known for a scandalous love affair with the Meiji feminist Hiratsuka Raichō, which culminated in an unsuccessful double suicide in March 1908. It was through Sōseki's patronage that Sōhei's fictionalized account of the affair, a *succès de scandale* entitled *Baien* (Smoke), appeared in *Asahi* serialization in 1909.[24] Although Sōhei long enjoyed his mentor's patronage, a penchant for outlandish behavior was known to incite Sōseki's ire.[25]

Suzuki Miekichi (1882–1936), who hailed from Hiroshima, entered the English division of the Imperial University in 1904, where he was among Sōseki's students. Suzuki aspired to a literary career and sought Sōseki's patronage for his early attempts at fiction. A work entitled *Chidori* (The Plover, 1906) earned Sōseki's praise and served as his entrée into the Thursday Club, at its inception. Following Sōseki's death, Suzuki went on to establish himself as a leading exponent of children's literature, through his editorship of the influential journal *Akai tori* (Red Bird).[26]

But it was Komiya Toyotaka (1884–1966) who can be said to have earned primus inter pares stature as Sōseki "protégé in chief." Komiya met Sōseki in 1905; together with Morita and Suzuki, they formed the first cadre, so to speak, of Mokuyōkai regulars. They remained on close terms thereafter. Like

Morita, Komiya would occasionally test Sensei's patience, but he remained a reliable right-hand man throughout his mentor's life.[27]

There would be others whose connection was more tenuous—aspiring writers, for example, who wished to be "taken in" but failed to establish themselves; unexpected callers with something to offer or some request to make; and the occasional eccentric who would merit a cameo appearance in a literary anecdote. As we've seen, such episodes tended to play on the victimization motif.

The Sōseki circle was for the most part a fraternal organization. But several women figured as well. Notwithstanding certain allegations of misogyny, Sōseki fostered the work of talented women writers—most notably, Nogami Yaeko and Ōtsuka Kusuo[28]—and in several *danwa* accounts he expresses the view that gifted literary women were more than capable of outdoing their male counterparts.[29]

Having noted an uneasy complementarity in the *shōhin* between the spheres of writer and family man, let us now examine the manner in which the author portrays the comings and goings of those in his literary family.

Mokuyōkai: The Thursday Sessions

As godfather to his younger charges, Sōseki cultivated an affectionate voice for recalling their time together. For the last ten years of his life, until shortly before his death in December 1916, Sōseki hosted his Thursday soirées, which would begin at about three in the afternoon and continue into the night. Visitors were welcome, but the in-group predominated. The following episodes suggest something of the relationship he established with his surrogate family of writers, who were a fixture in the Natsume home.

NEW YEAR'S DAY

I had partaken of the traditional New Year's breakfast and repaired to my study when three or four of the young men came by to visit. One had on a formal frock coat.[30] The others were in their everyday Japanese garb—not at all in keeping with the festive occasion, I might add. Frock must not have been accustomed to the formal getup, given how uncomfortable and fidgety he appeared. When the others took one look at Frock, they let out with a chorus of amazed exclamations, to the effect of "Get a load of him!" My own expression of amazement came as the last in the series of gibes.

For no apparent reason, Frock took out a white handkerchief and began wiping his face. Then he started in on the festive spiced sake, with a vengeance.[31] The other fellows were liberally partaking of the various dishes that had been set out. Things were in full swing by the time Kyoshi showed up. In his black *haori* coat and formal kimono, he epitomized the traditional look.

"Given your outfit," I remarked, "you must have come prepared to work on a *yōkyoku* piece."

"Yes, I have. Shall we do one together?"

"I'd be happy to."

And so the two of us joined in a rendition of *Tōboku*, a Noh play I'd once studied but hadn't practiced in years.[32] Consequently, it was very rough going, and I must admit that my voice sounded weak and hesitant. When we finally finished the piece, our small audience, as if by prearrangement, unanimously declared my own performance to have been abysmal. For his part, Frock remarked that my voice had been halting and unsteady. I knew only too well that none of these fellows had the slightest familiarity with Noh recitation and therefore lacked any basis for judgment. But I had to concede that being subject to criticism is perfectly natural. Hence I couldn't muster the nerve to get worked up about it.

Kyoshi then mentioned that he'd recently begun lessons on *tsuzumi*—the hand drum used in Noh. Hearing this, the group urged him on, notwithstanding their ignorance of the art.

Kyoshi turned to me. "I'll need you to do the chanting, then."

I'd never performed with any accompaniment before, so this would be a challenge. But I was tempted by the novelty of it all and agreed to take part.

First, though, Kyoshi had to send a rickshaw man to go and fetch his instrument. . . . Once the drum arrived and he had finished preparing it, Kyoshi removed his *haori* and positioned the drum under his arm, ready to begin. I asked him to wait a moment before we got started. For one thing, how was I to know when he'd be striking the drum? Wasn't there some need to coordinate our efforts? Referring me to the *utaibon* text, Kyoshi solicitously tried to clarify things for me. He pointed out exactly where he would come in with his *kakegoe* voicings,[33] where the drum would come in, and with what sort of beat.

"Let's get started, then," he said.

I was more confused than ever. But since we could hardly afford to spend hours trying to get things just right, I halfheartedly nodded my agreement. We would be performing an introductory section from *Hagoromo*. . . .[34]

And so I started in, rather unimpressively, and instantly regretted having agreed to go through with this. But I forged ahead, albeit with scant enthusiasm. Then all of a sudden—a piercing shriek, followed by a resounding whack on the drum. The ferocity of Kyoshi's attack came as a total surprise. The *kakegoe,* which I'd assumed would be something graceful and modulated, was instead rendered as an earsplitting scream, as though the man were engaged in mortal combat. . . .

I somehow managed to continue singing my part, when Kyoshi attacked from the flank with yet another deep-throated howl. And another. My own voice, gradually cowed into submission by the man's bellowing, became more frail and tentative with each successive foray. By this time, our little audience had started in with barely suppressed titters and giggles. What a fiasco, I thought to myself. Just then, Frock rose up, front and center, and broke into a fit of laughter. I could not help but follow suit.

This unleashed a torrent of gibes, with Frock delivering the most caustic blow. . . . The younger contingent had their turn as well. Even my wife joined in on the banter.

"And I must say," she added, "that whenever Mr. Takahama [referring to Kyoshi] beat the drum, I was able to see the sleeves of his under-kimono, which were fluttering about. What a lovely color!"

Frock immediately agreed. As for myself—I saw nothing lovely about any of it whatsoever.[35] (*Eijitsu* 1, 1909)

This New Year's essay, an auspicious choice for the first *Eijitsu* selection, appeared in the *Asahi* on January 1, 1909, although it recalls the prior year's festivities. It thus complies with the prevailing convention of publishing *ganjitsu* features to usher in the new year.[36] The essay creates a lively stage for the antics of Sōseki's circle. The informality that the author prized in his role as mentor is in evidence, and the contrast with the dour, peevish persona of the harried householder is obvious. Even the wife is assigned a minor role.[37]

Presumably, the *Asahi* readers would have been familiar with the cast of characters, of whom the only named individual is Takahama Kyoshi. Morita Sōhei, known for his flamboyant excess, appears as Frock—a dig, perhaps, at his penchant for formal wear on inappropriate occasions.

Self-parody, though, strikes the dominant chord here, playing on the narrator's clumsy *utai* rendition. As already noted, Sōseki was in fact a serious student of Noh recitation, having been originally encouraged by Kyoshi himself during their stay in Kumamoto many years earlier.[38] The episode provides a refreshingly unbuttoned glimpse of the Sōseki crowd in its earlier phase. Notwithstanding the spirit of camaraderie, though, the self-mockery here is undercut by a slightly bitter edge, as Sōseki's narrator appears unwilling entirely to abandon his pride when made the object of ridicule.

Again, the Mokuyōkai was by no means an exclusive club. In contrast with the above portrayal of the inner circle, other *shōhin* tell of unexpected callers. The following concerns one such individual, who came bearing an unusual gift:

THE PHEASANT

A group of us were gathered around the hibachi one day, engaged in conversation, when a young man arrived—a total stranger, with no letter of introduction—asking for an audience. When he was shown into the parlor, the young man stood before us—carrying a pheasant! Following an exchange of formalities, he presented the bird to us. "I've brought this for you. It was sent by my family back home."

It was a cold day, and in no time we were all feasting on pheasant stew. The young man had gone straight into the kitchen to pluck the feathers, take charge of the cooking, carve the meat, and dispose of the bones. He was short of stature, and his pale, elongated face was adorned with a thin mustache and a pair of thick eyeglasses, which glinted in the light. But most remarkable of all was the *hakama* that he had on—a garish, thick-striped garment that no self-respecting student would want to be seen wearing. "I'm from up north," he announced, with both hands placed upon the *hakama*.

The young man returned a week later, this time with a manuscript. "Please tell me if you think it's not very good," he remarked. "I'll gladly rewrite it." With that he left. The next week he came by with another manuscript. Whenever he visited, he'd bring along something he'd written. There was even a magnum opus in three volumes, which turned out to be the worst of the lot.

On several occasions I picked through the assorted manuscripts and sent the most promising to one of the literary journals, requesting their kind consideration. Out of charity's sake, the editor would see to it that the piece got published, but this never earned the lad a penny's worth of remuneration. By and by I learned of his financial difficulties. "From here on out," he mentioned, "I intend to eke out a living through my writing."

The young man was in the habit of bringing some unusual item for the group. One day it was thin sheets of dried chrysanthemum....A younger member of our circle who happened to be on hand took the stuff in to be soaked in water and boiled, and we partook of the dish with some sake. On another occasion, he brought a decorative bunch of artificial flowers—lilies of the valley, to be exact. "My younger sister made it," he proclaimed, twirling the wire branch around with his fingers. I learned that he was living with a sister and that the two were renting a room on the second floor of a firewood shop. The sister was taking lessons in embroidery.

The next time, he brought a grayish-blue necktie with embroidered white butterflies, wrapped in newsprint. "This is yours to keep," he said, presenting me with the tie, "provided you'll actually wear it." When the young man left, Yasuno told me that he wanted the tie. I was more than happy to have him take it off my hands.

Whenever the young man visited, he would have some tale to tell about his native region—its scenery, folklore, festivals. He also mentioned that his father was a scholar of Chinese studies and a seal engraver of some note. His grandmother had been in the service of the local daimyo. She'd been born in the year of the monkey, he said, and the daimyo had taken such a fancy to her that he set about presenting her with things associated with monkeys. One such item was a hanging scroll by Kazan, depicting a gibbon. "I'll bring it by for you to have a look at."

But his visits stopped after that.

Spring came and went, and summer was upon us. I'd all but forgotten about the young man. Then, one hellishly hot day, he unexpectedly reappeared. Dressed in my lightest summer garb, I sat reading a book in my shaded room; the heat was unbearable. And there he was before me, wearing the same outlandish outfit, busily wiping the sweat from his pallid brow. He seemed to have lost weight.

"It truly pains me to ask, but could you possibly loan me twenty yen? You see, a close friend suddenly took ill and I've had him hospitalized. But at present I'm hard up for money. I've come to you out of dire need."

I put down my book and looked long and hard at the young man, as he sat with both hands placed decorously upon his knees. "I beg of you," he pleaded in a low voice.

"Is your friend's family really all that poor?"

"No, it's just that they're far away and can't come up with the money in time. It should arrive in two weeks, though, at which point I'll repay you immediately."

When I agreed to the loan, the young man opened up a parcel he had with him and took out a mounted scroll. "This is the Kazan piece that I'd mentioned the other day." He spread it out for me to see. I couldn't tell if it was fine art or junk. As for the artist's seal, it didn't resemble any of those used by either of the famous Kazans—Watanabe or Yokoyama.[39]

"I'd like to leave this with you."

"There's really no need to," I responded. But he insisted that the scroll be left in my care. The next day he returned for the money. And after that he was heard from no more. The two weeks passed, and no trace of the man. It would appear, I concluded, that he'd pulled one over on me.

And so with the arrival of autumn, the gibbon scroll continued to decorate the wall. By and by it was time to take out the heavier garments, and with the bracing weather came a renewed determination to get down to work. Then one day Nagatsuka showed up, wanting to borrow money yet again.[40] Time and again I'm loaning out money. I'd come to hate it.

Just then I recalled the young man and his scroll.

"Look, there's twenty yen of mine that I've loaned out, and it's long overdue. If you can manage to get it back, that sum is yours on loan."

Nagatsuka hesitated, anxiously scratching his head, but he agreed to take me up on my offer. I wrote a note asking that the money be handed over to the bearer and gave it to Nagatsuka, together with the gibbon scroll. He returned the next day, and immediately proceeded to remove something from his pocket and hand it over to me. It was the note I'd written, in its unopened envelope.

"So you didn't go after all?"

"I did go," Nagatsuka said, frowning. "But what a wretched situation they're in over there! The place is absolutely filthy. The wife is working on her sewing. The man of the house is sick. I couldn't very well broach the subject of money. So I assured them that there was nothing to worry about, that I'd just come by to return the scroll." This took me quite by surprise.

The next day a postcard arrived. "The scroll is back in my possession. I must apologize for lying to you." I bundled up the postcard with some other correspondence and placed it in a basket. And once again I put the young man out of my mind.

Winter arrived, and with it the busy New Year season. I was taking advantage of a lull in the parade of well-wishers to get some work done when the maid brought in an odd package wrapped in reinforced paper. The thing was round and made a thumping sound when put down. It had been sent by the long-forgotten young man. I tore open the wrapping and out came a pheasant! A letter was attached: "Circumstances have dictated that I return home. But I fully intend to repay the loan when I visit Tokyo this coming March." The letter was stuck to the congealed blood of the pheasant, and it was no easy matter to peel it loose.

It was a Thursday, the day when my protégés gather to spend the evening. On that occasion, the group of us sat down at a large table and dined—once again—on pheasant stew. And we all expressed our best wishes on behalf of the wan youth in the garish *hakama* who had been our companion. Later that night, after the others had left, I wrote a note of thanks to our young friend. "As for the twenty yen," I added, "consider the matter forgotten."[41] (*Eijitsu* 12, 1909)

The *bundan* annals are well represented by accounts of good, decent folk who are down on their luck and deserve a helping hand. Money is a perennial problem, and its recurrence as a motif in Sōseki's work should not be dismissed as a nagging peccadillo. Rather, it points to the sad reality of Meiji youth who struggled to write for a living—against considerable odds and often with unfortunate consequences.[42] In this instance, Sōseki used his good offices on the lad's behalf, but to no avail.

A similar situation, somewhat closer to home, concerns one Nishimura Tōin (1885–?), an aspiring writer with little talent and limited resources. Nishimura eagerly sought Sōseki's patronage but failed to make the grade, at which point he was taken into the Natsume home as a *shosei* (live-in houseboy), in 1909. A handful of diary entries, tinged with compassion and exasperation, touch upon the young man's desperate circumstances and Sōseki's efforts to help the fellow out with the occasional proofreading job. Tōin's younger sister, too, was taken in to work as a housemaid, but she eventually turned to prostitution, while his own literary aspirations met with repeated failure and disappointment.[43]

Thursdays with Sensei

Inevitably, the Thursday Group would not remain the same over its ten-year course—a situation noted in several of the transcribed interviews. In one, a "Sōseki Chat" that appeared in the April 16, 1914, issue of *Hankyō* (The Echo), the interviewer—none other than Morita Sōhei—took the liberty of inserting some personal remarks. "It was a Thursday," Morita notes, "and the *monkasei* were assembled for their weekly session of gossip and small-talk *(mudabanashi)*. How the group has changed, though, over the years. A number have graduated; some have gotten married. Many have stopped coming altogether. The new ones are all into foreign literature—German, French, English. And they'll show up, rain or shine."[44]

It was on November 16, 1916, that the Mokuyōkai gathered for the last time. Sōseki sensei passed away some three weeks later.

It may go without saying that "Thursdays with Sensei" calls to mind Mitch Albom's best-selling *Tuesdays with Morrie,* a memoiristic account of life lessons learned from one's beloved former professor through weekly visits over the course of the man's terminal illness. Evoking a sentimentalism in the mode of *Goodbye, Mr. Chips,* Albom's eulogy to a wise and beautiful soul is both memorable and moving. Sōseki's protégés, for their part, viewed Sensei from diverse perspectives. Some came to regard the man as an irascible prig, while others affectionately recalled this or that idiosyncracy. None, though, would bear witness to sitting reverentially at the man's feet and basking in his august presence. What they shared, in their own personal writings, was a nostalgic recollection of those Thursdays with Sensei.

Here I would like to mention a film—the final work of Kurosawa Akira. Entitled *Mādadayo* (Not Just Yet! 1993), it is a cinematic retelling of the life of scholar-author Uchida Hyakken (1889–1975). Hyakken was one of the young newcomers to Sōseki's Thursday group—and the one, mentioned above by Morita, with the German literary training.[45] Following Sōseki's example, Hyakken himself would give up teaching in order to take up writing as a career, but he retained his identity as Sensei among his own circle of devoted former students and admirers. The film, a beautiful (if unabashedly sentimental) evocation of the bonds of affection and loyalty forged between this good-natured eccentric and his "boys," extends as well to the community of discipleship that Hyakken experienced, as a young man, in Sensei's company. The continuity of the mentor-disciple relationship is an easily overlooked facet of the Sōseki saga, one that points to a traditionalist quality of Japanese culture that many—myself included—have found especially moving.

Tsuitōbun: Memorial Remembrance

Remembering the deceased, in some form or fashion, is an anthropological given. Death obliges a ritual acknowledgment—be it religious or merely journalistic. In the latter regard, the obituary is our mode of public notice. A line or two of print may suffice in most cases, but the passing of prominent individuals will naturally warrant a wordier account.

In late-Meiji Japan, the celebrity demise would call forth memorial features in the periodical press, special memorial issues, and finally the publication of memoir and reminiscence in book form. In all cases, the epitomizing anecdote—typically informal and off-the-cuff—would ostensibly point to the "real" person, and to human qualities concealed behind the public face and reputation.

The term *tsuitōbun* refers to the memorial essay genre—a subgenre, in effect, of reminiscence narrative. Within the *bundan,* the death of a notable writer would send literary editors and reporters scurrying for material for their special issues—the content, size, and sales of which might arguably serve as a crude index of one's reputation. Not surprisingly, the living notables would be among the first responders to the call for memorial reflection and reminiscence. Sōseki would dutifully hold forth on those literary folk who passed away during his lifetime—as he himself would be memorialized, lavishly, following his own demise. And as with all biographical writing, his *tsuitō* remembrances will reflect as much upon himself as on his subject.[46]

In fact, Sōseki remarks upon this very thing in the course of his *Garasudo* musings:

> Over the past several years, I've been seriously ill at least once a year, and each time I've been bedridden for a month or so.... When I am up and about, I'll occasionally find one of those black-bordered obituary notices sitting on my desk. Like someone casting his fate to the winds, I'll don my silk hat and rush off to join the funeral procession. The deceased naturally tend to be elderly folk, but among them are those even younger than myself, who'd proudly boasted of their excellent health....
>
> It is curious to note that I rarely receive obituary notices during my periods of convalescence. Last autumn, having recovered from a bout of illness, I attended three or four funerals in quick succession. One of these was for Satō Hokkō, a colleague on the *Asahi* editorial staff. I recalled the banquet at which Satō was honored by the newspaper. He came over, bringing with him the silver cup he'd been presented with, and offered me some sake. I still remember the bizarre little dance he regaled us with on that occasion.
>
> I normally have little difficulty in accepting the fact that I should outlive a robust, energetic man like Satō. But it does occasionally cross my mind that it's an unnatural state of affairs for me still to be alive. I suspect that fate might be playing tricks on me.[47] (*Garasudo* 22, 1915)

The rationale behind Sōseki's memorializing is not always clear. An earlier opportunity to reflect upon the death of someone close to him—namely, Masaoka Shiki—yielded a surprisingly disjointed and dispassionate remembrance.[48] In a 1908 interview, he remarks upon Shiki's unusual eating habits and other idiosyncrasies; and a 1911 essay concerns a painting by Shiki and the curious artlessness that was his stylistic signature. One would have expected more.

As a rule, Sōseki's memorial remarks tend to be pro forma exercises. This would be expected in the case of individuals whom he did not know well.[49] But on occasion he would hold forth in an uncharacteristically personal voice.

Such was the case with writer Futabatei Shimei (1864–1909), the pen name of Hasegawa Tatsunosuke.

Futabatei/Hasegawa

Futabatei ranks among the more intriguing figures in Meiji literature.[50] Having made his mark on the emerging *bundan* scene with the novel *Ukigumo* (Drifting Clouds, 1887–1889), he abandoned a promising literary career in favor of diplomatic and journalistic pursuits, exploiting his fluency in Russian. Futabatei reentered the *bundan* at about the time that Sōseki embarked on his *Asahi* career. Before that, however, he had himself entered the employ of the *Asahi,* as a political writer and, eventually, foreign correspondent. Posted to Russia in 1908, Futabatei took ill and passed away, on May 10, 1909, somewhere in the Bay of Bengal, aboard a Japan-bound ship.

Futabatei Shimei was a much admired, if elusive, figure, whose skepticism regarding the ultimate worth of literary endeavor struck a responsive chord with Sōseki. In this sense, there is a certain irony in the efforts made by several *bundan* colleagues—Uchida Roan and Tsubouchi Shōyō—to edit what became an impressive memorial volume. Sōseki's contribution to the volume is as follows:

HASEGAWA AND I

Hasegawa and I had merely known one another by name. Indeed, I hadn't even realized that he was on the staff of the *Asahi shinbun* when I myself was hired.[51] I've forgotten how I happened to learn that we were colleagues. In any event, our paths did not cross for a period of time. Moreover, since our homes were so close to each other—like myself, Hasegawa lived in Nishi-katamachi, on land that had been part of the great Abe estate[52]—it would have only been a common courtesy to pay him a call. But I was hopelessly remiss, neglecting even to inquire as to his whereabouts.

Then one day I attended a dinner at a club in Yūrakuchō, at the invitation of Ikebe Sanzan, together with a number of *Asahi* colleagues. The occasion was the visit of Torii Sosen, chief editor of the Osaka edition of the *Asahi.*[53] As a relative newcomer to the staff, this was my first occasion to dine with the company's upper echelon. As it turns out, Hasegawa was among those in attendance.

When we were introduced, I was stunned at the discrepancy between the individual as I'd imagined him and the person standing before me. Judging from the impression he gave when first entering the room, and the easy familiarity with which he greeted everyone, I assumed that he represented the *Asahi* management. Who would have guessed that this was

Hasegawa himself. . . . I never imagined he would be so tall, so powerfully built. I never imagined such burly breadth to his shoulders, such an angular set to his chin. Indeed, his entire appearance struck me as a set of right angles. Even his head seemed to be square—quite comically so, in retrospect.

At the time I hadn't yet read Hasegawa's recent novel, *Sono omokage*.[54] But for such a sensual, romantic tale to have been written by the man before me seemed hard to fathom. How could someone with his commanding presence be the sort to languish away at a desk, with pen in hand? I was dumbfounded.

What surprised me even more was Hasegawa's manner of speaking. I'd frankly imagined that he would sound nervous and fidgety. Quite the contrary, his voice was deep and relaxed. There wasn't a hint of edginess. When we were introduced, we had a brief exchange of greetings. Hasegawa's exact words escape me, but I recall that he didn't resort to the standard pleasantries. Then there was a curt exchange of bows. Who could have anticipated such a brief encounter? We didn't converse any further on that occasion. I merely listened to Hasegawa talk, and found myself much taken with his dignified, gentlemanly manner. He conveyed a certain bearing, a gravitas that I sensed was both an inborn trait and the product of personal cultivation. . . .

Hasegawa embarked on a discussion of Russian party politics with Ikebe. Evidently engrossed in the subject, the two of them went on and on—an impressive verbal display that bespoke an extraordinary breadth of knowledge on Hasegawa's part. He'd hold forth on a certain Mr. This-or-that-ski from one party, and another Mr. Something-or-another-ski from the opposing party. It was as though he had just returned from Russia with the most up-to-date political intelligence. But strange as it may seem, there wasn't the slightest hint of pedantry or bombast in his remarks.

By nature indifferent to things political, I found little of interest in Hasegawa's conversation with Ikebe. Truth be told, I wouldn't have known whether the Russians even *had* a legislature! And so I took my leave while the two were still at it. This, then, was my first meeting with Hasegawa.

Several days later, I happened by the *Asahi* offices on some business. Climbing the filthy stairway to the editorial department, I entered the room to find a group of staff sitting around a table by the window. I recognized all of them except for one who had his back to me—a large man in a gray suit, whose hefty torso bulged out from the chair back. Wondering who this might be, I moved to the side and had a look. It was Hasegawa.

181

"I was thinking of paying you a visit," I said, trying to catch his attention. But he responded before I could even finish.

"Sorry, but I've been under the weather. I'm not receiving any callers." Not knowing Hasegawa, I couldn't gather the meaning of his being "under the weather." But it was perfectly clear that he did not want me to visit. And so I chose not to pursue the matter, surmising that the expression he'd used was a clever way of indicating that he was somehow out of sorts. I would later discover that Hasegawa was actually suffering from a serious condition, which for its duration was the cause of acute pain.

For the time being, then, I hung up my own No Visitors sign. And since we'd yet to establish the wherewithal to bring down our mutually imposed barriers, we lost our chance to become better acquainted.

Then one afternoon I went to the public bath. I undressed and walked into the washroom area. And there, on the far end of the room, was Hasegawa. Facing the other way as he washed himself, Hasegawa had not noticed me entering. When I called his name, he turned to me. "Hello, there!" This was the extent of our conversation for the time being.

It was a very hot day, I recall. I got out of the bath, dried off, and went out on the veranda, where matting had been spread out, to sit down and fan myself off. By and by, Hasegawa left the bath. Putting his eyeglasses back on, he spotted me from across the way and we began chatting. Both of us were bare naked. I noted that Hasegawa's manner of speech was indistinguishable from his discourse on Russian party politics that first time we met—the same resonant, calm, deliberate style. Quite at odds with our current environs!

This time, though, Hasegawa openly discussed his medical condition, in considerable detail. He'd apparently undergone a fainting spell a year earlier and had spent some time recuperating in a facility near Tabata. Things had evidently improved somewhat.

"What about that No Visitors sign, then?" I ask, half in jest.

"Well, I'm afraid that..."

"I see. In that case, I'll hold off visiting for the time being."

And with that, we parted company.

It was that autumn when we moved from Nishi-Katamachi to Waseda, which further distanced me from Hasegawa. To make amends, I went out and bought a copy of his novel, *Sono omokage*. It impressed me greatly.... I sent him a letter praising the work—a gratuitous gesture, perhaps, but one that might suggest my concern regarding Hasegawa's condition. Quite unaware that he was at the time loath even to consider himself a literary person, I flattered myself with the assumption that the words of a fellow writer might provide a degree of comfort. This was a needless impertinence, in view of his antipathy toward the literary life.[55]

The last time I saw Hasegawa was several days before his departure for Russia, when he came by to say farewell. This would be the first and only time that Hasegawa would set foot in my house. Ushered into the sitting room, he remarked that it had the look of a Buddhist retreat.[56] The occasion being a formal leave-taking, our conversation involved nothing out of the ordinary. Before leaving, though, he reminded me of my agreement to look after several of his literary protégés—Miss Mozume and the young man from up north.[57]

Several days later, I went to pay a return visit to Hasegawa, but he was not at home. Nor was I able to see him off on his trip. I would never see him again. He did send a postcard from St. Petersburg, mentioning how brutally cold it was. I sympathized, but assumed with amused detachment that the cold certainly wouldn't kill him. Apparently it did. Hasegawa passed away before we could get to know one another. Had he lived, we may well have kept our distance. Then again, the opportunity might have arisen for us to become close. He thus remains a far-off friend whom I know only through memories of our few encounters. As for his protégés—I occasionally see Miss Mozume, but there has been no word at all from the young man.[58]

Despite the evident admiration for Hasegawa/Futabatei—the man and his work—Sōseki's memorial essay appears more an account of one's misapprehensions than an attempt to epitomize the man and his place in the Meiji literary world. A wistful, possibly cautionary tale of opportunities missed—two like-minded souls who have every reason to be on close terms yet fail to connect.[59]

One is struck by the narrator's dumbfounded reaction to the surprisingly masculine presence before him and the incongruity he senses in the image of this man scribbling away at a desk. Psychoanalytic readings aside, the essay is a curious variant of the *shosai* persona—the naive, self-deprecatory writer-type contrasted with the self-assured, imposing man of affairs. The calculated distancing of oneself from politics and affairs of state—here rendered in comic overstatement—strongly marks this persona.[60]

Sōseki remains a passive player in this little drama of unexpected meetings and unexplored possibilities. Death does foreclose options. As for Hasegawa's final bequest—namely, his young protégés—Sōseki merely notes that he occasionally sees the Mozume girl.[61]

Other memorializations would elicit more than the perfunctory gesture. For instance, Sōseki wrote movingly of his colleague Ikebe Sanzan, who passed away in February 1912. After all, it was Sanzan, as noted in the *Omoidasu* reminiscence, who had hurried to the author's side at Shuzenji when he was barely clinging to life. And as with the Hasegawa essay, there is the expression of regret for having failed to maintain closer ties.[62]

Kusuo

Let us turn, in conclusion, to an individual whose relationship with Sōseki has given rise to much speculation—Ōtsuka Kusuo (1875–1910), the wife of his old college friend Ōtsuka Yasuji.[63] Tokyo-born Kusuo was an unusually gifted woman, whose literary proclivities were evident in childhood. A published tanka poet, she branched out into free verse *(shintaishi)* and the literary essay. She also published literary criticism and translation, while at the same time pursuing voice and piano training. Then, emulating the example of Higuchi Ichiyō, she began publishing fiction in 1895, receiving plaudits that heralded her as a successor to Ichiyō within the top echelon of Meiji women's literature *(joryū bungaku)*.[64] It was through her fiction that Kusuo began associating with Sōseki, whom she met through her husband's introduction, and her work is said to bear the marks of Sōseki's mentorship.

Literary credentials aside, Ōtsuka Kusuo was by all accounts a beauty. *Bundan* gossipmongers have hinted at Sōseki's infatuation with Kusuo and at an unsuccessful rivalry, with his friend Yasuji, for her affections—the emotional consequences of which were said to be severe.[65] Some have concluded that Kusuo is the model for the "mystery woman" *(nazo no onna)* who appears, in different guises, in Sōseki's work. The following episode from *Garasudo* has helped fuel such speculation.

A RAINY NIGHT'S ENCOUNTER

The following incident occurred one rainy night many years ago, while I was living in Sendagi.[66] On my way back from a walk, I turned down a less-traveled side road.... Wherever I looked, gloom and darkness greeted me, and my mood mirrored the foul weather and dreary surroundings. Lodged inside me is the ugly, tumorlike mass of cheerlessness, which always threatens to poison my spirit.

And so I listlessly plodded along through the pouring rain, wearing a dismal expression. Just as I passed by the *yose* theater in Hikage-chō,[67] a rickshaw approached. It was equipped with a rain canopy, but I was close enough to notice that the passenger was a woman. Since this was before the advent of celluloid windows, I had an unobstructed view of an

astonishingly beautiful face, the skin almost white in its pallor. Captivated
by her beauty as I walked on through the rain, I assumed that she must be
a geisha. I was convinced of it, in fact, but when the rickshaw approached
within arm's length, the woman who had so transported me smiled and
made a polite bow in my direction as she passed by. It was only then that I
recognized her—Ōtsuka Kusuo!

When we had occasion to meet several days later, Kusuo touched upon
our recent encounter. I took advantage of this opening to speak my mind.

"You looked so beautiful that I took you for a geisha."

I don't recall her exact response, but Kusuo appeared not in the least
flustered or put out by my candid remark. She accepted it with perfect
equanimity.

Quite some time passed, and one day Kusuo stopped by the house
to pay a call. Unfortunately, I'd just had a quarrel with my wife and had
retreated to my study, where I remained at my desk in a foul mood. Kusuo
ended up chatting with my wife and then left.[68]

Nothing further transpired that day, but soon thereafter I visited the
Ōtsuka residence to apologize for my behavior.

"The fact is, I'd been quarreling with my wife. She must have been
rather unsociable as well. As for myself, I thought it best not to expose you
to my ill humor, and so I made myself scarce."

As for Kusuo's response—I'm afraid that her words, now relics of the
past, are submerged in the recesses of my memory, from which I cannot
retrieve them.

News of Kusuo's death reached me while I was in the Nagayo Clinic.[69]
I recall having been phoned to inquire if I objected to having my name
included in the obituary. While in the clinic, I composed a haiku in
Kusuo's memory: "Take every last chrysanthemum and throw them in her
coffin."[70]

A certain fellow with a penchant for haiku was so taken with the
verse that he asked me for a *tanzaku* rendition. This, too, was long ago.[71]
(*Garasudo* 25, 1915)

The episode incorporates three separate recollections of Ōtsuka Kusuo:
the first, a dreary scene from the past, enlivened by the gorgeous white vis-
age—an apparition of beauty that is none other than Kusuo; the second, a
more recent encounter, spoiled by a marital spat and the strategic retreat into
one's study; and the third, hearing of Kusuo's death, five years earlier, as he
himself convalesces in a Tokyo clinic, and the memorial haiku that he wrote.
What these three share is the narrator's dominant viewpoint. Walking the

185

dismal, rain-swept streets—a scene reminiscent of the bleak cityscape of his London walks—he encounters a spectral beauty that stops him in his tracks.[72] Then, it is his wife, ironically, who ends up receiving Kusuo when she calls; and when he recalls having gone to apologize for his antisocial behavior, Sōseki's narrator cites *his* exact words to Kusuo, but confesses that hers have become forgotten "relics of the past, submerged in the recesses of memory." He then recalls the obituary and the haiku, but in the end there is no vestige of the woman in whose memory he composed it.

A curious memorial, one is tempted to conclude, for someone assumed to have been so dear. But as we've seen, Sōseki was not one to wax sentimental, and the *Garasudo* series is marked by a reluctance to portray individuals (especially family members) in a negative light. Even the reference here to marital discord stops short of assigning blame to his wife.

On Sōseki and the Telling Episode

As the above examples suggest, Natsume Sōseki's memorial narratives are a blend of convention, invention, and self-presentation. The genre itself dictated certain constraints and caveats, but what threatens to become a merely decorous exercise is enlivened by a concern for mise en scène and dramatized incident. Yet the narrator's point of view is predominant, and a standard refrain concerns the "reluctant survivor" lament—one lives on, in the face of advancing decrepitude, while others continue to die off.

In the broader *shōhin* framework, what has Natsume Sōseki "told" in these telling portrayals of literary lives? Recalling Lopate's notion of the personal essay as free-form literary ramble, how inventive has Sōseki been? I've noted the early experimentation with fictional narrative, which extended to the *Eijitsu* episodes. This is less evident with the later *shōhin*, where the reminiscent attitude predominates.

In one sense, the literary portraits can be regarded, collectively, as a Meiji cultural document—a *bundan* cross-section via personal reminiscence. At the other interpretive extreme, these accounts can be read as *shishōsetsu*—the famous literary nebulosity composed of writing that ostensibly channels the true authorial self in some essential way.[73]

Again with an eye to Lopate's schema, I would call attention to a commonality among the "told lives" in this chapter and elsewhere in this book. Literary caricature is prevalent, as with the Craig portrayal, although the overall effect is not comic. Sōseki's subjects tend to be those on the margin—minor lives written out of the "official" record. Again, given the gritty Grub Street reality of the Tokyo *bundan* and the sheer excess of supply over demand, many who struggled to gain a foothold in the literary marketplace were relegated to the shadows. Following upon contemporaries such as Uchida Roan, Sōseki has effectively contributed to the salvage of these individuals, through his *shōhin* portrayals.[74] And the *shōhin* genre itself, by definition on the margins, is most worthy of reclamation. In the hands of a master craftsman, such literary morsels become a feast for the attentive reader.

Zōshigaya and Beyond

Re-membering Sōseki

T his book has traced Natsume Sōseki, through his many literary reflections, from B to Z—the B of his Babashita roots in the early years of
Meiji to the Z of his final resting place in Zōshigaya. While drawing
heavily upon the *shōhin* collections, I have included other literary personalia
as well—diary entries, poetry, published interviews, and autobiographical fiction. These writings, which strain against their respective genre categories, are
stylistically and thematically diverse. They coalesce, I would argue, through
the predominant personal voice. At times introspective and intense, at times
light and fanciful, Sōseki's narrator also traces connections with many individuals, both living and dead, and he recreates scenes and incidents drawn
from memories of the past. Throughout, he thinks about things and ponders
his own presence in the here and now.

Natsume Sōseki's iconic stature will incline some to read this book as
displaced biography, cobbled from selected *auto*biographical episodes.[1] The
author has been so strongly identified with his time that the collected writings may be likened to a great *Meiji monogatari,* and his convincing literary
portrayal of Meiji life and manners is surely representative, in the Emersonian
sense of the term.[2] But the cobbling together of *shōhin* incident and episode was never intended as a summation of this celebrated literary life. The
"B to Z" synopsis, in other words, belies many lacunae in the alphabetical
sequence.

My chief concern has been with the *shōhin* as literary narrative and the narrator per se—specifically, the manner and method of his reminiscence. Sōseki's
reminiscing narrator speaks in different voices—the workaday writer, the bedridden invalid, the skeptic, the dreamer, the poet. I've pointed to the bond
between *shōhin* narrator and fictional protagonist—each a crafted voice reflecting upon one's private circumstances and the world at large. This is a crucial
concern, raising as it does the fraught issue of Japanese literary genres and their
peculiar taxonomy. Despite readers' expectations regarding genre integrity and

differentiation, the borders between fictional and essayistic narratives are permeable, if not illusory, and a priori claims to a concrete distinction between "fiction" and "essay" as discrete genres must be regarded with caution.

Nonetheless, faced with the uncontested preeminence of Sōseki's novels, I have wanted to claim the personal essay as a bona fide literary genre, and I have treated each of the *shōhin* vignettes—however modest in scope—as a carefully wrought narrative. I have also pointed to the larger integrative artistry of literary miscellanies such as the *shōhin* collections.³ Unlike the fiction, which bears the burden of psychological portrayal and extended plot development, the *shōhin* episodes, in sequence, tap into a literary aesthetic that privileges discursive freedom and stylistic play.

It may go without saying that I have adopted here a belletristic approach to Sōseki's personal writing, approaching his essay style as an amalgam of casual informality and formal elegance, quotidian specificity and lyrical transcendence. While underscoring the dominant role of memory and melancholy in the author's literary design, I have also pointed to his playful, puckish voice and the wry, ironic tones that it evokes.

What is more, I have wanted my *own* writing to reflect something of the belletrist spirit, which a recent handbook of literary terms defines, pointedly, as a species of writing "free of the laborious, inert, jargon-ridden habits indulged by professors."⁴ Having worn deep grooves in the decades-long path of my academic travels, I have tried to cultivate fresh approaches and new directions—and, most important, a voice that invites rather than excludes the reader. While Natsume Sōseki is anything but "new," the *shōhin* project has opened many doors—a serendipity that I suspect the author himself experienced over the course of years spent writing newspaper fiction on the installment plan.

Kodokusei

Sōseki's is a richly thematic literature. I have singled out a particular theme—*kodokusei* (aloneness)—as emblematic of the *shōhin* and, to be sure, the later novels.⁵ The loner persona emerged early on, and an atmosphere of alienation and disaffection permeates much of the personal writing. But we need to recognize the bivalence of the *kodokusei* theme in the *shōhin* and beyond. For Sōseki, confinement signals both the pain and burden of self-centeredness and the hope of connecting with others and being restored to a wholeness of spirit, if not body.⁶ Here I join with Angela Yiu in calling attention to the author's lyrical voice—in particular, his *kanshi* verse—as a meditative exercise

189

to which he returned periodically, one that drew inspiration from the deep well of private reflection.[7]

Kodokusei, in other words, stands at a thematic intersection. And Sōseki's personal writings, as presented here, point to other intersections as well—the domestic, family realm versus the public, and publicized, author; Meiji Japan versus its Edo/Tokugawa roots; the reality of Tokyo in the late Meiji versus evocations of an early-Meiji past; and—with a nod to the "glass doors" motif—the private self versus the larger world. To put it differently, Natsume Sōseki—the man and his work—versus the collective memory of Meiji Japan.[8] The humble trope of the reclusive thinker has generated a world of signification. But to my mind, Sōseki's literary lights most meaningfully intersect with—and illuminate—the social and spiritual anxieties of our own time.

Sōseki Re-membered

The Meiji era is dead and gone, but its great literary chronicler lives on. The nearly century-long history of Natsume Sōseki's resurrection and "re-membering" of course hinges upon the continued relevance and readability of his work, which has never been out of print and remains a mainstay of the "lit paperbacks" *(bunkobon)* shelves in the bookstores. But there is more here than meets the eye. Let me connect some Sōseki-related dots that begin with Zōshigaya and end with our not-so-new century.

The tale of Sōseki remembrance begins, in a sense, with a dismembering. On December 10, 1916, a day after the author's death, an autopsy was performed, at his wife Kyōko's request, by Dr. Nagayo Matao. The very next day, detailed reports of the autopsy began appearing in the press, competing with what would be a rising tide of the more routine eulogizing. Among other things, it was revealed that the great author's brain was abnormally— and impressively—large, and substantially heavier than the average human brain. What is more, it was described in glowing terms as a superb specimen, quite at odds with the fact of its having been extracted from a disease-ravaged corpse.

The superlative brain, together with the diseased stomach that hastened Sōseki's demise, have been preserved in the medical college of the Imperial University. It has periodically been on display, as well. And like Einstein's brain, also liberated from a famous cranial enclosure, it has inspired its own literary re-membering.[9]

In the midst of the media hoopla, Sōseki's funeral was conducted on December 12, in Aoyama. Later that month, on the twenty-eighth, his remains were interred in Zōshigaya. The *bundan*-based memorial reminiscence commenced with the New Year. The January 1917 issue of *Shinshōsetsu* published a special *tsuitō* issue, containing some fifty essays. Other journals followed suit. Shortly thereafter, an editorial committee consisting of the senior protégés set to work on the first *Sōseki zenshū*—the collected works, which appeared in 1919, in fourteen volumes. Three subsequent *zenshū* editions would be published over the next ten years.[10] A vast number of collectanea have been published since then.

The final gathering of the Mokuyōkai was on November 16—a matter of weeks before Sensei's death. Thereafter, the erstwhile *monkasei* vied with one another as custodians of the Sōseki legacy, all the while continuing to visit the widow at her Waseda residence as a sign of respect.[11] Komiya Toyotaka emerged as the chief legatee. It was Komiya who had a major editorial role in the early *zenshū* projects, and his monumental *Natsume Sōseki* (1938) stood as the authoritative literary biography for decades. And it was he who most actively promoted the myth of *sokuten kyoshi*, in effect a campaign aimed at Sensei's beatification.[12]

The personal relationships established with *Sōseki sensei* would deeply color the outpouring of *monkasei* reminiscences and literary appreciations. Veneration, though, was generally not the point. Rather, the remembered episodes were meant to convey authenticity and intimacy, even when the resulting portrayal was not at all flattering. Having been a stock-in-trade of Sōseki's own *shōhin* reminiscence, the telling episode would survive his passing and attract a growing audience.[13] This was the case, as well, with memoirs written by family members, which both complement and contrast with the *monkasei* reminiscence.

Of the many accounts of Sōseki as husband, father, and grandfather, Natsume Kyōko's 1929 memoir, *Sōseki no omoide,* affords an intimate and comprehensive view of Sōseki the man.[14] This work has served here as an invaluable commentary upon, and corrective to, her husband's recounting of events and episodes. Interestingly, Kyōko's memoir bears the imprint of one of her husband's protégés—Matsuoka Yuzuru (1891–1969)—who had married into the family. A younger writer earlier associated with the *Shinshichō* coterie, Matsuoka was one of Sōseki's "latter-day" disciples.[15] His marriage to Fudeko, the eldest Natsume daughter, meant that he could claim dual citizenship, in effect, within the *monkasei* ranks and as a Natsume son-in-law. As a family insider, it was Matsuoka who, years after Sōseki's death, served as transcriber of his mother-in-law's spoken narrative and editor of the subsequent manuscript. His own position was decidedly sympathetic with Kyōko's.[16]

Weathering the vicissitudes of scholarly trends and literary politics, Sōseki reminiscence has retained its popular appeal. Hundreds of volumes have appeared over the years—a virtual library of Sōsekiana that invites comprehensive study. Fortunately, the most recent *Sōseki zenshū* contains an appended volume of reminiscence, which yields a composite profile of the author through the testimony of over seventy acquaintances and family members.[17] Several oddities deserve mention. For example, Terada Torahiko (1878–1935), who belonged to the inner circle of protégés, crafted a poetic reminiscence—a series of twenty tanka composed during the year following the author's death.[18] Uchida Roan, writing for the *Shinshōsetsu* memorial issue, sets about refuting rumors of Sōseki's being curt and antisocial, then confesses that he hasn't read the recent novels, preferring the earlier work instead—especially the *shōhin*.[19] And Kyōko, whose memoir is a landmark of the reminiscence literature, is given surprisingly short shrift—in the form of a short, nondescript essay regarding letters to her husband while he was in England.[20]

The second generation of family reminiscence was essentially co-opted by Natsume Shinroku, who published no fewer than four book-length memoirs between 1943 and 1967. His best-known work, the 1956 *Chichi Natsume Sōseki* (My Father, Natsume Sōseki), presents a *katei*-based anecdotal portrayal that situates his father at his desk in the study, interacting with *monkasei* and dealing with this or that domestic circumstance. Reflecting the spirit of his mother's memoir, Shinroku's work seeks to capture the habits and moods of a complex and conflicted man.

In recent years, Sōseki reminiscence has moved on to a third generation. Two of the grandchildren have written extensively of an individual they knew only indirectly—and in part through the earlier memoirs. Yōko Matsuoka McClain, daughter of Matsuoka Yuzuru and Natsume Fudeko, has written of Sōseki as "tragic father," relating tales she had heard from her parents, her grandmother, and her aunts and uncles—especially Shinroku. Synopsizing the hearsay testimony, she portrays her grandfather as a deeply troubled man and a failure as a parent—a tragic figure, in short, insofar as his keen intellect and deep sensitivity to human psychology could neither compensate for nor help overcome the terrible loneliness and isolation.[21]

Yōko McClain's cousin, Natsume Fusanosuke—son of Natsume Jun'ichi —has written two memoirs that play upon the "famous grandfather" motif. A reference to the first of these—a 2002 memoir based on his visit to London— concludes chapter 1. A more recent work, *Mago ga yomu Sōseki* (A Grandson Reads Sōseki, 2006), presents a synopsis of the novels in a breezy personal voice. A free spirit with an obvious distaste for academic pretense and sham,

Fusanosuke accompanies each of his essays with an original cartoon.[22] His wry, ironic voice recalls Sōseki's *Neko* narrator, who knowingly comments on his master's peccadilloes.

To my knowledge, the family reminiscence has not yet advanced to the fourth generation, although this would come as no surprise. Be that as it may, Natsume Sōseki is very much alive and well in the twenty-first century, despite recent developments that suggest decanonization—for instance, the Education Ministry's decision, in 2002, to eliminate Sōseki literary excerpts from middle-school readers.[23] Beyond the scholarly domain, where Sōseki interpretation and analysis remain a thriving enterprise, how is the author appropriated by his literary descendants? The question merits a more probing study, but one can point, for instance, to Murakami Haruki's recent *Kafka on the Shore*—whose teenage runaway protagonist, Kafka Tamura, holes up in a library and immerses himself in Sōseki's collected works.[24] Then there are the many sequels to Sōseki's novels, which pursue various narrative tangents. In *Zoku Meian* (1990), for example, Mizumura Minae produced an ending for the famously incomplete final novel, *Meian,* and in so doing crafted a version of Sōseki's style that some critics have hailed as an improvement on the original. Okuizumi Hikaru, for his part, has reconstituted Sōseki's first novel in the form of his *Wagahai wa neko de aru satsujin jiken* (I Am a Cat—the Murder Mystery, 1996). This postmodern literary romp resurrects the dead feline and resituates him in Shanghai, where he learns that his erstwhile master, Kushami, has been murdered.

Okuizumi's novel points to a proud lineage of Sōseki parody in the *wagahai* vein. The figure of Sōseki's famous feline was turned upon the author, during his own lifetime, as a stock epithet. And the parodying of the original cat parody—perhaps *the* great Japanese literary satire—through the famous *wagahai* branding of the original title, lives on. In addition to Okuizumi's recent work, *Neko* parodies have been written, over the years, by Uchida Hyakken and Inoue Hisashi, among others. Not surprisingly, grandson Fusanosuke, a whimsical soul, has also gotten into the act.[25]

Then there is the tried-and-true *sokuten kyoshi* trope, which sagely counsels us to reject the trammels of our ego obsessions and follow a higher path. On the very day that Sōseki's brain was being celebrated in the Japanese press, articles were appearing that linked the dead author with this exalted epigram.[26] Here I should acknowledge my own complicity in promoting this notion, if only through repeated mention. What interests me is the phenomenon of seemingly reverential discipleship, whereby the mantra of *sokuten kyoshi* has emerged, in some quarters, as a kind of "Rosebud" encapsulation of the man's essence.

As a diadem adorning the brow of an important cultural property, the epithet may well honor the public figure, but it cannot fathom the man or his work. Recently, though, the term has taken on a new, pop-cultural cachet—serving, for example, as the title of trendy music albums, anime features, and TV shows. Google lists tens of thousands of *sokuten kyoshi* sites, and these are a far cry from earnest literary homage. While I cannot gauge the larger cultural significance of this phenomenon, the proliferation of such pop-culture dross will understandably rankle the purist.[27] Then again, I suspect that for a large segment of the Japanese public, Natsume Sōseki is understood simply as "the cat author."

Another avenue of Sōseki appropriation concerns the self-help market, and books that promote the inspirational and healing powers of the man's writings. Here, Nagao Takeshi has emerged, on the strength of nearly ten such volumes, as a Deepak Chopra–style proponent of enlightenment through exposure to the sayings of the wise man. In fact, though, Nagao began as a Sōseki anecdotalist and triviac, and has only recently moved into his role of ministering to a public in need of edifying passages from the master.[28] A recent book contains one hundred aphorisms and epigrams—drawn from the fiction, poetry, letters, diaries, and *shōhin*—that promise spiritual succor.[29] In a similar vein, Yajima Yukihiko has published an annotated selection of Sōseki's letters, from which the reader is invited to derive deep insights and personal healing.[30]

Leveraging a healthy market for feel-good (or feel-better) books, such works present Natsume Sōseki as a once-tormented man who managed to quell his inner demons and achieve a heightened awareness. Stranger things have been done with our cultural icons—living and dead. Yet whatever shape the author assumes, whatever niche he occupies in the cultural marketplace, the literature itself remains—as a well from which one is invited to draw pleasure, wisdom, and inspiration freely, and in full measure.

Afterword

Tokyo, June 2003

A sultry early summer's day on the campus of K University, and I am in the library, at my usual spot, working on a chapter of the *Omoidasu* text. The translation is not going well. Sōseki's reflections on mortality weigh upon my mind. Touched by the death and dying hovering in the textual air, it occurs to me that I've yet to pay my respects at the author's grave site in the Zōshigaya. What better excuse to take a break from this ponderous section of the *Sōseki zenshū,* volume twelve. I round up my camera, a water bottle, and a Tokyo map and set out on an impromptu urban pilgrimage.

First I must find the temple, which occupies a major chunk of Tokyo real estate, albeit off the beaten track. I walk down to Shibuya and take the Yamanote train to Mejiro. I head east, on foot, past the campus of the Gakushūin—the site of Sōseki's famous lecture on individualism and the modern temper. I soon lose my bearings; the map is playing tricks on me. But thanks to instructions provided by a policeman at the local *kōban,* I turn left at a convenience store, turn right at the tracks of the last remaining Tokyo trolley line, the Toden, head into an old, wooded residential neighborhood— and there before me is the west wall of the Zōshigaya.

It was fast approaching dusk. The cemetery is vast and empty—of living souls, that is. The office was closed. There was no one to ask about the Sōseki site. I'd assumed that there would be appropriate signage—after all, shouldn't Japan's national author merit at least a directional arrow? But there was nothing. A sea of stones, and I had no idea where to begin.

I decided to put my karmic bond to the test. In the half an hour or so of remaining daylight, I'd wander the Zōshigaya grounds and "gargle stones"— as the Sōseki pen name tells me to do—in hopes of coming across the right one. Time was wasting, and I feared the consequences, karmically speaking, of a futile search.

Up and down row upon row of headstones. Down and up. It was almost pitch dark when I turned down a row much like all the others. And there it was—site number 1-14-2—the final resting place of Natsume Sōseki. No special sign, no commemorative anything—just one of thousands and thousands of stones erected at the Zōshigaya. I let the moment sink in, trying to coax a frisson of communion with the spirit of my long-dead writer. Instead, I felt thirsty.

A woman strolled by, walking her small dog. A jogger ambled by from the opposite direction, casting a sideways glance at the loitering gaijin. I took a drink from the water bottle, then snapped three pictures of the Sōseki stone—two vertical, one horizontal—in the fading light. I put my hands together in a prayerful gesture, bowed my head in the direction of the barely visible headstone, and walked away.

London, March 2005

During Spring Break week, Ginger and I went to visit our son Danny, who was doing a study-abroad semester at University College, London. This was where Sōseki himself had a brief stint as an auditor, before cloistering himself in his flat on Flodden Road. Thankfully, Danny had a better time of it than his predecessor.

Our time in London was short, and it was essential that I fit in a visit to the Sōseki Museum, together with Ginger and Danny. There were competing tourist destinations, but I held firm, and we managed to find the place, in south London, without too much trouble. The weather was seasonably unpleasant. The museum, which occupies a flat in the middle of a long block of row-house residences, is directly across the road from the one Sōseki had occupied. A minimalist institution, as museums go, it is under the directorship of Mr. Sammy Tsunematsu, a Sōseki devotee and translator of many of the personal writings. Officially named the Sōseki Museum in London, it takes up one floor of the building at 80a The Chase and serves as a modest repository of Sōseki memorabilia. Mr. Tsunematsu's wife Yoshiko was there to greet us—her husband having gone back to Japan, as I recall. Non-Japanese visitors were rare, Yoshiko remarked, as we received the grand tour of the rooms. But various Japanese dignitaries had found their way there—members of the imperial family, government officials, and of course the scholarly and arts crowd.

We didn't stay long. The collection, such as it was, could be surveyed in five or ten minutes. One of the portraits that adorned the walls caught my eye—it was William Craig, Sōseki's tutor and subject of the *shōhin* vignette. I was reminded of the man's own London flat, high up in a similar building somewhere across the River Thames.

But I was inevitably drawn to the oil painting that dominated the museum's main room—a portrait of the author himself, with a serene expression that seemed to belie the madness and melancholy so closely connected with his life in that city, and with much of his subsequent literature.

It was only when we left the building, thanking our guide for her kind attention to this unlikely threesome from the American Midwest, that I had a look at the museum brochure, which came with the four-pound admission. It featured a prominent, bold-face rendering of the iconic epigram—*sokuten kyoshi.*

St. Louis, August 2007

I'm now in my sixties, having managed to outlive the authorial subject of this book by well over a decade. The time I've spent chipping away at this single task corresponds roughly to the entire literary career of its subject, whose work comprises nearly thirty imposing volumes in the standard edition. Then again, Natsume Sōseki was under contract to write—every day. It was his job. I've had the luxury of ruminating about this man and his work, of sharing my thoughts with students and colleagues at Washington University in St. Louis and elsewhere, of taking literary detours and putting things on back burners. But I've managed not to lose my bearings. The man and his work have been my lodestar, a fixed point on the compass.

Yet here is a writer who has been studied to death, by a virtual army of scholars, specialists, and devotees. Little has escaped their collective gaze. What could I presume to add, of any substance, to the great accretion of Sōsekiana? Under the sway of a certain scholarly chutzpah, together with an equal and countervailing dose of inertia, this "work-in-progress" progressed in very small increments, consuming a longer time than I've cared to admit.

I recall our year at the Inter-University Center in Tokyo, in the late 1970s, trying to learn enough Japanese to survive in grad school. I had a tutorial class that was to focus on a writer of one's choice. I opted for Sōseki, since this name virtually exhausted my knowledge of modern Japanese literature at that early stage. But my mentor steered me in a different direction—toward Mori Ōgai, having sensed in me some affinity with this other literary luminary. Not wishing to challenge Sensei's judgment, I duly embarked on studies that would last many years and that culminated in my first book, *Paragons of the Ordinary.*

The detour proved unexpectedly fortuitous, having brought me back, along many scenic byways, to the writer who had initially attracted me.

I appear to have "a thing" for enshrined writers. These two—Sōseki and Ōgai—have long stood as twin pillars of modern Japanese literature. And the pairing of this book with *Paragons* (and the two are well matched) is gratifying on many levels. As an "ephemerist" by inclination, I managed to orient the Ōgai book in this general direction. And I was even more strongly drawn to Sōseki's work in this vein. The recluse persona, with its comic and sardonic edges, proved most congenial, insofar as my own preferred habitat is the book-shelved enclosure, and my own view of the world is, truth be told, congenitally ironic.

But there is much more. In an obvious sense, Sōseki's personal writings are a modest labor. His concerns are ordinary; his anxieties and fears, utterly human. He thinks about what it means to be a writer, a father, a husband. He looks at his world, at the sort of person he has become, and shakes his head, often despairing of making sense of things. On occasion he is moved to laughter, to tears, to some dawning sense of comprehension. And then he moves on.

———————

A century ago, in Tokyo, Natsume Sōseki looked out beyond the glass doors of his study and into the world inside his head. As a fellow traveler in territories of memory and melancholy, and a fellow trafficker in words, I've come to share the concerns of this Japanese writer, and I've learned much from his attempts at reconciling the past with the insistent and often maddening demands of each day. His *shōhin*, these modest reflections upon matters large and small, have moved me to laughter and tears, bemusement and—just perhaps—a new comprehension of things.

As with *Paragons*, this book is a token of a literary kinship deeply felt, if only imperfectly understood.

A Sōseki Chronology

1867

Feb. 9   Natsume Kinnosuke born in Edo, the fifth son and youngest of eight children (father, Kōhe: 1818–1897; mother, Chie: 1827–1881).

1868

Nov.   Adopted by Shiohara family (Shōnosuke and wife, Yasu), who were in Kōhe's circle.

1875   Returns to natal home from Shioharas late in the year (exact date unknown), following the couple's divorce. Keeps Shiohara surname, though, until January 1888.

1878   Excels in school, winning several awards.

1879   Enters First Middle School, in Hitotsubashi.

1880   Babashita house burns down. Family moves to Ushigome.

1881

Jan. 9   Mother dies. Enters Nishō Academy, with its traditional Chinese curriculum.

1882

Spring   Leaves Nishō Academy.

1883   Growing interest in literature. Enters Seiritsu Academy in Kanda, to prepare for matriculation into the university preparatory school *(daigaku yobimon)*. Meets Ōta Tatsujin; first experience of dormitory life.

1884   September: Enters *daigaku yobimon*. Classmates include Nakamura Zekō and Haga Yaichi in addition to Ōta.

1885   At *daigaku yobimon*. Shares lodgings with Nakamura. Focus on English composition (occupies him through 1892).

1886   *Daigaku yobimon* becomes First Higher School (college-level curriculum). Gets teaching position at Etō Academy, with Nakamura, to help defray living expenses.

July   Stomach problems.

1887

Mar., June — Death of two older brothers, Daisuke and Einosuke, both stricken with tuberculosis.

1888

Jan. — Officially retakes Natsume surname. Transfers to English literature program at First Higher School, having decided not to pursue architecture.

1889

Befriends Masaoka Shiki, a literarily gifted classmate. Growing interest in poetry; first ventures into haiku. Adopts pen name Sōseki.

1890

Graduates First Higher School and enters Tokyo Imperial University. Receives a Monbushō scholarship. Studies English literature. Writes and publishes haiku and *kanshi*.

1892

May — Lectures at Tokyo Senmon Gakkō (modern-day Waseda University).

Aug. — Visits Shiki, who had withdrawn from the university, in Matsuyama (Shikoku); meets and befriends Takahama Kyoshi.

1893

Active in literary translation and criticism. Studies aesthetics at university with Professor Koeber.

July — Graduates from the Imperial University, in English literature, and enters its graduate program.

1894

Experiences tubercular symptoms early in the year.

Aug. — Sino-Japanese war commences.

Oct. — Leaves university lodgings and moves to temple compound in Koishikawa.

Dec. — Moves to Enkakuji temple in Kamakura, intent on a regimen of Zen meditation.

1895

Apr. — Travels to Matsuyama to assume teaching position at the middle school. Shiki, a native of the city, returns from his correspondent post covering the war, having taken ill, and moves in with Sōseki for several months (August–September). Begins period of active haiku composition and publication.

Dec. — Returns to Tokyo. Becomes engaged to Nakane Kyōko, daughter of secretary to House of Peers.

1896	Active with Shiki's Negishi haiku circle in Tokyo.
Apr.	Assumes teaching post in Kumamoto (Kyūshū), at the Fifth Higher School.
June 9	Marries Kyōko.
1897	
Mar.	Publishes essay on Sterne's *Tristram Shandy.*
June 29	Father dies.
July	Kyōko suffers miscarriage, shows signs of depression. Spends summer in Tokyo, deeply engaged in haiku activity with Shiki and the Negishi circle.
Sep.	Returns to Kumamoto; continues to publish haiku.
1898	In Kumamoto.
Late June	Kyōko suffers from depression and attempts suicide by drowning; is rescued. Terada Torahiko becomes his student; would be a lifelong friend.
1899	In Kumamoto.
May	Eldest daughter, Fudeko, is born.
Sep.	Begins *utai* practice.
1900	
June	Notified of selection as one of three Monbushō Scholars in a new program that would entail a two-year period of foreign study, which would prepare one to assume a key university post. Stipend of 1800 yen per year.
July	Returns to Tokyo with pregnant wife and child.
Sep. 8	Boards the *Preussen* and sets sail for England, arriving in London on October 28.
Nov. 7	Audits Professor Ker's class at University College.
Nov. 22	First visit with Professor Craig; their weekly tutorial, on Tuesdays, would last until October 1901.
Dec.	Indications, in letters to Kyōko, of disenchantment with London life.
1901	
Jan.	Second daughter, Tsuneko, born.
Jan. 22	Death of Queen Victoria; funeral on February 2.
Feb.	Incidence of stomach ulcers.
July 20	Moves into his fifth and final London boardinghouse, at 81 The Chase.
Aug. 3	Visits Carlyle Museum, with Ikeda Kikunae.

1902	Serious psychological symptoms.
Sep.	On the advice of his landlady and doctor, takes up bicycling to help alleviate his mental disturbance.
Sep. 19	Shiki dies.
Oct.	Visits Pitlochry, in Scotland.
Dec. 5	Leaves England.
1903	
Jan. 24	Returns to Tokyo; moves in with his family in Ushigome.
Mar.	Moves into Sendagi house, which had been occupied by Mori Ōgai.
Apr.	Assumes joint posts at the First Higher School and the Imperial University.
May 22	Suicide of his student, Fujimura Misao, which proves very disturbing.
June	Publishes *Jitensha nikki*.
June	Serious episodes of psychopathology; Professor Kure provides *shinkei suijaku* (neurasthenia) diagnosis. Recurring marital problems.
July	Kyōko leaves, returning to her family; in September, when the situation improves, she returns home.
Oct.	Avid practice of watercolor and calligraphy.
Nov.	Third daughter, Eiko, is born.
1904	Russo-Japanese War (1904–1905). Active involvement in literary translation, poetry, criticism. Begins *danwa* interviews. Late in the year, encouraged by Kyoshi, starts composing *Wagahai wa neko de aru* (I Am a Cat).
1905	*Neko* (serialization in *Hototogisu*, 1905–1906).
Jan.	Publishes "Tower of London" and "Carlyle Museum."
Sep. 15	House is burglarized.
Dec.	Fourth daughter, Aiko, is born.
1906	Young protégés begin visiting the home on a regular basis.
Apr.	*Botchan* serialization begins.
Sep.	*Kusamakura* (The Three-Cornered World) serialization begins.
Oct.	First "official" session of the Mokuyōkai (Thursday Society).
Dec.	Moves from Sendagi to Nishi Katamachi.
1907	
Apr.	Resigns from the Imperial University and his other teaching posts.

May 3	Joins the staff of the *Tokyo Asahi shinbun,* as the highest-paid staff writer.
May	Jun'ichi, eldest son, is born.
June	*Bungakuron* (Theory of Literature) is published.
June	Serialization of *Gubijinsō* (The Poppy), first *Asahi*-based novel, begins. All subsequent novels would be serialized in the *Asahi.*
Sep. 29	Moves to Waseda, his final residence.

1908

Jan.	Serialization of *Kōfu* (The Miner) begins.
June	Serialization of *Bunchō* (The Java Sparrow).
July	Serialization of *Yume jūya* (Ten Nights of Dream).
Sep.	Serialization of *Sanshirō* begins.
Dec.	Second son, Shinroku, is born.

1909

Jan.	Serialization of *Eijitsu shōhin* (Spring Miscellany) begins.
June	Serialization of *Sorekara* (And Then) begins.
Sep. 6–Oct. 13	Trip to Manchuria and Korea, under the auspices of friend Nakamura Zekō, director of the Southern Manchuria Railway. Serialization of travel account, *Mankan tokorodokoro* (Here and There in Manchuria and Korea).
Nov.	*Asahi* literary column *(bungeiran)* is inaugurated, with Sōseki as editor.

1910

Mar.	Serialization of *Mon* (The Gate) begins.
Mar.	Fifth daughter, Hinako, is born.
June	Enters Nagayo clinic with serious ulcerative condition.
Aug.	Moves to Shuzenji, on Izu Peninsula, for convalescence.
Aug. 24	Near-death episode *(Shuzenji taikan).*
Oct.	Returns to Tokyo, for further convalescence in Nagayo clinic.
Oct.	Serialization of *Omoidasu koto nado* (Recollections) begins.

1911

Feb.	Refuses Monbushō honorary doctorate *(gakui).*
June	Travels to Nagano for a lecturing stint.
Aug.	Travels to Osaka and environs for a series of four lectures (published in 1913 as *Shakai to jibun* [Society and Self]).
Aug.–Sep.	Recurrence of ulcerative disorder; hospitalization.
Nov. 11	Sudden death of daughter Hinako, not yet two years old.

1912

Jan.	Serialization of *Higan sugi made* (To the Spring Equinox and Beyond) begins.
July 30	Death of Meiji emperor.
Sep. 13	Funeral of Meiji emperor, and ritual suicide *(junshi)* of General Nogi and his wife.
Dec.	Serialization of *Kōjin* (The Wayfarer); ill health would delay completion until November 1913.

1913

Jan.	Recurrence of depression and manic behavior *(seishin suijaku)*.
Mar.	Recurrence of stomach ailment; bedridden until May.
Nov.	Avid pursuit of watercolor.

1914

	Outbreak of First World War.
Apr.	Serialization of *Kokoro* begins.
Sep.	Recurrence of stomach ailment; bedridden for a month.
Nov. 25	"Watakushi no kojinshugi" (My Individualism) lecture at Gakushūin.

1915

Jan.	Serialization of *Garasudo no uchi* (Inside My Glass Doors) begins.
Mar.	Trip to Kyoto; takes ill.
June	Serialization of *Michikusa* (Grass on the Wayside) begins.
Nov.	Trip to Yugawara, with Nakamura.
Dec.	Akutagawa and Kume join the Thursday group as young protégés.

1916

May	Serialization of *Meian* (Light and Darkness) begins (ending on December 14, following Sōseki's death, with chapter 188). Finds solace and repose in poetic composition (haiku and *kanshi*).
Nov. 16	Final Mokuyōkai session.
Nov. 22	Stricken with serious gastric symptoms.
Dec. 2	Internal bleeding; condition worsens.
Dec. 9	Dies, at 6:45 p.m., in his Waseda home.
Dec. 12	Funeral.
Dec. 28	Interment in Zōshigaya.

Notes

Abbreviations

Cat	*I Am a Cat* (translation of *Wagahai wa neko de aru*)
Doors	*Inside My Glass Doors* (translation of *Garasudo no uchi*)
Dream	*Ten Nights of Dream* (translation of *Yume jūya*)
Equinox	*To the Spring Equinox and Beyond* (translation of *Higan sugi made*)
Gate	*The Gate* (translation of *Mon*)
Grass	*Grass on the Wayside* (translation of *Michikusa*)
Hearing Things	Translation of *Koto no sorane*
Kafū zenshū	Nagai Kafū, *Kafū zenshū*
"My Individualism"	Translation of "Watakushi no kojinshugi"
NSJ	*Natsume Sōseki jiten* (Gakutōsha, 1990)
NSJ/b	*Natsume Sōseki jiten* (Bensei shuppan, 2000)
Omoide	Natsume Kyōko, *Sōseki no omoide*
Recollections	Translation of *Omoidasu koto nado*
Rediscovering	*Here and There in Manchuria and Korea* (translation of *Mankan tokorodokoro*)
Spring	*Spring Miscellany and London Essays* (translation of *Eijitsu shōhin*)
SZ	*Sōseki zenshū* (Iwanami, 1993–1997)
Tower	*The Tower of London* (translations of *Rondon tō* and other London writings)
Wayfarer	*The Wayfarer* (translation of *Kōjin*)

Note: The place of publication, when Tokyo, has been omitted for books and articles in Japanese cited in full here.

Introduction

1. See Donald Keene, *Dawn to the West*, vol. 1, p. 305. The chapter on Sōseki (pp. 305–354) provides a comprehensive treatment. The banknote image

has of course been the ubiquitous Sōseki icon. I should note that several passages in this chapter have been taken from my introduction to the *Garasudo* translation by Sammy Tsunematsu (pp. vii–xvii).

2. See the appended Sōseki chronology. Sōseki criticism and commentary comprise a virtual subdiscipline of Japanese literary scholarship. For an overview of the trajectory and current state of Sōseki studies, see Angela Yiu, *Chaos and Order*, pp. 6–11. For extensive biographical essays, see Van Gessel, *Three Modern Novelists*, pp. 11–67; Edwin McClellan, *Two Japanese Novelists*, pp. 3–15; and Jay Rubin, "Sōseki," in *Modern Japanese Writers*, pp. 349–384. Here I should cite McClellan's study, which concerns Natsume Sōseki and Shimazaki Tōson, as a model of amalgamating translation and commentary. And Jay Rubin's many translations and scholarly interpretations of Natsume Sōseki and the contemporary novelist Murakami Haruki, arguably the "alpha and omega" of modern Japanese literature, stand as a major achievement in the field.

Sōseki's popularity among Japanese readers has been generally consistent but not entirely uniform. As noted by John Dower, his work enjoyed a remarkable resurgence in the immediate postwar years, ostensibly on account of its abiding concern with questions of identity and individuality in a changing world—a notion that resonated powerfully during the Occupation period. See *Embracing Defeat* (New York: W. W. Norton and Company, 1999), pp. 189–190.

3. For details, see Jay Rubin's essay on Sōseki in *Modern Japanese Writers*, pp. 349–350.

4. This was a routine career choice among Meiji-era graduates. The *inaka kyōshi* (rural teacher) figure is prevalent. See, for instance, Tayama Katai's novel *Inaka Kyōshi* (Country Teacher, 1909) and Shimazaki Tōson's *Chikumagawa no suketchi* (Chikuma River Sketches, 1912), a literary reminiscence of the author's experiences teaching in rural Komoro.

5. Like many of his contemporaries, Sōseki eschewed political connections and ties to officialdom. This avoidance he shares with figures such as Jane Austen and Charles Dickens.

6. It is often observed that Japan's first psychological novel, and by consensus its great literary achievement, is Lady Murasaki's *Tale of Genji*—a monumental work of the early eleventh century that was in effect rediscovered by Meiji readers, thanks to the availability of modern annotated editions.

7. *Makura no sōshi* (Pillow Book) and *Tsurezuregusa* (Essays in Idleness) have long stood as the tandem classics of the *zuihitsu* genre of Japanese literary essay. For an excellent study of the *zuihitsu* genre in its classical mode, see Linda Chance, *Formless in Form: Kenko,* Tsurezuregusa, *and the Rhetoric of Japanese Fragmentary Prose* (Stanford, Calif.: Stanford University Press, 1997).

8. Saeki Shōichi, the leading scholar of Japanese literary selfhood, has written extensively on the emergence of narrative self-expression among Tokugawa literati. See, for instance, "The Autobiography in Japan," *Journal of Japanese Studies* 11, no. 2 (Summer 1985): 357–368. Here Saeki surveys the domain of

what can be regarded as pre-modern Japanese autobiography, through exemplary works by three prominent samurai literati: Arai Hakuseki, Yamaga Sokō, and Matsudaira Sadanobu. In addition to many books on the subject of the Japanese literary self, Saeki has edited *Nihonjin no jiden* (Heibonsha, 1982), a twenty-five volume encyclopedia of Japanese autobiographical writing.

The Tokugawa period witnessed the proliferation of essay writing of every description, spanning historical and philological subjects, contemporary manners and customs, folklore, and philosophical reflection. The sheer volume of pre-modern *zuihitsu* is amply represented in the form of the massive *Nihon zuihitsu taisei* (Yoshikawa Kōbunkan, 1993–1996), a sixty-three volume compilation of Tokugawa-era discursive writing.

9. Arai Hakuseki (1657–1725) was a prominent Confucian scholar, administrator, and adviser to the Tokugawa shogunate. For a translation of his autobiography, *Oritaku shiba no ki,* together with extensive commentary on the author and his work, see Joyce Ackroyd, *Told Round a Brushwood Fire* (Princeton, N.J.: Princeton University Press and University of Tokyo Press, 1979).

10. In this regard, see Saeki Shōichi, *Kindai Nihon no jiden* (Modern Japanese Autobiography). See as well my essay "The Writer Speaks," pp. 232–249.

11. For an overview of the Meiji intellectual climate, see Bob Tadashi Wakabayashi, ed., *Modern Japanese Thought.*

12. Itō Sei's research on the *kindai bundan* has been extensive and authoritative. Its essence is distilled in Irena Powell's *Writers and Society in Modern Japan.* While purporting to be a sociological study, Powell's work pursues a chronological listing of leading figures and coteries, leaving many of the broader theoretical and institutional questions unanswered.

13. See ibid., p. 12.

14. A socioeconomic study of the *bundan* would inquire into how money changed hands, and among whom; it would pursue a "cost-benefit" analysis of coterie membership and explore the structure and function of the coteries as patronage system and social network. As revealed in Sōseki's many *bundan*-related writings, patronage entailed, for instance, writing book prefaces for one's protégés, subcontracting writing assignments, conferring assistant editorships, and the like. For a revealing study of the social history and structure of a literary community, see Nigel Cross, *The Common Writer.*

15. On the conventions of *bundan* journalism, see my *Paragons,* pp. 30–58, and "The Writer Speaks," pp. 239–249.

16. For a study of the *danwatai* conversational style and its debt to the advent of shorthand transcription *(sokkijutsu),* see J. Scott Miller, "Japanese Shorthand and *Sokkibon,*" *Monumenta Nipponica* 49, no. 4 (Winter 1994): 471–487.

17. Maeda Ai has written authoritatively on this matter, in *Kindai dokusha no seiritsu* (The Rise of the Modern Reader; Yūseidō, 1973). As in other modernizing nations, in Japan the emergent readership consisted of various regional and demographic subcategories—for instance, women and young people—each with

a grouping of periodicals catering to them. The role played by consumerism, advertising, and marketing is crucial. A survey of Maeda's work is available in *Text and the City: Essays on Japanese Modernity.*

18. Mori Ōgai's early experiments with romanticized fictional autobiography were based on his four-year stay in Germany, from 1884–1888. As for Shimazaki Tōson—his 1890s "new-style" poetry *(shintaishi)* in the Wordsworthian romantic idiom became a powerful vehicle for lyrical expressions of longing and loss.

19. Futabatei Shimei, a corruption of the vulgar expression for "drop dead," was the ironic pen name of Hasegawa Tatsunosuke. Paralleling Mori Ōgai's mastery of German language and literature, Futabatei built his career around a mastery of Russian. For an excellent literary biography, see Marleigh Ryan, *Japan's First Modern Novel.*

20. The goal of *genbun itchi,* which took decades of experimentation to fully achieve, was most forcefully promoted by the author and critic Tsubouchi Shōyō in his 1885 literary manifesto, *Shōsetsu shinzui* (The Essence of Fiction). The subsequent development involved an ebb and flow of progressive and conservative forces—most notably a "traditionalist" movement in the 1890s that privileged older literary styles. See Nanette Twine, *Language and the Modern State: The Reform of Written Japanese* (London; New York: Routledge, 1991), passim.

21. The cachet of unmediated self-presentation, which stands as a legacy of the Naturalist movement, fostered the emergence of the so-called I-novel *(shishōsetsu),* arguably *the* representative modern Japanese literary genre. Works in this famously problematic category, in spite of obvious fictional manipulation, have been understood to represent an author's essential selfhood. With its aura of spiritual elevation and integrity, the I-novel has been seen as transcending autobiographical and other "merely factual" accounts of a writer's life. But such claims cannot be corroborated, and the genre remains a "black hole" in the Japanese literary firmament—powerfully present, yet strangely unknowable. See Edward Fowler, *The Rhetoric of Confession,* passim.

22. In the Meiji, two related disciplines developed concurrently—first, the academic discipline of psychology, which in the nineteenth century had strong connections with philosophical speculation, on the one hand, and experimental science, on the other; and second, clinical psychiatry, which belonged within the medical domain. Kure Shūzō (1865–1932), the figure credited with having pioneered modern psychiatry in Japan, would be involved in Sōseki's own clinical diagnosis, as we will see.

While not formally trained in psychology, Sōseki was deeply influenced by the work of William James and Henri Bergson, vis-à-vis their studies of memory and psychological associationism. Moreover, Sōseki's techniques of psychological narration benefited from his readings of George Meredith (1828–1909), a novelist of great psychological depth.

NOTES TO PAGE 9

23. See Howard Hibbett, "Natsume Sōseki and the Psychological Novel," pp. 307–308. Here I should note the applicability in Sōseki's case of what William Sibley has termed, in connection with Shiga Naoya, an "intuitive psychoanalytical consciousness." See *The Shiga Hero,* passim.

24. The variant genres of literary personalia include *kansōbun* (reflections), *kaisōbun* (retrospection), *kaikoroku* (reminiscence), *inshōki* (impressions), *omoidebanashi* (recollections), *jijoden* (autobiography), *shaseibun* (literary sketch), and *shōhin* (literary episode). The overlap among these is obvious, as is the case with the corresponding Western genres.

25. Definitions of *shōhin* are notoriously vague. *Natsume Sōseki jiten (NSJ)* defines the genre as follows: "A special category of *kindai* literature—neither *shōsetsu* nor *kansō,* and occupying a position somewhere between short fiction and essay; freer narrative than more heavily plotted fiction; marked by fresh, keen emotional expression, whereby an author's true features emerge; a distinctly Japanese genre that differs from Western realist narrative" (p. 63). A number of the contemporary literary journals regularly published *shōhin,* and the genre enjoyed a heyday in the late Meiji.

The category of personal essay has been explicated and anthologized by Joseph Epstein and Phillip Lopate. In the introduction to *The Art of the Personal Essay,* Lopate calls attention to the following characteristics of the personal essay, each of which is further explicated: conversational element; honesty, confession, and privacy; self-belittlement; contrariety (going against the grain of popular opinion); egoism and its deflation; irony and impudence; the marginal/idler persona; retrospection on the past and on the local scene; melancholy, and often lyrical, voice. Lopate concludes by observing that the personal essay is a "mode of thinking and being" (pp. xlii–xlv). See also Graham Good, *The Observing Self,* especially pp. 1–25; and Margaretta Jolly, ed., *Encyclopedia of Life Writing,* passim.

26. For details regarding the Chinese literary roots, in the *xiao pin* (essays) of the Ming period, see Yang Ye, *Vignettes from the Late Ming* (Seattle and London: University of Washington Press, 1999).

27. Emerging as a featured literary genre in journals such as *Bunshō sekai,* the *shōhin* vignette attracted authors such as Sōseki, Tayama Katai, Izumi Kyōka, Masamune Hakuchō, and many others. The writer Mizuno Yōshū (1883–1947) in effect became a *shōhin* specialist—in addition to publishing a number of *shōhin* collections, Mizuno wrote a guidebook to proper *shōhin* style (*Shōhin sahō,* 1911). Reaching a zenith in 1910, with the publication of a massive ten-volume compilation, the *shōhin* as a discrete literary genre went out of fashion around the time of Sōseki's death in 1916, giving way to the more generic term *zuihitsu.*

28. As a literary genre, *kindai zuihitsu* has only recently become the subject of scholarly study. See, for instance, Rachel DiNitto, "Return of the *zuihitsu:* Print Culture, Modern Life, and Heterogeneous Narrative in Prewar Japan," *Harvard Journal of Asiatic Studies* 64, no. 2 (December 2004): 251–290. DiNitto calls attention to the essential ambiguity of the genre, which is typi-

209

cally conflated with the better-known—and even more amorphous—*shishōsetsu* (I-novel) genre (see note 21 above). She goes on to study the dramatic expansion of modern essay writing in the mid-1920s, in connection with the rise of mass media, consumerism, and popular culture. Much of De Nitto's study concerns the *kindai zuihitsu* genre as reconstituted by the journal *Bungei shunjū,* which promoted a middlebrow version of "lifestyle" essays that appealed to the urban middle class.

For a good cross-section of Japanese critical commentary on *kindai zuihitsu,* see the Summer 1992 issue of the literary journal *Bungaku,* which is devoted to the modern essay genre.

The rise of literary self-expression has interesting affinities with modes of self-expression in poetry, painting, drama, and the like. Many of Sōseki's literary contemporaries were deeply involved in the visual arts as well. Indeed, Sōseki himself was an accomplished watercolorist whose clever, ironic sketches nicely complement his *shōhin.* Of note, too, is Ishii Hakutei (1882–1958), a *shōhin* author who, as an artist, produced a number of self-portraits.

29. For details on Shiki's *shaseibun* sketches, see Janine Beichman, *Masaoka Shiki,* pp. 54–60. Sōseki's debt to Shiki has been widely attested. Over the years, the two engaged in a productive exchange of haiku and *shaseibun,* as well as *kanshi.* In connection with the preceding note, I would argue that Sōseki's *shaseibun* sketching strongly conditioned the style and shape of his *shōhin* vignettes.

Many have written of their admiration for Sōseki's *shōhin.* As early as 1911, Mizuno Yōshū wrote in praise of Sōseki's mastery of *shōhin* style. In 1938, Matsuoka Yuzuru remarked on the *shōhin* as pure stylistic gems, which represented the very height of Sōseki's literary art. By way of contrast, Hibbett has typified the *shōhin* as "reticent," and marked by a "bland, reflective tone" ("Natsume Sōseki and the Psychological Novel," p. 342).

30. In *Natsume Sōseki:* Yume jūya *ron* (Meiji shoin, 1986), an exhaustive study of the dream narratives, Sasabuchi Tomoichi argues that despite these having been regarded as actual dream content, the evidence points to only one of the ten—number three—as based on an actual dream. Sasabuchi stresses Sōseki's unique fictional creation here, cautioning against using the texts as clinical documents in support of a psychoanalytic reading.

31. The dream episodes are also literary miniatures that have long served in Japanese language and literature courses. Here I will take the liberty of including a dream narrative of my own: March 7, 2007—I've come across some books addressed to Natsume Sōseki and strangely left undelivered, until my chance discovery. These are beautiful books—three in all, and gilt-edged. Two are in English, one in Japanese. I fondle and caress these treasures—and awake, sadly empty-handed.

32. *Eijitsu* appeared in between the *Sanshirō* and *Sorekara* serializations in the *Asahi.*

33. The English translation of *Mankan,* by Brodey and Tsunematsu, was

preceded by a French translation, by Olivier Jamet and Elisabeth Suetsugu, entitled *Natsume Sōseki: Haltes en Mandchourie et en Corée* (Paris: La Quinzaine Littéraire, 1997). Also, note a subsequent Manchuria travel account, *Man-Mō yūki*, by the renowned Meiji poet and essayist Yosano Akiko (1878–1942). Joshua Fogel's translation of the 1928 text is *Travels in Manchuria and Mongolia: A Feminist Poet from Japan Encounters Prewar China* (New York: Columbia University Press, 2001). Yosano's lively and engaging travelogue contains many fascinating vignettes and observations.

34. There have been allegations of Sōseki's complicity with Japan's imperial and colonialist projects, yielding an interpretation of *Mankan* as a "politically incorrect" work and, hence, something of an embarrassment in the context of Sōseki's oeuvre. See, for instance, James Fujii, *Complicit Fictions*, pp. 103–150.

35. This format is reminiscent of the classical convention of *kotobagaki*, whereby a poem is given an often quite elaborate narrative context.

36. The notion of Sōseki's literature as a subject for psychoanalysis was promoted by Doi Takeo, the Japanese psychiatrist whose 1972 study, *Amae no kōzō* (Anatomy of Dependence), proposed *amae*—dependency, indulgence—as the defining Japanese character trait. Essentially claiming Sōseki as Japan's answer to Sigmund Freud—*before* the advent of Freudian psychology—Doi treats the fictional characters as clinical case studies. In *Sōseki no shinteki sekai* (The Psychological World of Natsume Sōseki, 1969), Doi psychoanalyzes ten of Sōseki's novelistic protagonists, thus delving into the author's psyche, albeit at a certain remove, through the textual evidence of literary surrogates. His schema could surely be applied to the narrating persona of the *shōhin* as well.

37. Paul Eakin emphasizes the notion of remembered pasts—indeed, *any* narrativization of the past—as a fictional construct; and that memory, far from being a repository of lived experience, is an ongoing creative and integrative process, essential to a sense of self as a coherent entity. Eakin goes on to note that the very fallibility of human memory enables the narrative assertion of one's identity. See *Touching the World*, pp. 66–67.

38. Several studies that present the literary personalia of individual authors have served as models. Kenneth Henshall's *Literary Life in Tokyo* presents an exhaustively annotated translation of Tayama Katai's 1917 *bundan* reminiscence, *Tōkyō no sanjūnen* (Thirty Tokyo Years). Parenthetically, of the hundreds of figures mentioned in this work, Sōseki is conspicuous in his absence. (As Henshall notes, Katai evidently disliked the man [p. 13].) David Magarshack's *Turgenev's Literary Reminiscences and Autobiographical Fragments* (London: Faber and Faber, 1959) was a welcome discovery and revealed many parallels with the *shōhin*. Finally, Angela Yiu's mix of illustrative passages and interpretive commentary in her *Chaos and Order* has been very useful.

39. This stance accords with the "new historicist" agenda of privileging the intersection of literature and its many contexts and connections—especially material culture and the larger social and economic milieu.

Chapter 1: London Underground

1. *SZ* 10, p. 3; *Grass on the Wayside*, p. 3.

2. For a concise overview of the London years, see McClellan, *Two Japanese Novelists*, pp. 9–14. See also Flanagan's comments regarding Sōseki's London pieces in the Introduction to *Tower* (esp. pp. 9–16). Natsume Kyōko's memoir, *Sōseki no omoide* (Remembrances of Sōseki), serves as an invaluable complement to her husband's *shōhin* accounts.

3. Some of the "Sōseki's London" accounts showcase the city and its tourist attractions rather than the unremarkable life that the author led there. See, for instance, Deguchi Yasuo and Andrew Watt, eds., *Sōseki no Rondon fūkei* (Kenkyūsha, 1985), a profusely illustrated ramble through turn-of-the-century London, featuring the Sōseki-related highways and byways. One senses the irony in the high-gloss promotion of this city that had inspired such antipathy on Sōseki's part.

4. The diary entry, dated July 1, 1901, is in *SZ* 19, p. 89. Sōseki's London correspondences are contained in *SZ* 22, pp. 196–266. The narrative fragments can be found in SZ 19, pp. 104–130. These occupy the category of *danpen*—a miscellany of literary notes and personal observations. About half are in English—including the final one, a curious poetic fragment: "Japanese poetry / two partings / Friendship / Mount Aso / In the graves / A Twinkling Star / A dream / A bird of passage / Compensation / Artificiality (nudity) and Vulgarity (coarse)." In *SZ* 22, p. 130.

5. This material was published in the May 1901 issue of *Hototogisu*. It comprises three separate essays, crafted as letters, sent to his friends Shiki and Takahama Kyoshi. See *SZ* 12, pp. 3–31. The translations that follow are based on *Tower*, pp. 53–76.

6. *SZ* 12, pp. 11–14; *Tower*, pp. 60–62.

7. In the preface to his *Memoirs of Himself* (1880), Robert Louis Stevenson (1850–1894), a writer whom Sōseki greatly admired, remarks as follows: "I am living absolutely alone in San Francisco.... After weeks in this city, I know only a few neighboring streets; I seem to be cured of all my adventurous whims and even of human curiosity; and am content to sit here by the fire and await the course of fortune." In *The Works of R. L. Stevenson* (New York: Charles Scribner's Sons, 1923), vol. 26, p. 205. The memoir extends to p. 237. Whereas Sōseki's London experience led him to a productive yet alienating immersion in a foreign literature, Stevenson's experience of living alone in California would yield a moving memoir of childhood and youth.

Sōseki's library contained many of Stevenson's works. The latter's *Memories and Portraits* parallels the style and substance of the *shōhin*, in their reflections on boyhood and youth, sketches of college life, and the like.

8. *SZ* 12, p. 57; *Tower*, p. 77. The original, *Jitensha nikki*, was published in *Hototogisu* in June 1903. See *SZ* 12, pp. 57–70.

9. *SZ* 12, pp. 61–62; *Tower,* pp. 80–82.

10. *SZ* 12, pp. 68–69; *Tower,* pp. 87–88.

11. Kyōko comments on this in episode 16 of her memoir. She notes that her husband had evidently gotten quite good as a cyclist, but on his return to Tokyo he refused to resume his bicycling because the roads were frighteningly narrow and in generally deplorable shape.

12. Sōseki visited the Tower in late October 1900. The essay was published in the January 1905 issue of *Teikoku bungaku.* See *SZ* 2, pp. 1–29. Translated excerpts are based on *Tower,* pp. 91–116. Note the fine interpretive essay (pp. 16–22).

13. *SZ* 2, pp. 18–19; *Tower,* p. 107.

14. *SZ* 2, pp. 25–26; *Tower,* p. 113.

15. See *SZ* 2, pp. 31–44. For Tsunematsu's translation, see *Spring,* pp. 119–132. Here, again, my translation is based on *Tower,* pp. 117–129. Note the interpretive essay (pp. 22–26). Sōseki's affinity with Carlyle is apparent in an 1889 student composition, which includes an imagined run-in with Carlyle's ghost! Incidentally, Carlyle, too, suffered from chronic stomach problems (see *Tower,* p. 220).

16. *SZ* 2, pp. 40–43; *Tower,* pp. 126–128.

17. A similar description would be applied to the residence of Sōseki's mentor, William Craig. See chapter 6.

18. The Blue Plaque dedication was held on March 22, 2002—in effect marking the centennial of Sōseki's London stay. Years earlier, in 1984, the first floor flat of the building directly opposite, at 80b The Chase, was converted into the Sōseki Museum, thanks to the unstinting efforts of Ikuo "Sammy" Tsunematsu, a lifelong Sōseki devotee and translator of many of his personal writings.

A more recent homage to the author is the restaurant Soseki, situated in a plaza beneath the "Gherkin" skyscraper in London's financial district. According to its Web site, Soseki features a traditional Japanese cuisine that "Japan's favourite novelist missed as he trudged through the dank streets of the city…yearning for a refuge, a place where he could give sanctuary to his nostalgia."

19. *SZ* 14. The work is signed Natsume Kinnosuke—the author having chosen to distinguish it from his creative writings.

20. The *Bungakuron* manuscript went through a complex editorial process, as explained in the preface. The accumulated London research notes became the lecture notes for Sōseki's university course on English literature (taught 1903–1905). These, in turn, were meticulously recorded by one of his students, Nakagawa Yoshitarō, who collated them with several fellow students. This penultimate manuscript was then presented to Sōseki for editing. The final draft was published in 1907.

21. There has been a marked increase, of late, in critical attention. In the United States, scholarly conferences and panels on *Bungakuron* have commemorated the centennial of its publication.

22. Sōseki also held the book up as an expression of his belief that Japanese had no need to imitate Westerners. Cited by Rubin, in *Modern Japanese Writers*, p. 355.

23. See *SZ* 14, pp. 3–15. The preface is written in the formal *bungotai* style, but in the first person. It is signed "Natsume Kinnosuke."

24. The term *fuyukai* (unhappy, peeved, disconsolate) appears often in the *Bungakuron* introduction and elsewhere in Sōseki's writings. See *SZ* 28, p. 583, for a complete listing of appearances.

25. See *SZ* 14, pp. 14–15. *Yōkyoshū* (Drifting into the Void) is a 1906 compilation of seven shorter works, including *Rondon tō*, *Kārairu hakubutsukan*, and *Koto no sorane* (Hearing Things). *Uzurakago* (A Quail's Cage), published in 1907, included *Botchan*, *Nihyaku tōka* (The 210th Day), and *Kusamakura* (Pillow of Grass, translated as *The Three-Cornered World*).

26. Paul Eakin remarks upon sickness, solitude, and confinement as "enabling conditions" for the creative process and for achieving deeper, more nuanced levels of self-awareness. Here he cites the work of Edmund Wilson, Lionel Trilling, and Susan Sontag. See *Touching the World*, pp. 60–64.

27. Sōseki offered this course at the Imperial University from 1905 to 1907. The London material comprises part 2 of *Bungaku hyōron*, contained in *SZ* 15, pp. 56–173.

28. These are episodes 6, 7, 9, 10, 15, 20, and 25. Each is titled.

29. The descriptive passage here is a *shasei*-style correlative of the self-absorption that Sōseki would so often rail against in his "civilizational malcontent" voice.

30. Note the self-referential figures for "small" and "slow" here—terms such as noso noso *aruku;* kanman naru *ichi bunshi; noroi*. See *SZ* 12, p. 163.

31. *Eijitsu*, episode 9: *Atatakai yume*. *SZ* 12, pp. 164–165; *Spring*, pp. 52–55.

32. *Eijitsu*, episode 10: *Inshō*. *SZ* 12, pp. 165–168; *Spring*, pp. 56–58. The episode ends with the narrator finally arriving at Trafalgar Square.

33. *Eijitsu*, episode 15: *Kiri*. *SZ* 12, pp. 182–185; *Spring*, pp. 77–80.

34. Sōseki attended the performance on February 23, 1901, at Her Majesty's Theatre. For that day's diary entry, see *SZ* 19, p. 59.

35. In his penetrating analysis of this single episode, Haga Tōru remarks on Sōseki's appropriation of a dark fin de siècle modernist style, with its Kafkaesque sense of dehumanization. See Haga, "Sōseki no jikken kōbō." Remarking on the *Eijitsu* collection overall as an "experimental workshop," Haga speculates that the *Inshō* episode is based on the author's very first night in London—October 28, 1900.

36. The title of Dostoyevsky's 1864 work. Its protagonist is an "underground man" who philosophizes, reminisces, debates with himself, and laments the irrationality of man and the bankruptcy of positivist philosophy. An admiring reader of Dostoyevsky, Sōseki remarks, in episode 20 of *Omoidasu*, on Dostoyevsky's

"rapturous state" experienced in connection with his epileptic seizures. In the very next episode, he comments on Dostoyevsky's miraculous escape from death. Both references are in connection with his own brush with death.

37. Robert Alter, *Imagined Cities*. Alter's illuminating study centers on work by Flaubert, Dickens, Woolf, Joyce, Kafka, and the Russian novelist Andrei Bely (1880–1934).

38. *Omoidasu*, episode 32. *SZ* 12, pp. 448–451; *Recollections*, pp. 89–91. As for Heinrich Heine (1797–1856), the great German poet, it is clear that his five-month stay in London (1827) did indeed inspire a strong antipathy toward the British—in part because of his inability to speak their language. He could read the literature though, which he judged to be lamentably bad. See Louis Untermeyer, *Heinrich Heine: Paradox and Poet* (New York: Harcourt, Brace and Company, 1937), pp. 154–158.

39. *Michikusa*, ch. 58. *SZ* 10, pp. 174–175; *Grass*, p. 93.

40. *Michikusa*, ch. 59. *SZ* 10, pp. 178–179; *Grass*, p. 95. Chapters 57–60 concern Kenzō's reflections on his money woes, the financial straits that wife and family experienced during his absence, and the pitiful financial situation upon his return.

41. Note, by way of contrast, the more balanced tone that Sōseki adopts in his famous lecture on individualism, where he remarks as follows: "I am not very fond of England, to tell you the truth. As much as I dislike the country, however, the fact is that no nation anywhere is so free and at the same time so very orderly. Japan cannot begin to compare with her. But the English are not merely free: They are taught from the time they are children to respect the freedom of others as they cherish their own." "Watakushi no kojinshugi" (My Individualism), p. 307.

42. See *Omoide*, episodes 13–17. Kyōko's perspective is that of a single mother in Tokyo, with limited resources. Correspondence with her husband was infrequent; and despite their sharing respective concerns, the couple led virtually separate lives. The family turmoil that ensued following his return from London is detailed in episodes 18–21. This material, in other words, corresponds to the period dealt with in *Michikusa*.

43. Watanabe Shunkei's reminiscence, written at some point following 1937, was published in 1974. His circle of business acquaintances included, among others, Watanabe Watarō and Tanaka Kōtarō. They formed the Zai-Ei Nihonjinkai (Association of Japanese Residing in England). Although Sōseki had little involvement with the group, he was on good terms with Watarō (1878–1922)—a cultivated individual with whom he maintained a relationship back in Japan. For a biographical sketch of Watarō, see *NSJ/*b, pp. 418–419.

44. See *SZ bekkan*, pp. 110–121.

45. Okakura wrote on Sōseki in the context of a reminiscence centering on Haga Yaichi (1867–1927), who went on to become a pioneering scholar of Japanese literature. Haga had studied with Sōseki in the Yobimon Academy and

was on the same Europe-bound vessel, the *Preussen,* although his own destination was Germany, where he pursued literary research. Okakura's brother Kakuzō (Tenshin) was a distinguished figure in Meiji arts and culture.

46. See *SZ bekkan,* pp. 122–128. Fujishiro Teisuke (1868–1927) was among the contingent of Europe-bound Monbushō scholars aboard the *Preussen,* together with Sōseki and Haga Yaichi. Fujishiro was a student of German literature, and it was he who would be Sōseki's companion, upon his return from the Monbushō research stay in Germany. Sōseki corresponded with Fujishiro, both during their respective stays and thereafter. Several letters to his friend in Germany are revealing. February 5, 1901: "Come visit me in London, where I'm all alone with no friends." June 19, 1901: "These days, the very idea of going on to be a scholar of English literature seems totally ridiculous."

Fujishiro went on to a distinguished scholarly career. He and Sōseki simultaneously held professorships at the Imperial University. For further details, see *NSJ*/b, pp 303–304.

47. Having followed Kyōko's memoir serialization in the journal *Kaizō,* Doi strenuously denied certain allegations made in episode 16, which concerns her husband's "London madness." Intent upon setting the record straight, he embarks on a point-by-point rebuttal and calls for specific retractions on Kyōko's part. See *SZ bekkan,* pp 129–136.

48. See *SZ* 14, pp 14–15.

49. *Michikusa,* ch. 57. *SZ* 10, pp 171–172; *Grass,* p 91. There is no direct evidence of this incident having actually occurred, but it is in line with the reminiscences of Kyōko and son Shinroku.

50. Kure Shūzō was a pioneering figure in the introduction of psychiatry to Meiji Japan, and he wrote the first major treatise on the subject. The clinical diagnosis *shinkei suijaku*—neurasthenia—became identified with Sōseki in connection with his stay in England, and the author himself uses the term in various contexts—for instance, in letters he wrote between 1902 and 1906. Neurasthenia was an emblematic psychological disorder in nineteenth-century Europe.

On the introduction of psychology (both its academic and its medical and clinical aspects), see Satō Tatsuya, *Nihon ni okeru shinrigaku no juyō to tenkai.* Watarai Yoshiichi has written on *shinkei suijaku* as a distinctively Meiji "civilizational ailment." See his *Meiji no seishin isetsu* (Iwanami, 2003), pp. 155–194. Note also Oda Susumu, *Nihon no kyōki shi,* a "history of ideas" study of madness as a dominant Japanese cultural trope.

Interestingly, the development of clinical psychology in Japan is said to have been retarded by a move among some psychologists to study supernatural phenomena. In fact, the character Tsuda in Sōseki's *Koto no sorane* (1905) is a psychologist associated with this very school.

51. The detailed account comprises the bulk of episodes 19–21. Kyōko revisits the matter in episodes 49 and 51, vis-à-vis the recurrence, in 1913, of her husband's psychopathology. Note as well Sōseki's November 1914 diary episodes,

which point to emotional imbalance and irrationality. There are no entries for the periods specifically discussed by Kyōko.

52. See Karatani, "Sickness as Meaning," in *Origins of Modern Japanese Literature*, pp. 97–113.

53. A branch of Sōseki studies explores the psychopathology of the man and his literary creations. For a synopsis of this line of research, see *NSJ*, pp. 128–129. The psycho-biographical approach has been espoused by Etō Jun and others. They regard the London experience, with its bouts of depression, then the worsening physical condition, as having strongly conditioned both Sōseki's outlook and his creative endeavors. For an explicitly clinical analysis, see Chitani Shichirō, *Sōseki no byōseki*, which focuses on *Kōjin* as the key "case-history" document. Also, see Doi Takeo's psychoanalytical study of Sōseki via selected literary texts.

Among Sōseki's certifiably disturbed contemporaries, Akutagawa Ryūnosuke comes to the fore. Akutagawa's own clinical psychopathology (culminating in his 1927 suicide), and the family history thereof, are well documented. It can be argued that his modernist literary project brilliantly exploited this very condition.

54. As Chitani's book suggests, *Kōjin* is typically cited as the representative text, given the author's relentless probing of the inner torments of the character Ichirō.

55. Sōseki's critique of the excessively egocentric tendencies of modern civilization is cogently expounded in the 1914 "Kojinshugi" essay.

56. It should be noted that Kyōko herself had a history of mental disorder, one that deeply troubled her husband. Early on she displayed symptoms of hysteria and depression, evidently traceable to a traumatic miscarriage in July of 1897. The situation was such that in late June of 1898, in Kumamoto, evidently in a fit of despondency, she attempted suicide by drowning. She was rescued, but her husband, as he relates in his diary, would thereafter monitor her activities, going so far as to physically restrain her in her bed.

57. Natsume Fusanosuke (1950–). Professional cartoonist *(mangaka)* and son of Sōseki's eldest son, Jun'ichi, Fusanosuke and his cousin Yōko would write memoirs of the famous grandfather whom they'd never met. See chapter 7 herein.

58. *Sōseki no mago*, pp. 28–29. Overall, the memoir has more to say about the author's career in cartooning than the famous grandfather.

Chapter 2: Babashita Traces

1. The memory-related scholarly bibliography is vast. Setting aside the empirical work in neuroscience and experimental psychology, noteworthy sources pertaining to the intersection of literature, history, memory, modernity, and iden-

tity include the following: Patrick Hutton, *History as an Art of Memory;* Pierre Nora, "Between History and Memory: *Les Lieux de Mémoire, Representations* 26 (1989): 7–25; James Olney, *Memory and Narrative;* Paul Ricoeur, *Memory, History, and Forgetting* (Chicago: University of Chicago Press, 2004); Bruce Ross, *Remembering the Personal Past;* James Wertsch, *Voices of Collective Remembering* (Cambridge: Cambridge University Press, 2002); Eviatar Zerubavel, *Time Maps: Collective Memory and the Social Shape of the Past* (Chicago: University of Chicago Press, 2003). These and related works have both challenged my preconceptions and stimulated a broader engagement with the subject.

As attested by Sōseki's *shōhin* narrator, the unreliability of memory is a fraught issue on many levels. For instance, our legal institutions continue to credit witness testimony that is deeply flawed and unreliable, as attested by recent research on the ease with which memory can be "tricked" and manipulated. A good source here is Daniel Schacter, *The Seven Sins of Memory: How the Mind Forgets and Remembers* (New York: Houghton Mifflin, 2001).

2. Eric Hobsbawm and Terence Ranger, *The Invention of Tradition.* The "invented tradition" paradigm has been applied extensively across the cultural studies field. In the Japanese case, Stephen Vlastos's *Mirror of Modernity* bears noting. Among Japanese critics, Karatani Kōjin, in his seminal *Origins of Modern Japanese Literature,* posits the "invention" or "discovery" of essential epistemes of Japanese modernity—interiority, disease, childhood, landscape, and so forth.

3. "Memory politics" within and among competing ethnic, religious, and national groupings stands as a defining issue of our day. Competing claims to memory "turf," clashes of collective memory, the appropriation of collective memory by autocrats and elites, hybridized and confused identities (both individual and collective)—these have led to contestation and outright conflict on a broad scale and to a vast literature (literary, cinematic, artistic) of modern "memory-scapes."

4. For an analysis of late-Tokugawa *kokugaku* and *kokutai* discourse and the nativist project of the Meiji state, see, for example, Carol Gluck, *Japan's Modern Myths.* The essays in Vlastos's *Mirror of Modernity* are illuminating as well. Natsume Sōseki, who took a dim view of late-Meiji nationalist propagandizing, voices his own critique of *kokutai* discourse at the end of chapter 6 of *Neko* (*I Am a Cat,* pp. 212–213).

5. Late-Tokugawa literary styles and tastes—especially the so-called *gesaku* genre of popular fiction—survived well into the Meiji period. See Carol Gluck's enlightening essay, "The Invention of Edo," in *Mirror of Modernity.* It bears noting that much Tokugawa literature was in fact situated in the urban environs of Edo, Osaka, and Kyoto.

6. The claim that Sōseki was an "inventor" of modern Japanese literary self-consciousness must take into account his debt to precursors such as William James and Henri Bergson. In the *shōhin* context, James is especially significant.

His psychological explorations were of deep interest for Sōseki, whose later novels can be seen as a literary "enactment" of Jamesian introspectionism as a means of reflecting upon the past. Ogura Shūzō, in *Natsume Sōseki: Uiriamu Jēmuzu juyō no shūhen* (Yūseidō, 1989), has exhaustively studied the Jamesian influence on the novels. For a broader psychological perspective, see Bruce Ross, *Remembering the Personal Past,* especially chapter 2 ("Memory Observed by Introspection").

7. Kafū's literature of nostalgia was rooted in an idealized memory-scape of 1880s Tokyo. See Edward Seidensticker, *Kafū the Scribbler*—a superb study of the man and his work. As a counterpart to the nostalgic fiction, Kafū published a vitriolic critique of Tokyo urban design, in *Shinkichōsha nikki* (Diary of a New Returnee, 1909). See *Kafū zenshū* 4, pp. 175–248.

8. *Furusato* has been the subject of much recent scholarly attention. As represented in the Vlastos volume, Jennifer Robertson points to the notion of *kyōdōtai*, which, more so than *furusato,* conjures an essentialist Japanese quality of village collectivity (pp. 110–129). Hashimoto Mitsuru studies the key role of Yanagita Kunio (1875–1962) in the creation of a Japanese folk imaginary (pp. 133–143). Harry Harootunian expands upon the history of folk representation, including Orikuchi Shinobu (1887–1953) into his broad-ranging discussion (pp. 144–159). In his *Writing Home,* Stephen Dodd studies the figure of native place in modern Japanese literature. As Robertson has explained, the invention in modern Japan of an idealized rural topos, where traditional architecture and arts are on proud display, is part and parcel of a widespread marketing of nostalgia and "roots tourism."

9. As Karatani Kōjin argues, childhood in its modern sense was a "discovery" of the mid-Meiji. Here Karatani invokes Yanagita Kunio and the spread of romanticist notions of naivete/retracing roots/*furusato.* See *Origins,* pp. 114–135. One is reminded here of the author Shimazaki Tōson (1872–1943), who was raised in the rural hinterland and then sent off to Tokyo as a young boy, to receive a modern education. Turning to autobiographical fiction, Tōson constructed a literary idyll of growing up in the embrace of *furusato,* in contrast to the teeming metropolis in which he lived and wrote. Writing largely for the youth readership, he crafted tales of *furusato* virtues, conveyed in a voice of avuncular wisdom— hence all but unreadable to his target audience!

10. Pamuk's wonderfully moving memoir centers on the theme of *hüzün*— a species of lyrical melancholy reminiscent of the domain of *mujō/sabi/wabi* in Japanese aesthetics.

Maurice Halbwachs has advanced the notion of a topographical plane for memory formation—clearly delineated spaces and sites that are indispensable for remembered episodes. Cited in Hutton, *History as an Art of Memory,* pp. 80–84.

11. A nostalgia of place is prominent in *kindai* literature, especially concerning the ever-changing face of Tokyo—its topography of old districts and locales, gradually giving way to urban development. Here the flâneur figure—the nostalgic "man-about-town"—is a fixture of *kindai* literary narrative. Maeda Ai's

work is noteworthy here. See *Text and the City,* passim, and the prefatory essays by Harry Harootunian and James Fujii. For a Western literary perspective, see Mary Caws, *City Images.*

12. The two constituent episodes here, *Garasudo* 19 and 20, belong to a three-part sequential reminiscence of the old neighborhood. See *SZ* 12, pp. 562–567; *Doors,* pp. 54–59. Note the English translations of this material: *Doors,* pp. 54–62; Lawrence Rogers, *Tokyo Stories,* pp. 204–212. The Rogers translation is quite good, as is his introductory essay to the volume. Also see Angela Yiu, *Chaos and Order,* pp. 156–167.

13. *Kōshaku* and *kōdan* refer to a repertoire of historical and romantic tales and legends told by professional reciters and raconteurs. These were popular late-Tokugawa entertainments that survived well into the Meiji period.

14. Tanabe Nanrin (1855–1906). For details, see *SZ* 12, p. 739, note 565.11.

15. *Nishime:* vegetables boiled in soy sauce, standard "commoner" fare.

16. The original haiku text is: *hanshō to/narande takaki/fuyuki kana.* This early poem of Sōseki's dates from 1896. See *SZ* 12, p. 739, note 567.2.

17. The district's original name was Babashita. In 1869, the name changed to Kikui-chō.

18. This was the site of an old *bakufu zashiki.* See *SZ* 12, p. 740, note 572.9.

19. The crest is reproduced in *SZ* 12, p. 741.

20. For details of the *kuchō* office, and his father's service, see ibid., note 573.5.

21. Natsumezaka remains on the twenty-first-century Tokyo map, notwithstanding the transformations wrought by the passage of 140 years. Near the Waseda University campus, the site of Sōseki's Babashita birthplace is now a small office building with a commemorative plaque out front. Nothing remains of the house that the author and his family occupied during his novel-writing years. But the site, a patch of land within easy walking distance of the Babashita intersection, has been converted into Sōseki kōen—a small neighborhood park featuring some memorial statuary, several benches, and a dilapidated restroom. The stone bust of the author serves as a roosting spot for the local pigeons. And next to it is a bronze plaque with four Chinese characters rendered calligraphically: *sokuten kyoshi.*

22. As for the fate of the Kikui-chō house, upon the death of Sōseki's father in June 1897, his brother Wasaburō sold the house and divided the proceeds. At the time, Sōseki was teaching in Kumamoto. See *SZ* 12, p. 741, note 573.13.

23. The original haiku text is *kage shinshi/matsu sanbon no/tsukiyo kana.* Sōseki composed the verse in 1895.

24. *Garasudo,* episode 23. *SZ* 12, pp. 572–574; *Doors,* pp. 66–68.

25. The text evokes the quality of *mujō,* the classical trope of lyrical melancholy epitomized by the famous opening lines of the *Heike monogatari* (Tales of the Heike), with its lament for the vanished glories of the once-proud Taira clan.

26. *Michikusa,* ch. 69. *SZ* 10, pp. 209–211; *Grass,* pp. 111–112.

27. *Hearing Things* is anthologized in Natsume Sōseki, *Ten Nights of Dream, Hearing Things, The Heredity of Taste,* pp. 65–115. For the original text, see *SZ* 2, pp. 85–127. Sōseki's creation here of an otherworldly Tokyo landscape—in particular, the eerie landscape encountered in the narrator's long walk home—is quite evocative (pp. 86–93). See Michael Foster's study of *Hearing Things,* "Walking in the City with Natsume Sōseki."

28. Inevitably, Meiji writers would incorporate descriptions of the changing cityscape with evocative accounts of the "suburban" pastoral—the so-called *den'en fūkei*—an idyll of natural beauty and tranquility on the metropolitan fringes. The significance here of Kunikida Doppo's *Musashino* (The Musashi Plain, 1898) has been argued by Karatani and others. See *Origins,* pp. 22–26, 65–72.

29. This refers to kabuki theater, and the area corresponding to modern-day Asakusa where the kabuki houses were concentrated as of the Tenpō period (1830–1844). This was in line with Mizuno Tadakuni's plan to consolidate the formerly dispersed entertainment venues into one area. The three major kabuki theaters—the so-called Edo *za*—are the Nakamura-za, Ichimura-za, and Morita-za. For further details, see *SZ* 12, p. 739, note 567.9.

30. The original text mentions each of the stops along the way. See ibid., notes 567.13a, b. For details on Ageba, see note 567.13c.

31. The boat that they would take—the *yanebune*—was a roofed vessel rowed by one or two boatmen—an "Edo gondola" of sorts, used for excursions and entertainments. Yanagibashi was a major geisha district. The Sumida River, and the environs on either side, figure prominently as a Meiji literary topos. Note, in particular, Nagai Kafū's celebrated story *Sumidagawa* (The River Sumida, 1909).

32 A well-known restaurant on the Sumida River. See *SZ* 12, p. 739–740, note 568.3.

33. For details on the seating plan in the old kabuki theaters, see ibid., p. 740, note 568.5.

34. Reference to popular actors at the time, who happened to be brothers: Sawamura Tanosuke III (1845–1878) and Sawamura Tosshō III (1838–1886). For details, see ibid., notes 568.9a, b.

35. *Garasudo,* episode 21. *SZ* 12, pp. 567–569; *Doors,* pp. 60–62.

36. See *SZ* 12, p. 738, note 564.14. As noted above, the Tokugawa raconteur arts were widely popular and survived well into the modern period—to the present day, in fact. For an exhaustive study of the art of *rakugo*—its history, its subgenres, its celebrated performers, performative styles, and major repertoire—see Heinz Morioka and Miyoko Sasaki, *Rakugo.* For information on the *yose* halls, see pp. 1–10 and 240–248.

37. This avocation, also known as *utai,* was encouraged early on by Sōseki's friend Takahama Kyoshi, a practitioner in his own right.

38. See *SZ* 12, p. 745, note 604.2a. The original text contains further details regarding the exact location.

39. Tanabe is not to be confused with Nanrin (*Garasudo* 20). Tanabe Nanryū (?–1884) specialized in warrior episodes *(gundan)*, which he delivered in what was evidently a distinctive and unorthodox style. See *SZ* 12, p. 745, note 605.11.

40. *Garasudo*, episode 35. *SZ* 12, pp. 604–606; *Doors*, pp. 102–105. The name *yose* refers to the hall where performances were held.

41. *Yose* visits figure, for instance, in *Neko, Sanshirō, Kōjin*, and *Mon*. The character Sōsuke in *Mon* is cast as a devotee of *yose* (*Gate*, pp. 172–173). For details, see *NSJ*, p. 306. Also see *SZ* 28, p. 679, for all appearances of the term in the collected works.

42. It can be argued that such settings helped form a substrate of common experience for an emerging national readership. In addition to Sōseki's school-centered work, one can cite, for instance, Shimazaki Tōson's *Hakai* (Broken Commandment, 1906), whose drama is enacted in a rural school; Tsubouchi Shōyō's *Tōsei shosei katagi* (The Character of Today's Students, 1885); Tayama Katai's *Inaka kyōshi* (Country Teacher, 1909); and Mori Ōgai's *Seinen* (Youth, 1910).

43. Bearing the marks of Tokugawa Confucianist dogma, the *ryōsai kenbo* (good wife, wise mother) ethic sought to instill patriarchal authority and prerogative as a state-sponsored ethic. Research on modern Japanese education has been wide-ranging—in part a reflection of the "educational miracle" concomitant to the spectacle of Japanese economic power in the 1980s. While most of the studies concern the postwar educational scene, a number center on the Meiji, in particular, and on prewar education more generally. For example, Mark Lincicome, *Principles, Praxis, and the Politics of Educational Reform in Meiji Japan*, which focuses on the formative first two decades of the Meiji; Byron Marshall, *Learning to be Modern* (for Meiji coverage, see pp. 25–117); Donald Roden, *Schooldays in Imperial Japan*, which concerns elite education in Meiji-Taishō—hence, a useful historical and institutional context for Sōseki's school-related writings. Also see Wm. Theodore de Bary, Carol Gluck, and Arthur E. Tiedemann, eds., *Sources of Japanese Tradition*, 2nd ed. (New York: Columbia University Press, 2006), vol. 2, ch. 40 ("Education in Meiji Japan"), pp. 750–788.

44. In Sōseki's day, there were eight state-run higher schools. Each numbered, they are, in order, (1) Tokyo, (2) Sendai, (3) Kyoto, (4) Kanazawa, (5) Kumamoto (where Sōseki taught), (6) Okayama, (7) Kagoshima, (8) Nagoya. There were four imperial universities: Tokyo (1877), Kyoto (1897), Tōhoku (in Sendai, 1913), and Kyūshū (in Fukuoka, 1913). The sole woman's university was Nihon joshi daigaku, founded 1901; in addition, women could attend the college-level Joshi Eigaku-juku (Women's English Institute), founded in 1900 by the pioneering Tsuda Umeko.

45. For details regarding the *kugakusei* motif and its ties to the *risshin* ideal of striving and success, see Earl Kinmonth, *The Self-made Man in Meiji Japanese*

Thought, pp. 153–240. Sōseki's skepticism regarding the ethos of success-ism figures prominently in *Botchan, Sanshirō,* and *Kokoro.*

46. It was Naka Kansuke (1885–1965), one of Sōseki's younger protégés, who went on to produce a literary reminiscence that beautifully captures the child's point of view—*Gin no saji* (Silver Spoon, 1912–1913).

47. Ōta Nanpo (1749–1823), renowned Edo satirist, connoisseur, and literatus. His comic verse *(kyōka)* and chic comic narratives *(sharebon, kokkeibon)* enjoyed a large readership.

48. An 1814 collection of Nanpo's essays on assorted topics.

49. The prodigal son who sells off the scholar-father's books stands as a stock figure in Tokugawa personal writings. See Mori Ōgai's version of the story as he retells it in *Shibue Chūsai* (Marcus, *Paragons,* p. 114).

50. *Garasudo,* episodes 31–32. *SZ* 12, pp. 592–598; *Doors,* pp. 89–94.

51. See *SZ* 12, p. 744, note 592.

52. Ōta Tatsuto (1866–1945). A graduate of the Imperial University, in physics, Ōta befriended Sōseki at the university preparatory school *(daigaku yobimon),* 1884–1885. Ōta became principal of Akita Middle School; then, in 1913, he was appointed principal of Karafuto [Sakhalin] Middle School. In the text, Ōta is referred to simply by the first letter of his family name, O.

53. The temple, situated in the Hōraichō district of Komagome, was known for its impressive Kannon statue. See *SZ* 12, p. 735, note 537.4. Note the *kugakusei* motif here.

54. Refers to modern-day Sakhalin, controlled by Russia.

55. Note Ōta's version of this episode, as related in *Yobimon jidai no Sōseki* (Sōseki at the Preparatory School), a 1936 *danwa* reminiscence contained in *SZ bekkan* (pp. 15–26):

> When I returned to Tokyo from Karafuto, where I still served as Middle School principal, everyone was saying that something about me had appeared in the newspaper [a reference to the *Asahi* serialization of *Garasudo*]. And so I read the chestnut bun account. Well, here's what really happened. On the day of my visit to Sōseki's home in Waseda, I'd paid a visit earlier in the day to the residence of our former *han* domain lord, in Kudan. As it turns out, they happened to serve chestnut buns while I was there, and before I set out to see Sōseki, I wrapped one of the buns in my handkerchief to take with me.
>
> As you can read in the *Garasudo* episode, the very same sort of buns were served as refreshments at Sōseki's home. Later, when we were riding on the train, Sōseki noticed that I had something wrapped up in my handkerchief. When he asked me what it was, I told him it was a chestnut bun. He was surprised. "You mean that you took one of them with you from the house?" I never did mention having actually gotten that bun from the *han*

chief's home in Kudan. And to his dying day, Sōseki never did learn the true story. (*SZ bekkan*, pp. 25–26)

56. The name can also be read *tatsujin*—one who is expert, adept.

57. *Garasudo*, episodes 9, 10. *SZ* 12, pp. 535–540; *Doors*, pp. 25–31. Also, the episodes are translated in Yiu, *Chaos and Order* (pp. 144–147), in the context of the chapter focusing on *Kōjin* and its troubled protagonist Ichirō.

58. The matter of empty formalism—*kyorei*—appears as a concern in the Koeber reminiscence (see chapter 6 herein). In *Chaos and Order*, Yiu argues for Ōta as a Confucian paragon, citing passages from the *Analects* to make her case. To my mind, such a reading is overly idealized, especially given the brevity and overall lightness of the episode. I also take issue with Yiu's identifying *Garasudo* with a quality of "brooding solitude" (p. 148). This overlooks the variety of voice and mood that marks the collection.

59. The passage in question occurs while the introspective narrator is taking a walk one evening, when he chances upon an utterly inconsequential, yet strangely moving, scene:

Everything was a pale green; the touch of the air was chilly against the skin. The quiet made me strangely restless. There was a large mulberry tree beside the road. A leaf on one branch that protruded out over the road from the far side fluttered rhythmically back and forth. There was no wind; everything except the stream was sunk in silence. Only that one leaf fluttered on. I thought it odd. I was a little afraid even, but I was curious. I went down and looked at it for a time. A breeze came up. The leaf stopped moving. I saw what was happening, and it came to me that I had known all this before. (Donald Keene, ed., *Modern Japanese Literature* [New York: Grove Press, 1956], p. 276)

60. In the novel's climactic scene, the protagonist is left outside the gate, with no hope of entry:

Sōsuke had come here to have the gate opened to him.... But he had failed to summon up the power to achieve his purpose. He was standing now precisely where he had stood before having begun to search for a solution. Sōsuke stood facing the closed door, ignorant and impotent....—a poor unfortunate doomed to face the bolted gate, waiting for night to fall. (Based on *Gate*, pp. 204–205)

61. Sōseki's first school-related essay was actually a student composition, written *in English*, in June 1889. Signed Natsume Kinnosuke, the essay, entitled "My Friends in the School," recounts his experiences as a student at the prestigious First Higher School in Tokyo. Beginning with character sketches of several classmates, it reveals a good deal about mid-Meiji school life while pointing to

the nexus of literary and intellectual influences just at the point when the young man, having adopted his pen name, was embarking upon serious literary pursuits. Here are several representative passages from this clever, if somewhat contrived, composition:

A large school such as ours is nothing but a vast exhibition of human beings where we can easily form a fair conception of human nature. It is indeed full of remarkable young men whose careers and adventures are well worth careful study. Even the least observant reader of human nature, such as I, cannot fail to single out a few whose whims and eccentricities have constantly put him in mind of some odd animals he has met with in English novels.

The first of my friends is a robust, sturdy fellow, nicknamed the Duck, from his gait.... He has large owlish eyes, always goggling deep in their sockets; a heavy ill-cut mouth, with a set of big, sharp teeth, almost vying with those of a horse; a short flat nose turned a little up, rendering his expression somewhat comical. He is well known as the staunchest patron of all the ale houses in the neighborhood of the school; nor does he ever fail to signalize his omnivorous prowess, whenever he visits a so-called beef shop, often to the astonishment of his friends. (*SZ* 26, pp. 452–444)

62. Founded in 1877 by Mishima Chūshū (1830–1919), the academy focused on Chinese studies *(kangaku)*. The young Sōseki studied there from 1881 to 1882.

63. The *National Reader* series formed the basis of mid-Meiji English-language instruction.

64. The *daigaku yobikō*—of which there were several in Tokyo—provided focused instruction in preparation for university matriculation. It is the forerunner of today's "cram schools" *(juku, yobikō)*.

65. The five-year *yobimon* curriculum corresponds to our undergraduate program, constituting, in Sōseki's student days, the gateway to university entrance.

66. The reconstruction and expansion of the school facilities were for the purpose of reconstituting it as the First Higher School.

67. The three-year basic course at the *yobimon* followed a *sankyū/nikyū/ikkyū* (3-2-1) sequence of grades.

68. The classmates in question are Matsumoto Matatarō (1865–1943) and Komeyama Yasusaburō (1869–1897). Matsumoto went on to be a leading experimental psychologist, introducing the pioneering work of Wilhelm Wundt. For his part, Komeyama became a scholar of literature.

69. Notwithstanding Sōseki's dismissive remark, this episode has been cited as evidence of the author's keen sense of visual art and design, whose literary

manifestation may relate to the care with which he crafts interior spaces for his characters, which in turn mirror aspects of their personality and mood.

70. This is an abridged translation of the original text, entitled *Rakudai.* See *SZ* 25, pp. 161–166. The *danwa* was published in the June 20, 1906, special issue of *Chūgaku bungei,* entitled "Meishi no chūgaku jidai"—a collection of twenty-eight interviews with prominent individuals about their middle-school reminiscences.

71. This period witnessed a dramatic expansion of publications for the youth readership, which promoted the *risshin* ethic of achievement and advancement. Successful adults—literary figures and others—served as role models for the nation's budding *seikō seinen* (achievement-oriented youth). Again, Kinmonth's study *(Self-made Man)* is instructive here.

72. The account, entitled *Ikkan shitaru fubenkyō: watakushi no keika shita gakusei jidai,* appeared in the January 1909 issue of *Chūgaku sekai.* In *SZ* 25, pp. 317–325.

73. By way of comparison, consider several *danwa* interviews with Nagai Kafū, in response to solicitations on similar subjects. The first appeared in the October 1909 issue of *Bunshō sekai,* part of a series of reminiscences on one's life at age twenty; the second appeared in the May 1910 issue of *Chūgaku sekai,* on recounting one's late teens. See *Kafū zenshū,* vol. 27, pp. 39–48.

74. Entitled *Bunwa.* In *SZ* 25, pp. 377–381.

75. *Kanbun* studies in the Meiji eventually (and inevitably) declined in popularity. See *SZ* 25, p. 567, note 380.16. On the other hand, in line with the expanding youth-oriented journalism, which strongly promoted educational values and diligent study, there emerged special features and advice columns on pedagogical topics—especially with regard to writing technique and style. Sōseki's remarks span both areas.

76. Hashimoto Sagorō (1866–1952) was an authority on animal husbandry who had been invited by the Southern Manchurian Railway company to investigate the livestock situation in Manchuria. For details, see *NSJ*/b, pp. 287–288.

77. Ōta Tatsujin was among their number as well.

78. *Mankan,* episode 13. *SZ* 12, p. 257; Brodey and Tsunematsu, *Rediscovering,* pp. 57–58.

79. *SZ* 12, pp. 258–259; *Rediscovering,* p. 59.

80. Satō's dates are unknown. See *NSJ*/b, pp. 134–135.

81. A reference to *makanai seibatsu* (refectory chastisement). This was a custom—originating with the early Meiji and lasting into the 1930s—of boarding students banding together to trash the kitchen, smash up utensils, and generally run riot. See *SZ* 12, p. 692, note 276.8.

82. *SZ* 12, pp. 275–277; *Rediscovering,* pp. 72–73. Note Sōseki's many *shōhin* references to hair.

83. The issue concerns the proper kanji orthography for the holiday's name.

Two different *ki* characters have in fact been employed, but one became standard in the late Meiji. See *SZ* 12, p. 671, note 189.7. Also see explanatory note 35 in *Spring*, p. 86.

84. *Eijitsu*, episode 17. *SZ* 12, pp. 188–189; *Spring*, pp. 85–86. This very brief *shōhin* was originally published in the *Osaka Asahi* on February 11, 1909, to help commemorate the holiday, hence its journalistic origins. It was in 1893 that the holiday, meant to commemorate the accession of the mythical emperor Jinmu Tennō, became an official national observance, to be celebrated annually on February 11. It is a prime example of how "invented traditions" figured as a political objective of the Meiji oligarchs.

85. Sōseki graduated from the Imperial University in 1894; in 1895, he moved to Matsuyama to begin teaching.

86. The priest is a practitioner of divination techniques with ancient roots in Chinese culture, which had long since gained widespread currency in Japan.

87. *Omoidasu*, episode 28. *SZ* 12, pp. 437–440; *Recollections*, pp. 81–83. For details regarding the *kanshi* with which the episode concludes, see *SZ* 12, p. 720, note 44.5. See also *Recollections*, p. 83; note, p. 114. Sōseki recorded the poem in his diary on October 10, 1910. The entry goes on to discuss preparations to return to Tokyo, following the extended Shuzenji convalescence.

88. *Omoidasu*, episode 31, tells of the two older brothers, who died in their youth, sporting dark beards. See chapter 3 herein.

Chapter 3: *Shōhin* Episodes

1. Fukuzawa Yukichi (1835–1901) was the great Meiji exponent of *bunmei kaika* (civilization and enlightenment). His 1900 work, *Fukuō jiden*, is one of few that adopted the Western autobiographical mode. Interestingly, a number of others were written in English, and only subsequently "translated" into Japanese. See my essay "The Impact of Western Autobiography on the Meiji Literary Scene," pp. 371–389.

2. This term calls to mind an important essay—"Naibu seimei ron" (On the Inner Life)—by the pioneering intellectual Kitamura Tōkoku (1868–1894). Tōkoku was leader of the influential *bungakukai* (romanticist) coterie during the 1890s, and his essay is a hallmark of Meiji romanticism.

3. Takada Shōkichi was married to Sōseki's stepsister Fusa (1851–1915). The eldest son of his father's younger brother, Shōkichi was thus Sōseki's older cousin. He served as model for the character Hida in *Michikusa*. For details, see *SZ* 12, p. 737, note 554.11; and *NSJ*/b, p. 195.

4. In the original text, this refers to the many *machiai jaya* in the area— houses of assignation, to which geisha would be called.

5. Natsume Einosuke, 1858–1887.

6. The wastrel is a familiar character type in Tokugawa and *kindai* reminiscence. Note, for instance, the figure of Yutaka in Ōgai's *Shibue Chūsai* (see my *Paragons,* pp. 212–218).

7. For details concerning the store, see *SZ* 12, p. 737, note 558.7. Ōta Tatsujin (Tatsuto) is the subject of a *Garasudo* episode discussed in chapter 2 herein.

8. *Garasudo,* episodes 16–17. *SZ* 12, pp. 554–559; *Doors,* pp. 45–51.

9. The eighth dream episode from *Yume jūya* is set in a barbershop, with an interesting array of passersby and a mysterious dark-skinned woman who materializes. The barbershop *(tokoya)* figures as an important site for late-Tokugawa literary narrative, as epitomized by *Ukiyodoko* (Barbershop of the Floating World, 1813–1814), a stylish satire by the noted comic author Shikitei Samba (1776–1822). In Japan as elsewhere, barbershops served as neighborhood gathering places, where news and gossip would freely circulate.

10. Masujirō was the older brother of Shōhei and son of Sōseki's mother's older sister Hisa. He was evidently something of a misfit, who ended up in the postal service. See *SZ* 12, p. 742, note 580.2.

11. The Kaiseikō was founded by the Edo shogunate in 1863, to replace the old Bansho shirabesho; its focus was Western study *(yōgaku).* With the advent of the Meiji era, the school was renamed the Daigaku nankō, then simply Nankō in 1871. It would go through other renamings, all the while retaining its Western scholarly orientation. The school officially became Tokyo Imperial University in 1877.

12. Peter Parley was the pen name of Samuel Goodrich (1793–1860), American writer and author of widely used history texts. The Parley series was a standard in the early Meiji. See *SZ* 12, pp. 742–743, note 581.1.

13. The woman is referred to in the original as *perori no okusan,* a play on the onomatopoetic usage *perori-to.* Her Japanese-sounding phrase in the original is *anata yoroshii arigatō* (you fine thanks). *SZ* 12, p. 581.

14. *Garasudo,* episode 26. *SZ* 12, pp. 580–582; *Doors,* p. 74–77.

15. Note the depiction, in *The Fortune-teller,* of his *own* disheveled appearance. See end of chapter 2 herein.

16. *Omoidasu,* episode 31. *SZ* 12, pp. 446–448; *Recollections,* pp. 87–89. For details regarding the concluding *kanshi,* see *SZ* 12, p. 721, note 448.12; and *Recollections,* p. 89, and note, p. 117. The verse is recorded in Sōseki's diary (October 25, 1910). Note, too, the September 14, 1910, entry, regarding the brothers, with haiku accompaniment. See *SZ* 20, pp. 239–240, and pp. 203–204, respectively.

17. Sōseki's student composition, "The Death of My Brother," was delivered to the Eigo-kai (English Language Society) in February 1889. See *SZ* 26, pp. 40–42, with an accompanying Japanese translation. Of note is the depiction of the dying brother exhorting the younger lad to "be studious," thanks to which he is saved from a habitual self-indulgence. Note, too, the irony of the young man who, dutifully comforting his deathly ill brother, would himself go on to experience chronic ill health and periods of prolonged confinement.

18. Here is evidence pointing to relatively open homosexual practices in the late Tokugawa, with older individuals making advances toward the attractive *bishōnen* (younger men). See *SZ* 12, p. 746, note 607.3.

19. Modern-day Yamanashi Prefecture.

20. *Garasudo,* episode 36. *SZ* 12, pp. 606–609; *Doors,* pp. 105–108.

21. A similar incongruity will come to light regarding the father—the stiff, punctilious old man who is revealed to have been a denizen of the *yūkaku* (pleasure quarters) in his younger days.

22. *Nanushi* was a category of Edo official answerable to the local *machi bugyō* (city magistrate). For details, see *SZ* 12, p. 740, note 569.2 (material itself taken from Komiya Toyotaka's memoir, *Natsume Sōseki*).

23. The text identifies this as *itchūbushi,* a singing style popular in Edo, beginning early in the eighteenth century and extending through the Meiji. See *SZ* 12, p. 740, note 569.3.

24. *Genka* is a colloquialism for *genkan,* the now-standard entranceway into Japanese homes. This space would have served as an office of sorts for local officials such as Sōseki's father. See *SZ* 12, p. 740, note 569.7, which includes a relevant excerpt from Natsume Shinroku's memoir.

25. Excerpted from *Garasudo,* episode 21. *SZ* 12, p. 569; *Doors,* p. 62. The devices mentioned at the end of the episode—standard police issue used to nab and restrain suspected felons—were collectively known as the *mitsu dōgu* (the "three tools"). See *SZ* 12, p. 740, note 569.9.

26. Reference to Sawa (1846–1878) and Fusa (1851–1915).

27. For details concerning the custom of teeth-blackening, see *SZ* 12, p. 736, note 549.4.

28. During the largely anarchic *bakumatsu* period, citizens were often shaken down for money to help rogue bands procure weapons and sustain themselves. Note the parallel, in Ōgai's *Shibue Chūsai,* with the intruder incident involving Chūsai and his indomitable wife, Io (Marcus, *Paragons,* pp 186–189).

29. *Garasudo,* episode 14. *SZ* 12, pp. 548–551; *Doors,* pp. 39–42.

30. Here, again, one is reminded of Mori Ōgai's *shiden* project. *Shibue Chūsai,* for instance, includes the retelling of episodes told to the biographer-narrator by Chūsai's surviving son, Tamotsu, who had himself heard these from his mother, Io (his father having died when he was a small child). See Marcus, *Paragons,* passim.

31. *Michikusa,* ch. 15. *SZ* 10, pp. 43–46; *Grass,* pp. 24–25.

32. *Michikusa,* excerpts from chs. 38–44. *SZ* 10, pp. 114–134; *Grass,* pp. 61–71.

33. *Michikusa,* ch. 91. *SZ* 10, pp. 279–281; *Grass,* pp. 148–150.

34. The mother-son relationship, with its putative bonds of dependency and devotion, has a proud pedigree in Japanese literature and lore—most notably through the *Tale of Genji.* For a cultural-studies approach to this issue, see, for instance, Doi Takeo, *Amae no kōzō* (Kōbundō, 1971; John Bester, translator,

Anatomy of Dependence [Tokyo and New York: Kodansha International, 1973]); and Ian Buruma, *Behind the Mask* (New York: Pantheon Books, 1984).

35. *Garasudo,* episodes 37, 38 (both in excerpted translation). *SZ* 12, pp. 609–611, 611–614; *Doors,* pp. 108–114.

36. Hoashi Banri (1778–1852) was an important Tokugawa literatus and Confucian scholar of the Hiji *han,* widely versed in *rangaku* (Dutch studies)—economics, geography, and the like.

37. *Eijitsu* 21: *Koe. SZ* 12, pp. 197–199; *Spring,* pp. 96–98.

38. Ranging freely across the landscape of the author's imagination, the *Dream* series includes one—*The Ninth Night's Dream*—that centers on a mother and young child, and a father who will not return to the family. See *SZ* 12, pp. 124–127; *Dream,* pp. 56–59. This "sad tale, told to me by my mother in the dream" is reminiscent of Tanizaki Jun'ichirō's *Haha wo kouru ki* (Longing for My Mother, 1917), translated by Edward Fowler, in *Monumenta Nipponica* 35, no. 4 (Winter 1980): 467–478. In this hauntingly beautiful story, the adult narrator is reunited with his dead mother after wandering, as a child, through a surreal landscape.

39. His mother, Chie (1826–1881), was forty at the time of her pregnancy. The father was forty-nine.

40. *Garasudo,* episode 29. *SZ* 12, pp. 587–590; *Doors,* pp. 83–86. The published translations of the episode bear comparison. See McClellan, *Two Japanese Novelists,* p. 4. Yiu remarks on this episode as well (*Chaos and Order,* pp. 167–168). Also, note the two contrasting retellings of this episode in the memoirs of Natsume Kyōko (*Sōseki no omoide,* episode 7) and Komiya Toyotaka (*Natsume Sōseki,* ch. 4). The memoirs are divergent in many instances.

41. Note the parallel with the famous opening of *Neko,* in which the retrospecting feline relates a similarly hazy account of one's origins: "I am a cat, but as yet I have no name. I haven't the faintest idea where I was born. The first thing I do remember is crying out 'meow, meow' in some damp, gloomy place. It was there that I met a human being for the first time in my life" (Based on *I Am a Cat,* p. 1). Komori Yōichi calls attention to the displaced autobiographical subtext here, in *Sōseki wo yominaosu* (pp. 16–20).

Chapter 4: Burdens of Domesticity

1. The term *katei* first appeared, as a new Meiji coinage, in 1871. It took hold as a modern social institution in the 1890s. See Jordan Sand, *House and Home in Modern Japan,* which traces the rise of *kindai* bourgeois culture, with house and home as created modern spaces. Note, too, Ming-Cheng Lo and Christopher Bettinger, "The Historical Emergence of a 'Family Society' in Japan," *Theory and Society* 30, no. 2 (April 2001): 237–279, which studies the Meiji project of creating a "progressive" society through a uniform code of law while retaining the integrity of family hierarchy and traditionalist values.

2. Historians of Meiji Japan have commented widely on the Constitution, vis-à-vis the state-sponsored *kazoku kokka* notion of "subject-citizen." On these and related matters of Meiji myth making, see Gluck, *Japan's Modern Myths,* passim.

3. In "Sōseki Natsume and the Fluctuating Values of Property," Michael Bourdaghs studies Sōseki's *bunmeiron* critique of Japanese modernity through the author's writings on, and references to, property, money, and possessiveness. Here he remarks on Sōseki's interest in William James's notion of "possessive individualism," as articulated in *Principles of Psychology* (1890).

4. Marking a watershed in the emergence of the new *katei* family order, the 1890s witnessed a dramatic rise in readership among women and young people. The *katei shōsetsu* genre reflects this key trend. Noteworthy here is the work of Ozaki Kōyō and the *Ken'yūsha* coterie, which produced popular romantic fiction marked by sentimentalism and melodrama. See Ken Ito, *An Age of Melodrama.* The expanding female readership was served by a new category of housewife-oriented periodicals *(fujin zasshi, katei zasshi)* that appeared in the 1890s, promoting a "good housekeeping" gospel that incorporated edifying testimonials, practical tips and techniques, appropriate literary matter, and an aggressive consumerism. Circulations expanded dramatically in the early twentieth century.

5. Shimazaki Tōson addresses this question in *Ie* (The Family, 1911), an important analogue to Sōseki's novelizations of family life. Pursuing a more explicitly autobiographical tack than Sōseki, Tōson was sensitive to, and critical of, the corrosive influence of extended family and its pervasive sociopathology.

6. Sand, *House and Home in Modern Japan.* Sand notes that dining together as a family was a major sociological shift in the Meiji. For a study of Japanese writers and their literary depiction of domesticity, see Hosoya Hiroshi, *Bonjō no hakken* (Meiji Shoin, 1996), which explores the theme of domesticity in the work of Sōseki, Tanizaki, and Dazai Osamu. On the notion of *nichijōsei* (everydayness) in the context of Japanese modernity, see Harry Harootunian, *History's Disquiet,* passim. Note, too, the contrasting approach to domestic routine as a Confucianist "quotidian dignity." This virtue is epitomized by the subjects of Mori Ōgai's *shiden* biographies. See my *Paragons,* passim.

7. One space in the new Meiji home that promised a measure of privacy (typically, for the male head of household) was the study *(shosai).* As I have suggested, privacy was a problematic notion in Meiji social and literary discourse, reflecting the legacy of Tokugawa social control and conformist norms. In contrast, there is an extensive history-of-ideas literature on privacy in the West—for example, Philippe Ariès and Georges Duby, gen. eds., *A History of Private Life* (Cambridge: Harvard University Press, 1987–1991). Its five impressive volumes trace the conception and institution of private life from antiquity to the present day.

8. Maeda Ai has studied the marital relationship depicted in Sōseki's *Mon* as having been conditioned by the spatial dynamics of the couple's home. See Maeda's "Yamanote no oku" (In the Recesses of the High City: On Sōseki's *Gate;* in

Text and the City, pp. 329–350). Maeda extends his literary topology to *Sanshirō* and *Sorekara,* as well, calling attention to these works as literary constructions of a distinctive *"yamanote* space," where the specificity of detail, locale, streets, and shops is fully integrated into the novel.

In his groundbreaking *Toshi kūkan,* Maeda studies the significance of the second floor *(nikai no heya)* in *kindai* fiction, exemplified by Futabatei's *Ukigumo* and its famously introverted protagonist, Utsumi Bunzō. Maeda calls attention to protagonists for whom one's second-floor room serves as a private sanctuary—a space that also marginalizes them and reinforces their passivity, given the first floor as a more active—and interactive—social milieu.

9. The *shosai* persona—at least in its more comic aspect—is anticipated in the figure of the vain and socially inept Professor Kushami of *Neko.*

10. This refers to their second son, Shinroku, born on December 17, 1908. The events recorded here are thought to have occurred on January 8, 1909, when the baby would have been only several weeks old. See *SZ* 12, p. 661, notes 146.13 and 147.1.

11. *Eijitsu,* episode 5. *SZ* 12, pp. 146–150; *Spring,* pp. 33–37.

12. Shōno, who himself wrote on the uneasy terrain of family life and the domestic undercurrents of tension and failed communication, remarked admiringly on the hibachi essay and on Sōseki's *shōhin* overall. See his essay in the 1965 *Sōseki zenshū (geppō,* pp. 5–7).

13. Through his Kenzō alter ego, Sōseki underlines the corrosive impact of money concerns upon a marriage. Chapter 20 of *Michikusa* relates the family's straitened circumstances and Kenzō's jaundiced view of his wife's strategy of household economy. Such concerns likely reflect the author's deteriorating marital (and mental) situation just prior to the *Michikusa* serialization. His diary entries from December 1914 to March 1915 consist exclusively of household account ledgers—a detailed record of income and expenses, indicating that he had taken over this role from his wife. See *SZ* 20, pp. 453–463. Moreover, chapter 57 of *Michikusa* recounts Kenzō's self-pitying reflections on his failure to attain wealth and his resentment at being beset by money worries.

14. *Eijitsu,* episode 19: *Gyōretsu. SZ* 12, pp. 192–194; *Spring,* pp. 90–92.

15. The five daughters are portrayed in the text as follows: (1) *kū wo funde, tesuri no takasa hodo no* mono *ga arawareta,* (2) *Kondo wa sukoshi hikui,* (3) Dai san *no zukin wa,* (4) *Suru to, sugu ato kara masshiro na* kao *ga arawareta,* and (5) *Saigo ni deta* mono *wa, mattaku chiisai.* See *SZ* 12, pp 192–193. This passage suggests an analogy to the art of *emaki,* the well-known picture-scroll genre, which intertwines sequential pictorial scenes and accompanying narratives.

16. The modernist reading of such discourse, as noted in chapter 1, centers on the framed composition, and a strategy of repositioning, fragmentation, and defamiliarization. See Alter's *Imagined Cities* in this regard, vis-à-vis the construction of literary cityscapes.

17. From *Neko,* ch. 10. *SZ* 1, pp. 421–423. Based on *Cat,* pp. 337, 339.

18. The letter was written on September 11, 1910, as noted in that day's diary entry—a week following receipt of the girls' letters.

19. *Omoidasu,* episode 25. *SZ* 12, pp. 428–431; *Recollections,* pp. 76–78. A draft of the *kanshi* with which the episode concludes is contained in the October 7, 1910, diary entry. See *SZ* 12, p. 431; p. 719, note 431.9. See also *Recollections,* p. 78; note, p. 113.

20. See *SZ* 20, p. 60, for the July 18, 1909, diary entry.

21. *Michikusa,* ch. 81. *SZ* 10, pp. 246–249; *Grass,* pp. 131–132.

22. See, for instance, the *danwa* entitled "Katei to bungaku" (Home and Literature), which appeared in the February 1907 issue of *Katei bungei.* The interviewer was a literary acquaintance, Ikuta Chōkō. Sōseki discourses at length on household and family and on the need to foster literary values in the home. In *SZ* 25, pp. 224–233.

23. Nakamura Murao (1886–1949). Chapter 10 of his reminiscence, *Meiji Taishō no bungakusha* (Literary Figures of the Meiji-Taishō period), concerns his journalistic encounters with Sōseki, whom he regarded, tongue-in-cheek, as belonging to the "writer-in-his-study" coterie *(shosai-ha);* quotation, p. 116.

24. Kyōko's memoir relates her perspective on Hinako's death—and on the larger issue of her husband as father of their children. This will be compared with Sōseki's account. *Higan sugi made* is volume 7 of the *Soseki zenshū.* The "Rainy Day" chapter, comprising eight episodes, can be found on pp. 180–203.

25. *Equinox,* pp. 186–187.

26. *Equinox,* p. 186.

27. *Equinox,* p. 187.

28. *Equinox,* pp. 188–189.

29. *SZ* 20, p. 357. The Hinako-related diary entries, spanning November 29 to December 3, can be found on pp. 351–358.

30. *Equinox,* p. 190.

31. *SZ* 20, p. 358.

32. In fact, a final closure would occur on December 5, when Hinako's remains were taken to Honpōji temple for the required hundred-day period. Sōseki concludes the entry by noting that this has put an end to the matter *(kore de ichidanraku tsuita).* See *SZ* 20, pp. 359–360.

As for the rectal disorder (one of many gastrointestinal problems that plagued the author)—toward the end of 1911, he was being treated for an anal fistula by a certain Dr. Satō. Several diary entries suggest Sōseki's fascination with medical science, on the one hand, and point to his cordial relationship with the physician, on the other. Sōseki remarks on his rectal problems, which finally abated by mid-December of 1911, in an unusually matter-of-fact manner. At the risk of indulging my propensity for the comically deflating anecdote, allow me to note that Kyōko, too, exploited the anecdote in episode 47 of her memoir, entitled "Yabure shōji," which details the rectal surgery and her husband's rueful sense that his body was falling apart. Here Kyōko includes the slightly off-color

233

vignette *(shōshō kitanai ohanashi)* regarding the strange farting noises that he'd make, which sounded like torn shoji *(yabure shōji)*—presumably an anatomical result of the rectal surgery.

33. The Hinako reminiscence comprises episodes 48 and 49 of the memoir.

34. On November 29, Sōseki was visited by a writer friend, Nakamura Shigeru (1881–1952), who, having witnessed the scene of Hinako's death, would later write of the experience. See *SZ* 20, pp. 576–577. For his part, Sōseki's diary record of Hinako's death and its aftermath is entirely taken up with official matters—problems with completing the death certificate in the absence of a certifiable cause of death; arrangements to be made with the mortuary people, the local government office, and the Buddhist temple; and the various funeral details. It is a markedly detached, businesslike account.

35. Kyōko inserts an amusing anecdote regarding Sōseki's reaction to her exhortation regarding the wake. It closely parallels his own December 8, 1911, diary account: "This morning, my wife accuses me of being totally antisocial. 'People come over for Hinako's wake, and you tell them not to bother, that they should just go home.' 'Well, when *I* die, be sure not to plan any wake for *me*.' 'But in that case the mice will come out in the middle of the night and gnaw at the tip of your nose.' 'Fine with me—the pain would bring me back to life!'" *SZ* 20, p. 362.

36. Hinako was born on March 2, 1910; the "Rainy Day" chapter began in serialization on March 5, 1912. There is no Sōseki diary entry to corroborate Kyōko's claim that he began the chapter on March 2. The above, incidentally, is an excerpted version of *Omoide*, episode 48.

37. Kyōko notes that her husband took them on a family outing to collect seashells *(shiohigari)*, which was a first for him. Unfortunately, it was a stormy day, and they all ended up getting drenched. From *Omoide*, episode 49.

38. The following remarks are contained in episode 56 of *Omoide*, which focuses on the children's education.

39. This is noted by both Natsume Shinroku and Yōko McClain in their respective reminiscences.

40. Sōseki evidently had good facility with French. Here, it is unclear if the son in question is Jun'ichi (b 1907) or Shinroku (b 1908).

41. From *Omoide*, episode 56.

42. See *Omoide*, episode 21: "The Divorce Letter." Kyōko stops short of declaring any deep feeling—be it love or hate—toward her husband. But Komiya Toyotaka, Sōseki's quasi-official Boswell, makes the straightforward claim that he did indeed love his wife—"Sōseki wa Kyōko wo aishita." In *Natsume Sōseki*, p. 401.

For a study of divorce in late-Meiji Japan, see Harald Fuess, *Divorce in Japan: Family, Gender, and the State* (Stanford, Calif.: Stanford University Press, 2004). With the promulgation of the Meiji Civil Code in 1898, a Napoleonic Code–inspired approach to divorce was institutionalized; it established mutual consent as the criterion, and court adjudication only if the two parties could not agree. The relative laxity of the legal requirements resulted in high rates of divorce, but the *ie* system continued to privilege husbands over wives.

43. Based on the family situation in 1903, following Sōseki's return from England, the 1915 novel is thus a form of creative reminiscence. *Michikusa* can be regarded as a prototypical autobiographical novel, insofar as fictional technique and factual grounding are equally apparent and seamlessly integrated.

44. *Michikusa,* ch. 21. *SZ* 10, pp. 61–62; *Grass,* pp. 34–35.

45. *Michikusa,* ch. 54. *SZ* 10, pp. 162–163; *Grass,* pp. 86–87.

46. *Michikusa,* ch. 71. *SZ* 10, pp. 215–216; *Grass,* pp. 114–215.

47. *Michikusa,* ch. 102. *SZ* 10, pp. 317–318; *Grass,* p. 169.

48. Kenzō is especially solicitous and protective when his wife appears to be having a hysterical episode.

Chapter 5: Inside Glass Doors

1. Chapter 10, in particular, parodies the Kushami household through a frontal assault on the peccadilloes of the householder. See previous references to *katei* and modern domesticity, and to the rise of a materialist culture that stimulated changes in interpersonal relations. Again, Sand's *House and Home in Modern Japan* is instructive.

2. The conflict here can be seen as a reformulation of the well-known Tokugawa paradigm of *giri-ninjō*—social obligation versus personal feeling.

3. Note the parallel with *ai-kyōgen* vis-à-vis Noh theater. Serving almost literally as intermezzi, *ai-kyōgen* plays were meant to recapitulate—in vernacular, often comic language—the theme and story line of the plays with which they were associated.

4. *Yamanote* refers to the upscale "heights" neighborhoods of Western Tokyo (modern-day Bunkyō- and Shinjuku-ku), contrasting with the working-class *shitamachi* (downtown) district bordering the Sumida River. For a spirited and incisive cultural history of Tokyo's "high-city" district, see Edward Seidensticker, *Low City, High City,* pp. 236–251.

5. Among other things, literary personalia can serve as an inventory of material culture. The *danwa* are excellent sources, insofar as they center on the *bundan* as a subculture, accessible through "lifestyle" testimony of the contributing writers. For contemporary accounts of Meiji material culture by resident foreigners, see, for instance, Edward Morse, *Japanese Homes and Their Surroundings* (1887; Rutland, Vt.; Tokyo: Tuttle, 1972), and Basil Hall Chamberlain, *Things Japanese* (London: John Murray, 1905). Seidensticker's *Low City, High City* is an excellent source. Also see Susan Hanley, *Everyday Things in Premodern Japan* (Berkeley: University of California Press, 1997)—in particular, the coverage of material culture in the transition to Meiji (pp. 155–198).

6. Several iconic photographs of the writer in his study (see, for instance, figure 5) have helped memorialize Sōseki and his association with bookish reclusion and solitude. The question of how such images relate to a Japanese "collective memory" of the Meiji is of considerable interest.

7. *Garasudo,* episode 1. *SZ* 12, pp. 517–519; *Doors,* pp. 3–6.

8. The *Asahi* deal was struck, in effect, on March 15, when Ikebe Sanzan, the *Tokyo Asahi's* chief editor, visited Sōseki to discuss terms. The author had also received offers from Kyoto University and from the rival *Yomiuri shinbun.* Incidentally, the category of *bunshi*—writer—is not to be confused with *bunjin,* the "literatus" category associated with Tokugawa cultural elitism. With the Meiji period, the elevated cachet of *bunjin* gave way to the more workaday notion of "literary professional."

9. In this regard, an interview published in November 30, 1910, includes a memorably irreverent preface by the *hikkisha* (interviewer-stenographer), who sets the scene as follows: "Here is the famous *Cat* author, seated in his book-strewn study, smoking like a fiend—so much so that smoke seems to be coming out of his rear end!" See *SZ* 25, pp. 387–390.

10. Reference to the Sōseki residence in Waseda—the author's final residence.

11. One *tsubo* is equivalent to approximately forty square feet.

12. Billiards had been introduced into Japan during the Tokugawa era, via the Dutch trading mission in Dejima. Go and *shōgi* are time-honored East Asian board games that enjoyed widespread popularity in Japan and have since attracted players worldwide.

13. Like many of his literary contemporaries, Sōseki enjoyed curios and "antiquing." See Kyōko's remarks, in episode 49 of *Omoide,* on her husband's fondness for China curios *(Shina kottō),* which he'd delight in arranging on his desk to admire and fondle.

14. *Meisōjōki.* A Chinese classicism that had evident currency among Meiji writers.

15. Sōseki's distaste for empty formalism and meaningless ritual would be echoed in his portrayal of Professor Koeber. See chapter 6 herein.

16. The author would write this into the concluding passage of *Garasudo,* which appears later in this chapter.

17. Sōseki's *Bunshi no seikatsu* interview appeared in the *Osaka Asahi* on March 22, 1914. See *SZ* 25, pp. 425–430.

18. The *bunshi no seikatsu* series was a weekly Sunday feature during its month-long run. Others interviewed were Nagai Kafū, Suzuki Miekichi, and Morita Sōhei—an affinity grouping that centered on Sōseki. See *SZ* 25, pp. 425–430.

19. The interview, entitled *Bundan no kono goro* (Bundan Update), was published in the October 11, 1915, issue of the *Osaka Asahi*—a month after Sōseki completed his *Michikusa* serialization. See *SZ* 25, pp. 447–450.

20. *SZ* 25, pp. 382–383. The volume for which Sōseki was being interviewed is entitled *Meishi zen* (Notables Remark on Zen). The interviewee, notwithstanding his dismissive tone (and the smoldering-hair incident) in the comic prologue, does go on to remark at some length on Zen, concerning which he was quite well informed.

21. Kafu's remarks, published on April 5, 1914, nicely complement Sōseki's. The following excerpts are revealing:

> Literature may be a lofty calling, but making a living from it is something else again. Does someone who truly has to struggle to make ends meet as a writer really manage to get to the heart of the human condition *(jinsei)?* I make hardly anything from my writing; what one gets for fiction is a pittance.... My family supports me. Let's face it—I'm a parasite....
>
> I have strong dislikes when it comes to people. I'll decide to dislike someone just from hearing his name. But I'll just as easily take a liking to him once I get to know him. I absolutely hate dealing with my relatives. I never visit them on the formal occasions. And when relatives come to call, it's such an aggravation to have to make small talk; I'll just sneak out the back door.... There's nothing worse than being visited by some old aunt who has nothing better to do than go on and on about absolutely nothing. It truly shortens one's life.
>
> I'm very much a stay-at-home. But I do enjoy going out on walks— just letting my legs take me where they will. I'm an avid sleeper.... It's as though I was born to sleep. I'm in bed by eleven and stay fast asleep until nine in the morning. Nothing can wake me. Last year a burglar got into the house and robbed me—he stole things from the bedroom, and I didn't so much as budge.
>
> Like Natsume Sōseki, I believe in cultivating one's enclosed, private universe. I don't like going out in the world, loaded with ambition, running around all in a dither. I want nothing to do with formal meetings. In particular, I have no interest in taking charge of things. Living quietly in a small space—that's for me. I want my home to be bright, but my study shouldn't be overly illuminated. A slight gloom is much to my liking. (*Kafū zenshū,* vol. 27, pp. 80–85)

22. Sōseki did on occasion vent his spleen. He prefaced a February 1, 1912, essay with a simple invective: *"I hate journalists!"* This cathartic unburdening (quite possibly an insider's aside) set the stage for what would be a broad-ranging discussion, for his newspaper readership, of Henrik Ibsen's drama. See *SZ* 25, pp. 415–418.

23. The Carlyle episode is noted in chapter 1 herein. See chapter 7 herein for details on Sōseki's memorialization by his protégés.

24. Uchida Roan's privileged position at Maruzen, together with his editorship of the house journal, *Gakutō,* helped establish him as a leading authority on books and the book trade. Roan was deeply imbued with a sense of the civilizational value of books, concerning which he wrote extensively. With respect to writing implements, another of Roan's passions, it should be noted that the fountain pen *(mannenhitsu)* was an improvement upon the more ordinary Western pen, which one had to repeatedly dip in ink. The fountain pen was first introduced to Japan in 1880. For details, see *SZ* 12, pp. 727–728, note 501.2.

25. *Shūshū kyō* (collecting madness). Roan, himself an inveterate collector, wrote numerous essays on this "affliction" of acquisitiveness, which he regarded as a badge of honor. As for gourds and their status as collectibles, see Shiga Naoya's celebrated story *Seibei to hyōtan* (Seibei and Gourds, 1912), which has as its subtext a rage for gourd collecting. In Sibley, *The Shiga Hero*, pp. 138–142.

26. For further details on Pelican pens, a famous British make, see *SZ* 12, p. 728, note 503.12.

27. A reference to *Higan sugi made,* serialized January–April 1912.

28. Another English brand. See *SZ* 12, p. 728, note 505.9, which includes an illustration.

29. *Yo to mannenhitsu* (June 30, 1912). In *SZ* 12, pp. 501–505.

30. By way of contrast, see Roan's learned essay on the history of the fountain pen, published in *Gakutō* in April 1912 (*Uchida Roan zenshū,* vol. 6, pp. 535–546). This, too, was in connection with the Maruzen exhibit, which Roan had a hand in organizing.

31. However tempting it might be to impute some paranoid overreaction, one needs to recall that *bundan* writers were the target of predatory journalistic practices, and many of them (for instance, Ōgai, Tōson, and Kafū) played upon the motif of writer as victim, besieged by journalists and hounded by fans and literary aspirants. Also, as we've seen, burglary was relatively common at the time.

32. Reference to *Nikoniko* (Smiles), a third-tier journal whose aim was to provide a positive, cheerful cast to the otherwise stolid, competitive face of contemporary Japan by, among other things, publishing photographs of the featured personages smiling.

33. The special New Year's issues, with their expanded coverage and greater bulk, were meant to showcase the given periodical. Also, new literary serializations typically began with the January issue—in the case of newspapers, with the January 1 issue.

34. *Garasudo,* episode 2. In *SZ* 12, pp. 519–521; *Doors,* pp. 6–8. This episode, and the larger question of Sōseki as a *shosai* denizen, are examined in Kōno Kensuke's enlightening media-based study of *kindai* literary history, *Shomotsu no kindai,* passim.

35. As we have seen, *Neko* is rife with comic victimization. Note especially chapter 8, in which Kushami becomes an easy target of teasing and heckling by

students at the neighborhood school. Here, the feline narrator offers a learned disquisition on the psychology of teasing. See *Cat*, pp. 256–257.

36. Telephone technology was introduced into Japan in 1877—the year following Bell's invention. Telephone service was inaugurated in 1890, in Tokyo and Yokohama, and it spread rapidly thereafter, with demand far exceeding the supply of equipment and service. The telephone in the Natsume home was known to drive Sōseki to distraction, and during periods of mental instability he would ban its use entirely.

37. For details regarding the *Nikoniko* article, which appeared in the January 1915 issue, see *SZ* 12, p. 732, note 519.6. The smiling photo in question is reproduced. Sōseki's gullibility here is hard to fathom, given the title of the journal and its manifest aim of publishing only smiling faces.

Natsume Fusanosuke, Sōseki's cartoonist grandson, recalls a similar experience in the context of his remarks on *Garasudo*. Not only was he ordered by the photographer to smile—"You're a cartoonist, after all, so this shouldn't be too much to ask of you." He was then virtually forced to have his wife prepare a meal, whereupon the happy family was told to sit down at the table for the photo shoot! See *Sōseki no mago*, pp. 66–67.

38. *Garasudo*, episode 27. *SZ* 12, pp. 582–585; *Doors*, pp. 77–80.

39. Sōseki wrote the letter of apology to Iwasaki Tarōji on December 30, 1912. See *SZ* 24, p. 130.

40. A reference to the early-eighteenth-century Akō rōnin incident, the inspiration for countless dramatic works. The best-known dramatization is *Kanadehon chūshingura* (A Treasury of Loyal Retainers), which concerns the heroic—and intricately plotted—act of group vengeance wrought upon the villain responsible for the death of their liege lord.

41. *Garasudo*, episodes 12–13. *SZ* 12, pp. 543–548; *Doors*, pp. 34–39.

42. *Kijin* eccentricity is an established *kinsei/kindai* literary and cultural trope, with numerous examples in the work of Sōseki and others. As with other comic *shōhin* narratives, the Iwasaki episode is anticipated in chapter 9 in *Neko*, where Kushami, in the course of reading the day's mail, comes across a bizarre letter from one Tendō Kōhei, contained in an envelope "with red and white parallel stripes, like a stick of peppermint." The letter's author is later revealed to be a raving lunatic in the Sugamo asylum. See *Cat*, pp. 302–319.

As for *tanzaku* solicitation, Kyōko notes that about the time of the *Garasudo* serialization, it was not uncommon for total strangers to show up at the door, asking for a *tanzaku* inscription. If the mood struck, her husband would comply; if not, he would flatly refuse. See *Omoide*, episode 56.

43. The *danwa* in question was published in the April 16, 1914, issue of *Hankyō*, with Sōhei as interviewer. In *SZ* 25, pp. 434–436. Again, apropos the *tanzaku* matter, note an unusual diary entry, for June 15, 1911, regarding one Uchida Eizō, who came by that day requesting a *tanzaku* "autograph." When

Sōseki duly complies, the man nonchalantly observes that he is capable of moving his ears at will. "And they did indeed move," Sōseki notes. "Both of them, simultaneously." The man goes on to explain how he had come by this rare talent: "As a kid, you see, I'd get scolded at school, which would get me so angry that I'd grind my teeth together. Well, something felt strange, so I went and looked at myself in the mirror—and my ears were moving!" In *SZ* 20, p. 318.

44. For further insights, see David Goodman and Masanori Miyazawa, *Jews in the Japanese Mind: The History and Uses of a Cultural Stereotype* (New York: Free Press, 1995), especially pp. 16–35. Meiji-period stereotyping of Jews was widespread and persistent—as was the better-known (and more widely researched) prejudice against the so-called *eta* class of social outcastes, despite attempts at social reform.

45. The *Neko* narrator remarks as follows: "It is not often that my master does much donating. Once when there was a crop failure in the northeastern districts, he donated two or three yen, but later he would repeatedly complain that he had been deprived of a great deal of money because of the donation" (*Cat*, p. 301).

46. See Mark Schreiber, *The Dark Side: Infamous Japanese Crimes and Criminals* (New York and London: Kodansha International, 2001). For a different perspective, see Mikiso Hane, *Peasants, Rebels, and Outcastes: The Underside of Modern Japan* (New York: Pantheon, 1982); also Seidensticker, *Low City, High City*. Japanese sources include Aoki Tamotsu et al., eds., *Hanzai to fūzoku* (Crimes and Customs; Iwanami, 2000); and Wamaki Kōsuke, *Nippon dorobō-den* (Accounts of Japanese Burglars; Mainichi shinbunsha, 1993).

47. See *Hearing Things* (p. 103) and *Gate* (pp. 76–92).

48. *Eijitsu*, episode 3 *(Dorobō)*—a two-part episode. *SZ* 12, pp. 137–143; *Spring*, pp. 22–28.

49. Sōseki includes an interesting anecdote regarding house burglary in his diary entry of May 14, 1909. On that day, he notes having been visited by his friend Matsune Tōyōjō, who mentioned a relative who had ended up shooting some ruffian who'd assaulted him. "I've decided not to own a pistol or sword," Sōseki remarks, "given my irascible nature *(kanshakumochi)*. But when you are being burglarized, one does regret not having a weapon available." In *SZ* 20, pp. 36–37.

For Kyōko's account of the obi theft, see *Omoide*, episode 35. In contrast with the *Eijitsu* episode, her account centers on details regarding the lost obis. Note also episode 25 *(Arigatai dorobō)*, which concerns yet another theft of the family's clothing and the subsequent retrieval of the stolen items.

50. See *Cat*, pp. 151–169, 319–323.

51. *Garasudo*, episode 11. *SZ* 12, p. 541; *Doors*, p. 31.

52. *Garasudo*, episodes 6 and 7. *SZ* 12, pp. 530–533; *Doors*, pp. 18–21. See *NSJ*/b, pp. 394–395, for details of Sōseki's relationship with Yoshinaga Hide.

53. In episode 52 of her memoir, Kyōko touches upon the "disturbed

woman" *(nayanda onna)*, as she calls her. Noting her husband's solicitude, she points to her own skepticism regarding the woman and her story. Who in the world, she wonders, would go around advertising that they wanted to die; anyone seriously inclined would just go and commit suicide. Evidently perturbed by the episode, Kyōko remarks that her intuition would be vindicated when she came across an article in some journal that revealed the woman in question as a real operator, a regular Jezebel *(nakanaka no shitatakamono)*. "When I brought this to my husband's attention—and he realized that she'd been an impostor *(kuwasemono)* and that he'd been duped—he said nothing. But I can tell you that he looked quite put out." See *Omoide*, pp. 299–300.

54. In this regard, note Shimazaki Tōson's "Hōrōsha" (The Vagabond), from his 1909 essay collection, *Shinkatamachi yori* (From Shinkatamachi) (in *Tōson zenshū*, vol. 6, pp. 12–15). Here the author recounts an unannounced visit by a stranger, a young down-and-out vagabond, who wanted to sell his tale of woe to the author, to be used as literary raw material. Also, note Jay Rubin's perceptive reading of *The Miner*, one of Sōseki's less-reputed novels, in the Afterword to his translation of the work (pp. 165–181).

55. *Garasudo,* episode 33. *SZ* 12, pp. 598–600; *Doors,* pp. 95–98.

56. In Yiu's comparison of *Garasudo* and *Michikusa,* the former reduces to "order and peace," whereas the latter relates to "chaos and fear" (*Chaos and Order,* p. 156). I take issue with this simplistic formulation.

57. Reference to the fulling block *(kinuta)*, on which cloth is beaten with a wooden paddle to bring out its sheen.

58. *Omoidasu,* episode 18. *SZ* 12, pp. 409–412; *Recollections,* pp. 63–65. The concluding haiku reads as follows in the original: *Asasamu ya / ikitaru hone wo / ugokasazu. SZ* 12, p. 412; *Recollections,* p. 65; note, p. 100.

59. Shiki's sickbed narratives *(byōchūki)*, written toward the end of the poet's short life, are featured in Janine Beichman's fine literary biography. See *Masaoka Shiki,* pp. 116–144.

60. *Omoidasu,* episode 23. *SZ* 12, pp. 423–426; *Recollections,* pp. 72–74. For details on the *kanshi* that concludes this episode, see *SZ* 12, pp. 718–719, note 426.1. See also *Recollections,* p. 74, and note, p. 112.

61. Note, for instance, *Omoidasu,* episode 19, with its expression of gratitude.

62. Sōseki's well-known *Kojinshugi* lecture of 1914 expresses the author's skepticism regarding the tenor of modern civilization and its rampant egocentrism. The post–Russo-Japanese War milieu was marked by a sense of disillusionment *(genmetsu)* regarding the Meiji mission, together with concern within official circles regarding urban decadence and its baleful influence—especially among young people. This would give way to measures intended to bolster the nation's moral fiber and purge society of materials "injurious to the public morals." See Jay Rubin, *Injurious to Public Morals,* passim. It should be noted that Sōseki was drawn to Max Nordau's writings regarding civilizational degeneration.

241

63. The introspective attitude that this presupposes harkens back to the earlier *shōhin*, to Shiki and his *shaseibun* impressionism, and to the notion, inspired in part by William James, of literature as an inventory of one's perceptions and states of awareness.

64. Noted German philosopher and psychologist, 1863–1916.

65. Dr. Miyamoto Hajime (1867–1919). A graduate of the Imperial University College of Medicine and director of a Tokyo medical clinic, Miyamoto, together with Sōseki, had studied haiku with Shiki. See *SZ* 12, p. 709, note 367.4.

66. Translation based on *Recollections*. This *kanshi* verse has been cited as a masterful fusion of the spirit of Laozi and Zhuangzi (*Rōsō*, in the elliptical Japanese expression). The speaker's lyrical meditation upon reclusion and spiritual regeneration is enriched by several allusions—on the one hand, to the story of Tang monk Danxia and his burning a wooden Buddha in order to heat the temple; on the other hand, to the great poet-recluse Tao Qian and his "Peach Blossom Spring." For further explication, see *SZ* 12, pp. 709–710, note 367.8.

67. *Omoidasu*, episodes 4, 5. *SZ* 12, pp. 365–373; *Recollections*, pp. 35–40.

68. Nagayo Shōkichi (1866–1910). Details of his relationship with Sōseki can be gleaned from *NSJ*/b, pp. 244–245. As for William James, Sōseki mentions, in episode 3 of *Omoidasu*, that while at Shuzenji he completed James's *A Pluralistic Universe*—a work whose intellectual riches he gratefully savored. The narrator also notes the passing of Ōtsuka Kusuo; like the other deaths, this occurred during his convalescence.

69. This recalls the passage from the *Bungakuron* preface in which Sōseki's narrator credits his mental imbalance with having helped inspire his literary creations. See chapter 1 herein.

70. In the original text, the poetry produced in this "ecstatic state" is expressed in vivid terms—*yume no yō na atama no naka ni haimawatte, kōkotsu to dekiagatta mono*. For the actual poems, see *SZ* 12, pp. 371–372. Note the extensive commentary in *Recollections*, pp. 96–97.

71. Fostered by the Tokugawa literati, *fūryū* (in Chinese, *fengliu*) survived well into the modern period as a traditionalist icon of Japanese aesthetics and cultural elitism. It betokens a quality of traditional elegance, refinement, and poetic sensitivity. The term is akin to other essentialist aesthetic imponderables such as *aware, yūgen,* and *iki*. For Sōseki, *fūryū* evokes here both an explicitly Japanese poetic identity and a powerful nostalgic redolence.

72. From *Omoidasu*, episode 5. *SZ* 12, pp. 372–373; *Recollections*, pp. 37–40.

73. *SZ* 20, p. 196. This is from Kyōko's "proxy" entry for August 25.

74. *Omoidasu*, episode 16. *SZ* 12, pp. 403–406; *Recollections*, pp. 60–61. The concluding haiku reads as follows in the original: *Tsuyu kesa no/sato nite shizuka/naru yamai*. See *Recollections*, note, p. 99.

75. See *Omoidasu*, episodes 20, 21. *SZ* 12, pp. 415–420; *Recollections*, pp. 67–70.

76. Sanitation in late-Meiji Tokyo was relatively primitive, requiring regular removal of night soil *(koetori)*.

77. *Garasudo*, episode 39. *SZ* 12, pp. 614–616; *Doors*, pp. 114–117.

78. The passage is as follows: *Watakushi wa chotto hiji wo magete, kono engawa ni hitonemuri nemuru tsumori de aru.* Yiu's reading (*Order and Chaos*, p. 170) hinges upon her claim that *hiji wo magete* (bending one's elbow, as a "prop" for one's head) directly alludes to the Confucian *Analects* (p. 229, note 12). While the attribution is correct in the narrow sense, I take issue with the larger Confucian interpretation.

79. The final episode of *Garasudo* was published on February 23. It was during the subsequent hiatus, on March 22, that Sōseki would deliver his "Watakushi no kojinshugi" lecture.

80. See Yiu, *Chaos and Order*, pp. 156–157.

81. Leo Braudy, *The Frenzy of Renown: Fame and Its History* (New York: Oxford University Press, 1986).

Chapter 6: Literary Portraits

1. See my *Paragons* for a discussion of anecdotal characterization (pp. 76–77, 241–242). It bears noting that Ōgai's biographical project overlapped with the final years of Sōseki's own career.

2. For details regarding Ker, see *Tower*, p. 11, and *NSJ*/b, pp. 98–99.

3. Sōseki's first diary reference to Craig—on November 21, 1900—remarks upon the man's terrible handwriting. This would be noted as well in E. V. Lucas's eulogistic essay, cited below.

4. Edward Dowden, 1843–1913, noted British literary scholar and Craig's contemporary.

5. *Eijitsu*, episode 25: *Kureigu sensei* (three parts). *SZ* 12, pp. 208–217; *Spring*, pp. 110–118; and *Tower*, pp. 152–159. Note, too, Flanagan's perceptive remarks on the Craig essay (*Tower*, pp. 31–35).

6. Sōseki himself would pass away almost exactly ten years later—on December 9, 1916.

7. Excerpted from the Lucas essay, in *Character and Comedy* (London and New York: Macmillan, 1907), pp. 14–17. Lucas was an important literary journalist and prolific essayist. He had an editorship at Methuen, which published many of his essay collections. Hirakawa Sukehiro has compared Lucas's essay on Craig with Sōseki's. See his "*Kureigu sensei* futatabi."

8. One is reminded of Sōseki's description of Thomas Carlyle's London study, in connection with his visit there years earlier. The study is described as a

cocoonlike space built on the top floor of the flat, so as to distance oneself from the noise and clamor of the world below. See chapter 1 herein.

9. Based on *Tower,* p 165. Yamada's story, *Kiiroi geshukunin,* was published in 1953. A very different send-up of the Craig piece is contained in a poem by Anthony Thwaite, entitled "Sōseki," which appeared in the April 6, 1984, issue of the *Times Literary Supplement:*

> I sat with Craig for an hour this morning
> Hearing him mumbling Shakespeare through his beard
> And gave him seven shillings in an envelope—due fee
> For pedagogic drudgery

It should also be noted that Lu Xun (1881–1936), the great Chinese writer, was much taken with the Craig essay. An avid reader of Sōseki's *Asahi* serializations during his years of study in Japan, Lu Xun translated the essay into Chinese. He also wrote a reminiscence of his Japanese tutor in Sendai, which was evidently modeled on the Craig portrayal. Entitled "Tengye xiansheng" (Fujino Sensei), the account has been translated by Gladys and Hsien-yi Yang, as "Mr. Fujino." See *Dawn Blossoms Plucked at Dusk* (Beijing: Foreign Languages Press, 1976), pp. 80–88. See also *Tower,* pp. 161–162.

10. Koeber is credited with having advanced the level of Western philosophical studies in Japan, and he fostered many protégés. Koeber was also a gifted pianist and served as a Russian-language instructor during the Russo-Japanese War. For details, see *NSJ*/b, pp. 101–102.

11. One would suspect an ironic intent here, insofar as all of these cultural outlets were certainly available in Tokyo. In fact, the July 10 diary entry indicates that Koeber had vented his spleen regarding the sorry state of the arts scene in Japan.

12. See *SZ* 12, pp. 461–466: *Kēberu sensei.* The essay, published in the *Asahi* on July 16–17, 1911, was based on the diary entry for July 10 (in *SZ* 20, pp. 328–331). It was initially categorized as an *inshōki* (a literary "impression"). Koeber resided in Ochanomizu.

13. The diary notes that Koeber spoke, among other things, of his fondness for owls and bats; of liking only apples among Japanese fruits; and of his dislike for the works of Browning, Wordsworth, and Andreev. He expressed admiration for Hoffmann and Chekhov.

14. Kubo Masaru (1883–1972), who would go on to become a noted Platonist, was living with Professor Koeber at the time of Sōseki's visit. Kubo himself published a Koeber reminiscence, in 1951, based on their long acquaintanceship, and he also translated and edited a collection of Koeber's essays and personalia. See *SZ* 20, p. 633, note 329.

15. There is an impressive body of *bunmeiron* critiques of Japan's modernization in the late Meiji period. In addition to Sōseki's, one can point to signifi-

cant work in this vein by many writers, including Mori Ōgai, Shimazaki Tōson, and Nagai Kafū.

16. Published in the *Tokyo Asahi,* August 12, 1914. See *SZ* 12 , pp. 511–513.

17. The original title is *Sensō kara kita yukichigai.* See *SZ* 12, p. 515.

18. James Murdoch (1856–1921) was Sōseki's instructor in English in 1890. Sōseki presented his thesis, "Japan and England in the Sixteenth Century" (in *SZ* 26, pp. 68–98), to Murdoch on June 15, 1890, in effect as a farewell gift on the occasion of his graduation. The thesis is a remarkably sophisticated synopsis of comparative Japanese and English society and civilization. Murdoch remained in Japan until 1918, when he moved to Australia to teach at Melbourne University. He lived in Australia until his death.

19. This is manifestly the case with *Kokoro,* whose protagonist—Sensei— exerts a profound influence upon his younger protégé.

20. For a definitive listing of the various circles of affiliation, see *NSJ,* pp. 262–280.

21. For details on the *shaseibun-ha,* see *NSJ,* pp. 263–265. Owing to this connection, Sōseki had a reliable outlet—the *Hototogisu* journal—for much of his early work (most notably, *Neko*).

22. The traditionalist nuance of the term conjures a premodern (not to say feudalistic) model of mentorship that implies a structure of in-group loyalties and bonds.

23. *NSJ* contains separate entries for each of these individuals, who are presented in order of their length of association with Sōseki. See pp. 266–272.

24. The incident, duly recorded in the annals of *bundan* scandals, is known as the *"Baien jiken,"* based on the title of Sōhei's novel. Fitting squarely within the naturalist domain of sordid confessionalism, *Baien* is a fictionalized account of Sōhei's unhappy marriage and the scandalous affair with Hiratsuka Raichō (1886–1971). Raichō, who emerged as leader of the Seitō (Bluestocking) group, a pioneering women's liberation coterie, was renowned as a model of strong-willed, sexually liberated, and intellectually engaged modern Japanese womanhood.

25. Sōhei and Komiya enjoyed the status of "loyal retainers," to whom Sōseki would assign various tasks and responsibilities. For instance, he turned over his *Asahi* literary column to them.

26. *Akai tori* was the most progressive and sophisticated outlet for literature aimed at young readers, and it attracted serious work by major writers.

27. See Waki Akiko, *Natsume Sōseki to Komiya Toyotaka* (Kindai bungeisha, 2000). As one indication of Sōseki's righteous indignation in the face of Komiya's rather loose morals, note his letter of December 14, 1910, written while convalescing in the Nagayo clinic: "Kindly spare me the details of whom you've been boozing with and the geisha that you and your buddies have been visiting."

28. Nogami Yaeko (1885–1985) was a gifted writer introduced into the Sōseki circle through her husband, Toyoichirō. She achieved renown as a literary essayist, in which capacity she wrote extensively of her relationship with Sōseki.

See *NSJ*/b, pp. 266–268 for details regarding the Nogamis. Kusuo, the subject of several *shōhin,* is dealt with later in this chapter.

For her part, Nogami reveals a less attractive side of Sensei in a 1928 reminiscence. She remarks on a visit to the Waseda house to deliver a gift, a gesture of thanks for a recent favor. The gift was a decorative wooden box containing a set of recitation texts *(utaibon),* something that would surely please Sensei. It was a hot day, and the rickshaw man had inadvertently perspired onto the box, leaving unsightly stains. Evidently perturbed, Sōseki tried to wipe them off, but to no avail. He then vented his anger and frustration upon the unsuspecting Yaeko, who was thoroughly mortified by the experience. Entitled *Omoide futatsu* (Two Recollections), the reminiscence can be found in *SZ bekkan,* pp. 382–385.

29. This point is made, for instance, in interviews published in October 1906 and February 1909 (*SZ* 25, pp. 188–189 and 346–347, respectively). However, the fact that his remarks appear in women's journals may be interpreted as a patronizing gesture. On the subject of neglected Meiji women writers, see Rebecca Copeland, *Lost Leaves,* passim.

30. "Frock" was none other than Morita Sōhei, who was soundly ribbed by the group for showing up in such an outfit. (Kyōko notes that this irked him, whereupon a round of good-natured jibes ensued.) The frock coat was a formal Western-style garment—a double-breasted garment with tails. Given Sōhei's penchant for unconventional behavior, it is likely that this getup was an intentional affectation.

31. Spiced sake—*toso*—is a traditional New Year's treat.

32. Noh play of unknown authorship, composed during Zeami's lifetime. This is a *mugen* (dream) play, featuring the spirit of Izumi Shikibu, who speaks of the art of poetry and then dances, whereupon the dreaming monk *(waki)* awakes. See *SZ* 12, pp. 659–660, note 131.12.

33. *Kakegoe* refers to the staccato shouts and voicings produced by the player of the hand drum *(tsuzumi)* in conjunction with the drum beats, according to long-standing rules regarding timing and articulation.

34. *Hagoromo* (The Feathered Robe), one of Zeami's best-known plays, is a standard of the Noh repertoire. Owing to the play's auspicious celestial theme, the name was recently given to a Japanese lunar orbiter spacecraft.

35. *Eijitsu,* episode 1: *Ganjitsu. SZ* 12, pp. 131–134; *Spring,* pp. 13–17.

36. Sōseki published a sequel to this—namely, another *ganjitsu* piece—precisely one year later, on January 1, 1910, also in the *Asahi.* See *SZ* 12, pp. 353–355. This one, however, is a broadside against the very convention of *ganjitsu* special features, which "are guaranteed to produce sheer garbage." Yet despite the invective, the author ultimately gives in to the demand.

37. For her part, Kyōko would comment on the New Year's antics in episode 33 of *Omoide.* She mentions the general merriment, and her husband's indifferent performance having been made fun of. She then discusses the tutelage with

Hōshō Shin (1870–1944) and her husband's insistence on continuing his lessons, even after being advised by his doctor to give them up for health reasons.

38. Sōseki would occasionally remark on the progress of his lessons with Hōshō Shin, which formally began in November 1907—shortly before the events recorded in this episode. For instance, a *danwa* entitled *Keiko no rekishi* (A Chronicle of My Lessons; in *SZ* 25, pp. 412–414) traces the course of his *utai* training. The lessons with Shin were on Fridays, at a cost of five yen per session. Sōseki would also practice at home with Kyoshi.

References to *utai* in Sōseki's fiction can be found in a number of his novels—most notably, *Kōjin.* See *Wayfarer,* pp. 177–183, 193–198.

39. Watanabe Kazan (1793–1841) was a noted painter in the *bunjinga* (literati) style and a proponent of Western-oriented "Dutch learning" *(rangaku).* Yokoyama Kazan (1784–1837) was a well-known Kyoto painter, who specialized in flora and fauna.

40. Nagatsuka Takashi (1879–1915) was a Sōseki *monkasei* and author of the well-known novel *Tsuchi* (Earth, 1910).

41. *Eijitsu,* episode 12: *Yamadori* (two parts). *SZ* 12, pp. 172–177; *Spring,* pp. 64–69. See Sōseki's January 7, 1909, letter to the young man, Ichikawa Fumimaru of Aomori Prefecture, thanking him for the pheasant he'd sent as a gift. In *SZ* 23, p. 241.

42. This refers to the *bungaku seinen* mentioned earlier. See Kinmonth, *Self-made Man,* passim. See also Cross, *The Common Writer,* for a study of the corresponding phenomenon associated with the British literary scene, which parallels the *bundan* in many respects.

Here we are reminded of others who had come by with material for the author to use—the suicidal neighborhood woman, for instance, who confided her sad tale, only to have it expunged in Sōseki's *Garasudo* account (episodes 6–8). Then there is the lad who had visited in November 1907 with a harrowing story of working in the Ashio mines—a story largely lost in its retelling in the novel *Kōfu* (The Miner). See chapter 5 herein.

43. See Sōseki's 1909 diary entries for March 5, May 6, and May 20. See *NSJ*/b, p. 261, for a biographical sketch of Tōin. It should come as no surprise that Sōseki's diarist narrator vents in a far more unbridled fashion than his *shōhin* counterpart.

44. Sōhei goes on to explain that he had asked Sensei for a manuscript to grace the inaugural issue of this new journalistic undertaking. But contractual obligations at *Asahi* prevent this, so he must make do with the *danwa* transcription. He notes that Sensei dislikes being interviewed and that he (Sōhei) wouldn't normally go to these lengths, but he is intent on getting this project off to a good start.

Sōhei undertook joint editorship of the new journal, *Hankyō,* together with Ikuta Chōkō (1882–1936). The venture was not successful—only sixteen issues were published between April 1914 and September 1915. See *Nihon kindai bun-*

gaku daijiten, vol. 5, p. 331 for details. The *danwa* can be found in *SZ* 25, pp. 431–432.

45. Akutagawa was the one with the background in English literature. He and Hyakken joined the Thursday group in its final years, and both went on to write of the experience.

46. For an exhaustive treatment of *tsuitōbun* narrative, together with elaborate details on the memorial volumes for the major *kindai* writers, see Okano Takeo, *Meiji bungaku kenkyū bunken sōran,* pp. 135–192.

47. *Garasudo,* episode 22. *SZ* 12, pp. 569–572; *Doors,* pp. 63–65. Satō Hokkō (1868–1914) served on the *Asahi* staff. In this episode, Sōseki employs the familiar figure of himself as "decaying wreck."

48. Shiki died in September 1902, while Sōseki was still languishing in his London flat. In April 1901, some months before his friend's death, Sōseki sent a series of three "letters" to Shiki and Kyoshi, ostensibly "to console Shiki in his illness." As noted in chapter 1 herein, these epistolary essays, entitled *Rondon shōsoku* (Letters from London), appeared in the May 1901 issue of *Hototogisu.* They were *shaseibun* sketches, written in the style favored by the *Hototogisu* coterie. One can only wonder how these accounts of straitened circumstances and pained self-consciousness were expected to console the friend dying of tuberculosis.

49. For instance, responding to a *danwa* solicitation following the death of the writer Kunikida Doppo in July 1908, Sōseki remarked at the outset that he could say nothing about the man, since they did not know one another. The interview appeared in the July 15, 1908, issue of *Shinchō.* See *SZ* 25, pp. 268–272.

50. See Marleigh Ryan's fine literary biography of Futabatei, which precedes her translation of *Ukigumo.* For details of Sōseki's relationship with Futabatei, see *NSJ*/b, pp. 307–308.

51. Sōseki joined the *Asahi* staff in April of 1907, with a monthly salary of 200 yen—the highest of any *Asahi* staff employee. Hasegawa had been hired in 1904 as a correspondent on East Asian affairs, Russia being his area of expertise. His salary was 100 yen. For further details, see *SZ* 12, p. 679, note 219.2.

52. The Abe clan, which ruled over the erstwhile Fukuyama *han,* had a large estate in this area of Edo.

53. Torii Sosen (1867–1928). For details of Torii's relationship with Sōseki, see *NSJ*/b, pp. 230–231. The Tokyo and Osaka editions of the *Asahi* were under separate editorships and management. Torii Sosen was clearly interested in having Sōseki based in Osaka. But it was Sanzan, representing the Tokyo office, who succeeded in getting him under contract.

54. Futabatei's novel (translated as *An Adopted Husband*) was serialized in the *Asahi* from October to December 1906. Futabatei had earned a major reputation as a writer of fiction, yet he had no connection with the *Asahi* literary staff.

55. Three essays, in particular, express this skeptical attitude. Published between February and July 1908, on the very eve of Futabatei's departure for Russia, they constitute, in effect, his *vale* to the *bundan.*

56. Futabatei is said to have remarked, *"Nan da ka* garan *no yō da ne"* (Somehow it seems just like a monastic retreat). This is the same expression used by Sōseki in *Garasudo* to describe his study.

57. Futabatei had as protégées two literarily gifted daughters of Mozume Takami, a professor of Japanese literature at Tokyo University—the third daughter, Yoshiko (1886–1960), and the fourth daughter, Kazuko (1888–?). As per their agreement, Sōseki took Yoshiko as his own protégée, following Futabatei's departure. See *SZ* 12, p. 681 note 225.9. The identity of the "young man from up north" is unclear.

58. *Hasegawakun to yo* (August 1909; in *SZ* 12, pp. 219–226). The essay is included in the memorial volume, *Futabatei Shimei,* coedited by Uchida Roan and Tsubouchi Shōyō (rpt.; Nihon Kindai Bungakkan, 1995). This volume covers the range of *bundan* notables, and its sixty-two *tsuitō* essays beg a comparative study of reminiscence narratives on a single subject.

59. For further details, see Etō Jun, *Sōseki to sono jidai,* vol. 4, pp. 95–107.

60. In "The Sense of an Ending," Dennis Washburn remarks on the Futabatei essay as an ironic swerve away from the ostensible memorialization in favor of a projection of the narrator's own *kodoku* persona. In his opinion, the essay is among the most contrived in the Futabatei memorial volume (*The Dilemma of the Modern,* pp. 164–165).

61. Both Mozume girls eventually married and went their respective ways. See *NSJ*/b, pp. 377–378, for details on Sōseki's occasional contact with the two sisters.

62. Ikebe Sanzan (1864–1912). For the memorial essay, see *SZ* 12, pp. 497–500.

63. Ōtsuka Yasuji (1868–1931). Sōseki had known Ōtsuka ever since their graduate student days at the Imperial University. Together with Nakamura Zekō, they remained lifelong friends. A ranking scholar of Western philosophy and aesthetics, Yasuji was evidently instrumental in Sōseki's appointment to the professorship in English literature, and he himself went on to assume Koeber's position on the faculty—the first Japanese to occupy a professorship in Western philosophy at the Imperial University. See *NSJ*/b, pp. 54–55, for further details on Yasuji and his relationship with Sōseki.

64. Higuchi Ichiyō, who died in 1894, quickly earned a reputation as *the* great woman writer of the Meiji. Recent efforts have sought to reclaim neglected lesser lights among Meiji women writers. See Copeland, *Lost Leaves.* There is no mention here, however, of Ōtsuka Kusuo.

65. It has been conjectured that Sōseki's decision to accept the teaching post in remote Matsuyama was in part motivated by his lovelorn state following an abortive romance with Kusuo.

66. Sōseki lived in Tokyo's Sendagi district from March 1903 to December 1906, having moved there following his return from England. The stay in Sendagi overlapped with his professorship at the Imperial University. See *SZ* 12, p. 741, note 577.9.

67. Note the interesting coincidence of the narrator's gloomy mood and the name of the quarter—*hikage* (in the shadows).

68. There is abundant evidence of serious marital problems in the Natsume household late in 1914—in other words, just before the *Garasudo* serialization. Indeed, this very episode provides corroboration.

69. Kusuo died on November 9, 1910, shortly after Sōseki had left Shuzenji and returned to Tokyo for further convalescence (as related in *Omoidasu*). As the curiously impersonal diary entry of November 13 relates, he read of her death in a November 13 newspaper article, which mentioned the funeral, to be held in Tokyo. There is one single word of emotional reaction: *odoroku* (surprised). See *SZ* 20, p. 248. Kusuo had been serializing a novel, *Un'ei* (Cloud Shadows) in the *Osaka Asahi* earlier that year, but she came down with a bad case of flu and had to suspend the serialization. When she became sicker in late July, she went to Ōiso to convalesce, but her symptoms only worsened. Note the parallel with Sōseki, whose own brush with death in August 1910 had a very different outcome.

70. The original haiku, composed on November 15, is as follows: *Aru hodo no / kiku nageireyo / kan no naka*. See Sōseki's diary entry for that date (*SZ* 20, pp. 248–249; two versions of the haiku are included). Sōseki's *Omoidasu* narrator remarks, "As I pondered these things, I became terribly depressed and disappointed. And so as a restorative to my mood, I thought of Ōtsuka Kusuo, who had recently passed away in Ōiso, and I composed a haiku in her memory: *Aru hodo no...*" In *Omoidasu*, episode 7. *SZ* 12, p. 381.

71. *Garasudo*, episode 25. *SZ* 12, pp. 577–579; *Doors*, pp. 71–74. My translation omits details regarding locale.

72. Note here the *kodoku* rhetoric of isolation and melancholy—*kurai, wabishii, in'utsu*—and the *fuyukai na katamari* (tumor-like mass of cheerlessness) lodged inside him.

73. For instance, Miyoshi Yukio has likened the *shōhin*, collectively, to Sōseki's *shishōsetsu*. See *NSJ*, p 64. The related category of *shinpen shōsetsu*—fictionized accounts of an author's "social surround"—is a more appropriate categorization in this case. Both, though, point to a reading that minimalizes the gap between an author and his work.

74. Anecdotal biography in Western literature is often traced to the work of John Aubrey (1626–1697), who in 1667 began writing brief biographical sketches of individuals both famous and obscure. His hundreds of portrayals, which hinge upon the "telling anecdote," first appeared in a standard edition, entitled *Brief Lives*, in 1898. See my *Paragons*, pp. 289–290.

Chapter 7: Zōshigaya and Beyond

1. See Eakin's argument regarding the indispensable role of autobiographical texts in biography (*Touching the World*, pp. 54–70).

2. Ralph Waldo Emerson's 1850 work, *Representative Men,* is a series of essays (based on lectures) that reflect upon great individuals who came to represent and symbolize the world in which they lived.

3. As for the art of literary miscellany, the *shōhin* collections can be said to reflect an important Japanese literary complementarity—namely, fragmentation/integration. Originating in studies of the great imperial *waka* anthologies *(chokusenshū)* and their complex mode of compilation, collateral research has studied the manner in which small literary (and artistic) "fragments," which have intrinsic value in and of themselves, may be combined with others of their kind to achieve a higher-order integration on a narrative and aesthetic level. I've suggested that the *shōhin* collections may be said to have inherited something of this "classical" legacy, but this is open to interpretion.

4. David Mikics, *A New Handbook of Literary Terms* (New Haven, Conn.: Yale University Press), p. 39.

5. Miyoshi Yukio's authoritative listing of Sōseki themes includes, among others, money, death, time, women, existence, illness, quietude, egocentrism, and transcendence. See *NSJ*, pp. 109–217. Precisely two pages are devoted to an explication of each theme. Here I should note that in spite of my having condemned some of its interpretive excesses, I have pursued, implicitly at least, a psychoanalytic reading of the personal literature.

6. Eakin points to confinement and isolation—typically brought on by disease—as a sine qua non of autobiographical art. See *Touching the World,* p. 61.

7. Again, in her final chapter, aptly entitled "In Quest of an Ending," Yiu focuses on the daily *kanshi* regimen that began in August 1916 as a therapeutic corrective to the tiring and trying novelistic serialization of *Meian.* See *Chaos and Order,* pp. 182–196. The *kanshi* incorporated into *Omoidasu* have been of particular interest.

8. Here one is again reminded of Yiu's "order and chaos" paradigm—yet another binary intersection. Such is the character of the Meiji period itself, which Sōseki's work has come to epitomize.

9. The brain was reported to weigh 1,425 grams—fully 75 grams heavier than average. Encased in its formaldehyde jar, it was on display in 1995, in the Tokyo National Science Museum, and remains housed in the Tokyo University Medical College. In *Sōseki no nō* (Sōseki's Brain; Kōbundō, 1995), Saitō Iwane has written a series of essays inspired by the famous brain. (I wish to thank Sarah Frederick of Boston University for alerting me to this and other cerebral sources.) See Hirano Seisuke, *Shinbun shūsei: Natsume Sōseki zō,* vol. 2, pp. 263–384, for the series of autopsy-related reportage.

As for Einstein's brain, it was removed during an autopsy at Princeton Hospital by the staff pathologist, Thomas Stolz Harvey—against the family's wishes. Dr. Harvey ended up absconding with the brain, which he placed in a mason jar and kept in his home for years. Its whereabouts only came to light in 1978. See Michael Paterniti, *Driving Mr. Albert: A Trip across America with Einstein's*

Brain (New York: Random House, 2000), which tells of the author's driving Dr. Harvey and the brain from Princeton to Berkeley, in the late 1990s, in order to reconcile with Einstein's family, in the person of his granddaughter. The brain, incidentally, is safely back at Princeton.

10. For an exhaustive listing of all of Sōseki's publications through the late 1920s, including the collectanea, see *SZ* 27, pp. 458–591. For details regarding the four *zenshū* published between 1919 and 1929, see pp. 556–563. The recent Sōseki *zenshū*, published by Iwanami between 1994 and 1997, consists of twenty-nine volumes. It has been my indispensable primary source. Volume 12—the *shōhin* volume—has been the centerpiece of this study.

11. In episode 28 of her memoir, Kyōko notes that some of the *monkasei* were still visiting as of the time of her writing (1928).

12. See *NSJ*/b, pp. 125–126. Komiya's remained the standard account until the postwar period, when it was challenged and in effect displaced by the work of Etō Jun, whose revisionist program (in effect set forth in his 1965 biography, *Natsume Sōseki*) sought to desacralize the author and subject the work to a more rigorous and dispassionate analysis. Etō's work has in turn been challenged by a new generation of revisionist critics.

13. For instance, Morita Sōhei remarks on Sōseki's abusive treatment of himself and other *monkasei*. See, for instance, his 1919 memoir, *Bunshōdō to Sōseki sensei* (Sōseki Sensei and the Writer's Craft) (Shun'yōdō), pp. 11–19.

14. Among wifely memoirs of *kindai* writer-husbands, note, for instance, *Tōson no omoide* (Chūōkōronsha, 1950), by Tōson's second wife, Shimazaki Shizuko. Also, Kunikida Haruko (Doppo's wife) and Mori Shige (Ōgai's wife) wrote fictionalized accounts of their respective husbands.

15. Sōseki took several of the *Shinshichō* writers under his wing, and they became regulars at the Thursday sessions late in his life. In addition to Matsuoka, there are some who went on to literary prominence—notably, Akutagawa Ryūnosuke, Kume Masao, and Kikuchi Kan. For details, see *NSJ*, pp. 276–278.

16. Matsuoka authored five Sōseki-related memoirs between 1934 and 1967. As we will see, his daughter Yōko would continue the family's memoirist legacy.

17. The *SZ bekkan* volume contains nearly six hundred pages of reminiscence narratives, divided into specific categories—old friends, London acquaintances, school acquaintances, *Asahi* colleagues, *monkasei, bundan* contemporaries, and family members. Coverage is restricted to accounts of those who knew Sōseki personally.

18. Tanka, the traditional 31-syllable verse form, is also known as *waka*. For details, see *SZ bekkan*, pp. 63–65. Terada is also represented in the form of a 1932 essay recalling Sōseki as his literature teacher in Kumamoto. See *SZ bekkan*, pp. 66–78.

19. See *SZ bekkan*, pp. 454–458. Overall, Roan expresses high regard and genuine affection for Sōseki.

20. This 1928 essay is found in *SZ bekkan,* pp. 512–515. Other family reminiscence includes an excerpt from Natsume Shinroku's 1956 memoir (*Chichi Natsume Sōseki,* pp. 535–547), and a 1966 essay by Fudeko that recalls her fictionalized depiction in *Neko* (pp. 516–534). The essay originally appeared in the March issue of *Bungei shunjū.*

21. See Yōko McClain, "Sōseki: A Tragic Father." Note also her essay collection, *Magomusume kara mita Sōseki* (Sōseki, from a Granddaughter's Perspective). Yōko McClain had a distinguished scholarly career in Japanese language and literature at the University of Oregon.

22. Natsume Fusanosuke remarks on *Garasudo* as the very first of Sōseki's books that he found interesting. See *Mago ga yomu Sōseki,* pp. 227–238.

23. In 2002, both Sōseki and Mori Ōgai were dropped from middle-school readers—which spurred debate among educators and a special feature in the May 2002 issue of the journal *Bungakukai,* regarding the current state of literature in the standard school texts (see pp. 110–198). Then, in 2004, the author's image on the thousand-yen note was replaced, following a twenty-year run, with that of the renowned bacteriologist Noguchi Hideo (1876–1928).

24. *Kafka on the Shore* (Umibe no Kafuka) (New York: Vintage, 2005). Note the brief dialogue between the quizzical librarian, Ōshima, and the young runaway: 'What are you reading these days?' 'Natsume Sōseki's complete works.' 'You like him enough to want to read everything he wrote?' I nod" (p. 105).

25. In an unpublished conference paper, Irena Hayter has studied Okuizumi's novel, which she regards as quintessentially postmodern. Hayter identifies no fewer than forty parodies of Sōseki's *I Am a Cat,* including, notably, Uchida Hyakken's 1949 *Gansaku: Wagahai wa neko de aru* (I Am a Cat: The Parody; Rokkō shuppan, 1959) and Inoue Hisashi's *Wagahai wa Sōseki de aru* (I Am Sōseki; Hakusuisha, 1982). Natsume Fusanosuke has entitled the introduction to his 2006 memoir "Wagahai wa mago de aru" (Your humble servant is [the author's] grandson). In the Japanese blogosphere, Katō Shigeaki writes from the perspective of a cat named Wagahai. Incidentally, Ichikawa Kon directed a film version of *Neko* in 1975.

26. In a newspaper interview published on December 11, Morita Sōhei calls attention to this epigram as epitomizing Sōseki's way of thinking late in life. See *Shinbun shūsei,* vol. 2, pp. 285–286.

27. Note, for instance, the Sōseki feature in a recent issue of *Sarai,* an upscale monthly magazine. The feature, with the exalted title *Sokuten kyoshi tenkaichi no bungō no sugao* (The True Face of This Unparalleled Literary Giant of *sokuten kyoshi* Fame) ends up focusing on Sōseki's favorite foods, hobbies, and other lifestyle tidbits. In this regard, note Fujimori Kiyoshi's *Sōseki no reshipi* (Sōseki's Recipes; Kodansha shinsho, 2003)—a series of short episodes on food in Sōseki's work, including a number of Sōseki-inspired recipes. The irony of this author's being the vehicle for pop-gastronomy books is inescapable: he died of chronic gastrointestinal disease.

28. A 1993 book is entitled, simply, *Sōseki goshippu* (Sōseki Gossip); it is a veritable trivial pursuit of the author's life and work.

29. *Jibun no kokoro wo takameru: Sōseki no kotoba* (Uplifting Words of Sōseki; PHP Kenkyūsho, 2000). The *shōhin* selections here include seven from *Garasudo* and eleven from *Omoidasu*. Paralleling Nagao's work is Dale Ahlquist's *G. K. Chesterton: The Apostle of Common Sense* (San Francisco: Ignatius Press, 2003), which presents examples of Chesterton's edifying prose. Ahlquist makes no bones about his admiration for this English author (1874–1936), whom he proclaims "the best writer of the twentieth century" and "the most unjustly neglected writer of our time" (p. 12).

30. Yajima Yukihiko, *Kokoro wo iyasu: Sōseki kara no tegami* (Letters from Sōseki, to Heal the Spirit; Seishun shuppansha, 1999).

Selected Bibliography

Note: The place of publication, when Tokyo, has been omitted for books and articles in Japanese. Works by Natsume Sōseki are listed separately at the end of this bibliography.

Alter, Robert. *Imagined Cities: Urban Experience and the Language of the Novel.* New Haven, Conn.: Yale University Press, 2005.

Ara Masahito. *Sōseki kenkyū nenpyō.* Shūeisha, 1984.

Auestad, Reiko Abe. *Rereading Sōseki: Three Early Twentieth-Century Japanese Novels.* Wiesbaden: Harrassowitz Verlag, 1998.

Beichman, Janine. *Masaoka Shiki.* Tokyo and New York: Kodansha International, 1986.

Bourdaghs, Michael. "Sōseki Natsume and the Fluctuating Values of Property." *Japan Foundation Newsletter* 28, no. 3–4 (June 2001): 8–11.

Caws, Mary Ann. *City Images: Perspectives from Literature, Philosophy, and Film.* New York: Gordon and Breach, 1991.

Chitani Shichirō. *Sōseki no byōseki: Byōki to sakuhin kara.* Keisō shobō, 1963.

Copeland, Rebecca. *Lost Leaves: Women Writers of Meiji Japan.* Honolulu: University of Hawai'i Press, 2000.

Cross, Nigel. *The Common Writer: Life in Nineteenth-Century Grub Street.* Cambridge: Cambridge University Press, 1985.

Dodd, Stephen. *Writing Home: Representations of the Native Place in Modern Japanese Literature.* Harvard University Asia Center, 2004.

Doi Takeo. *Sōseki no shinteki sekai.* Shibundō, 1969. William Tyler, translator. *The Psychological World of Natsume Sōseki.* Cambridge: Harvard East Asian Research Center, 1976.

Eakin, Paul John. *Touching the World: Reference in Autobiography.* Princeton, N.J.: Princeton University Press, 1992.

Ellis, David. *Literary Lives.* Edinburgh: Edinburgh University Press, 2000.

Epstein, Joseph, ed. *The Norton Book of Personal Essays.* New York: W. W. Norton and Company, 1997.

Etō Jun. *Natsume Sōseki.* Keisō shobō, 1965.

————. *Sōseki to sono jidai.* 5 vols. Shinchōsha, 1970–1999.

Foster, Michael Dylan. "Walking in the City with Natsume Sōseki: The Metaphorical Landscape in *Koto no sorane.*" In *Landscapes: Imagined and Remembered,* ed. Paul S. Atkins, Davinder L. Bhowmik, Edward Mack. Proceedings of the Association for Japanese Literary Studies, vol. 6 (Summer 2005): 137–146.

Fowler, Edward. *The Rhetoric of Confession: Shishōsetsu in Early Twentieth-Century Japanese Fiction.* Berkeley: University of California Press, 1988.

Fujii, James. *Complicit Fictions: The Subject in the Modern Japanese Prose Narrative.* Berkeley: University of California Press, 1993.

Gessel, Van. *Three Modern Novelists: Sōseki, Tanizaki, Kawabata.* Tokyo and New York: Kodansha International, 1993.

Gluck, Carol. *Japan's Modern Myths: Ideology in the Late Meiji Period.* Princeton, N.J.: Princeton University Press, 1985.

Good, Graham. *The Observing Self: Rediscovering the Essay.* London and New York: Routledge, 1988.

Haga Tōru. "Sōseki no jikken kōbō: *Eijitsu shōhin* ippen no yomi no kokoromi." *Bulletin of the International Research Center for Japanese Studies,* no. 16 (September 1997): 187–209.

Hardacre, Helen, ed., with Adam L. Kern. *New Directions in the Study of Meiji Japan.* Leiden; New York; Köln: Brill, 1997.

Harootunian, Harry. *History's Disquiet: Modernity, Cultural Practice, and the Question of Everyday Life.* New York: Columbia University Press, 2000.

Henshall, Kenneth, translator. *Literary Life in Tōkyō 1885–1915: Tayama Katai's Memoirs.* Leiden: E. J. Brill, 1987.

Hibbett, Howard. "Natsume Sōseki and the Psychological Novel." In *Tradition and Modernization in Japanese Culture,* ed. Donald Shively. Princeton, N.J.: Princeton University Press, 1971.

Hirakawa Sukehiro: "*Kureigu sensei* futatabi: Sōseki no shōhin to Rūkasu no zuihitsu." *Shinchō* 87, no. 11 (November 1990): 222–224.

Hirano Seisuke. *Shinbun shūsei: Natsume Sōseki zō.* 6 vols. Meiji Taishō Shōwa shinbun kenkyūkai, 1979–1984.

Hobsbawm, Eric J., and Terence O. Ranger, eds. *The Invention of Tradition.* Cambridge: Cambridge University Press, 1983.

Hutton, Patrick. *History as an Art of Memory.* Hanover, N.H.: University Press of New England, 1993.

Ishihara Chiaki. *Sōseki no kigōgaku.* Kōdansha, 1999.

Ito, Ken K. *An Age of Melodrama: Family, Gender, and Social Hierarchy in the Turn-of-the-Century Japanese Novel.* Stanford, Calif.: Stanford University Press, 2008.

Jolly, Margaretta, ed. *Encyclopedia of Life Writing.* 2 vols. London and Chicago: Fitzroy Dearborn Publishers, 2001.

Karatani Kōjin. *Origins of Modern Japanese Literature*. Translated by Brett de Bary. Durham, N.C.: Duke University Press, 1993.

Keene, Donald. *Dawn to the West: Japanese Literature in the Modern Era.* 2 vols. New York: Henry Holt, 1984.

Kinmonth, Earl. *The Self-made Man in Meiji Japanese Thought.* Berkeley: University of California Press, 1981.

Komiya Toyotaka. *Natsume Sōseki.* 3 vols. Iwanami, 1953.

Komori Yōichi. *Sōseki wo yominaosu.* Chikuma, 1995.

Kōno Kensuke. *Shomotsu no kindai: media no bungakushi.* Chikuma, 1992.

———. *Tōki to shite no bungaku: katsuji, kenshō, media.* Shin'yōsha, 2003.

Lincicome, Mark. *Principles, Praxis, and the Politics of Educational Reform in Meiji Japan.* Honolulu: University of Hawai'i Press, 1995.

Lopate, Phillip, ed. *The Art of the Personal Essay.* New York: Anchor Doubleday, 1994.

Maeda Ai. *Text and the City: Essays on Japanese Modernity.* Edited by James Fujii. Durham, N.C.: Duke University Press, 2004.

———. *Toshi kūkan no naka no bungaku.* Chikuma shobō, 1982.

Marcus, Marvin. "The Impact of Western Autobiography on the Meiji Literary Scene." *Biography* 15, no. 4 (Fall 1992): 371–389.

———. *Paragons of the Ordinary: The Biographical Literature of Mori Ōgai.* Honolulu: University of Hawai'i Press, 1993.

———. "The Writer Speaks: Late-Meiji Reflections on Literature and Life." In *The Distant Isle: Studies and Translations of Japanese Literature in Honor of Robert H. Brower,* ed. Thomas Hare et al. Ann Arbor: University of Michigan Press, 1996.

Marshall, Byron. *Learning to Be Modern: Japanese Political Discourse on Education.* Boulder, Colo.: Westview Press, 1994.

McClain, Yōko Matsuoka. *Magomusume kara mita Sōseki.* Shinchōsha, 1995.

———. "Sōseki: A Tragic Father." *Monumenta Nipponica* 33, no. 4 (Winter 1978): 461–469.

McClellan, Edwin. *Two Japanese Novelists: Sōseki and Tōson.* Chicago: University of Chicago Press, 1968.

Morioka, Heinz, and Miyoko Sasaki. *Rakugo: The Popular Narrative Art of Japan.* Cambridge: Council on East Asian Studies, Harvard University, 1990.

Nagai Kafū. *Kafū zenshū.* Iwanami shoten, 1962–1965.

Nakamura Murao. *Meiji Taishō no bungakusha.* Vol. 16 of Meiji Taishō bungaku kaisō shūsei. Nihon tosho sentā, 1983.

Natsume Fusanosuke. *Mago ga yomu Sōseki.* Jitsugyō Nihonsha, 2006.

———. *Sōseki no mago.* Jitsugyō no Nihonsha, 2003.

Natsume Kyōko. *Sōseki no omoide.* Iwanami, 1929.

Natsume Shinroku. *Chichi Natsume Sōseki.* Bungei shunjū, 1956.

Oda Susumu. *Nihon no kyōki shi.* Shisakusha, 1980.

Odagiri Susumu, ed. *Nihon kindai bungaku daijiten.* 6 vols. Kōdansha, 1977–1978.

Okano Takeo. *Bungaku no toporojii.* Kawade shobō, 1999.

Oketani Hideaki. *Natsume Sōseki ron.* Kawade shobō, 1983.

Olney, James. *Memory and Narrative: The Weave of Life-Writing.* Chicago: University of Chicago Press, 1998.

Pamuk, Orhan. *Istanbul: Memories and the City.* New York: Knopf, 2005.

Powell, Irena. *Writers and Society in Modern Japan.* Tokyo; New York; San Francisco: Kodansha International, 1983.

Roden, Donald. *Schooldays in Imperial Japan: A Study in the Culture of a Student Elite.* Berkeley: University of California Press, 1980.

Rogers, Lawrence. *Tokyo Stories: A Literary Stroll.* Berkeley: University of California Press, 2002.

Ross, Bruce. *Remembering the Personal Past: Descriptions of Autobiographical Memory.* New York: Oxford University Press, 1991.

Rubin, Jay. *Injurious to Public Morals: Writers and the Meiji State.* Seattle and London: University of Washington Press, 1984.

————. "Sōseki." In *Modern Japanese Writers,* ed. Jay Rubin. New York: Charles Scribner's Sons, 2001.

Ryan, Marleigh Grayer. *Japan's First Modern Novel:* Ukigumo *of Futabatei Shimei.* New York: Columbia University Press, 1967.

Saeki Shōichi. *Kindai Nihon no jiden.* Kōdansha, 1981.

Sand, Jordan. *House and Home in Modern Japan: Architecture, Domestic Space, and Bourgeois Culture, 1880–1930.* Cambridge: Harvard University Asia Center, 2003.

Satō Tatsuya, *Nihon ni okeru shinrigaku no juyō to tenkai.* Kyōto: Kitaōji shobō, 2002.

Seidensticker, Edward. *Kafū the Scribbler.* Stanford, Calif.: Stanford University Press, 1965.

————. *Low City, High City: Tokyo 1867–1923.* New York: Knopf, 1983.

Shimazaki Tōson. *Tōson zenshū.* Chikuma shobō, 1966–1967.

Sibley, William. *The Shiga Hero.* Chicago: University of Chicago Press, 1979.

Tanaka, Stefan. *Japan's Orient: Rendering Pasts into History.* Berkeley: University of California Press, 1993.

Uchida Roan. *Uchida Roan zenshū.* Yumani shobō, 1987.

Vlastos, Stephen, ed. *Mirror of Modernity: Invented Traditions of Modern Japan.* Berkeley: University of California Press, 1998.

Wakabayashi, Bob Tadashi, ed. *Modern Japanese Thought.* Cambridge: Cambridge University Press, 1998.

Washburn, Dennis. *The Dilemma of the Modern in Japanese Fiction.* New Haven, Conn.: Yale University Press, 1995.

Watarai Yoshiichi. *Meiji no seishin isetsu.* Iwanami, 2003.

Yiu, Angela. *Chaos and Order in the Works of Natsume Sōseki.* Honolulu: University of Hawai'i Press, 1998.

Yu, Beongcheon. *Natsume Sōseki.* New York: Twayne Publishers, 1969.

Works by Natsume Sōseki

Botchan (1906, in *SZ* 2). Translated by J. Cohn. Tokyo and New York: Kodansha International, 2005.

Eijitsu shōhin (1909, in *SZ* 12). *Spring Miscellany.* Translated by Sammy Tsunematsu. Boston; Rutland, Vt.; Tokyo: Tuttle Publishing, 2002.

Garasudo no uchi (1915, in *SZ* 12). *Inside My Glass Doors.* Translated by Sammy Tsunematsu. Boston; Rutland, Vt.; Tokyo: Tuttle Publishing, 2002.

Higan sugi made (1912, in *SZ* 7). *To the Spring Equinox and Beyond.* Translated by Kingo Ochiai and Sanford Goldstein. Rutland, Vt.; Tokyo: Charles E. Tuttle Company, 1985.

Jitensha nikki (1903, in *SZ* 12). *Bicycle Diary.* In *Tower,* pp. 91–116.

Kārairu hakubutsukan (1905, in *SZ* 2). *The Carlyle Museum.* In *Tower,* pp. 117–129.

Kōfu (1908, in *SZ* 5). *The Miner.* Translated by Jay Rubin. Stanford, Calif.: Stanford University Press, 1988.

Kōjin (1913, in *SZ* 8). *The Wayfarer.* Translated by Beongcheon Yu. Detroit: Wayne State University Press, 1967.

Kokoro (1914, in *SZ* 9). Translated by Edwin McClellan. Chicago: Henry Regnery Company, 1957.

Koto no sorane (1905, in *SZ* 2). *Hearing Things.* Translated by Aiko Itō and Graeme Wilson. In *Ten Nights of Dream, Hearing Things, The Heredity of Taste.* Rutland, Vt.; Tokyo: Charles E. Tuttle Company, 1974.

Kusamakura (1907, in *SZ* 3). *The Three-Cornered World.* Translated by Alan Turney. London: Peter Owen, 1965.

Mankan tokorodokoro (1910, in *SZ* 12). *Here and There in Manchuria and Korea.* Translated by Inger Sigrun Brodey and Sammy I. Tsunematsu. In *Rediscovering Natsume Sōseki.* Kent, UK: Global Oriental, 2000.

Meian (1916, in *SZ* 11). *Light and Darkness.* Translated by V. H. Viglielmo. Honolulu: University of Hawai'i Press, 1971.

Michikusa (1915, in *SZ* 10). *Grass on the Wayside.* Translated by Edwin McClellan. Chicago: University of Chicago Press, 1969.

Mon (1911, in *SZ* 6). *The Gate.* Translated by Francis Mathy. London: Peter Owen, 1972.

Natsume Sōseki jiten. Edited by Hiraoka Toshio et al. Bensei shuppan, 2000.

Natsume Sōseki jiten. Edited by Miyoshi Yukio et al. Vol. 39 of Bessatsu kokubungaku. Gakutōsha, 1990.

Omoidasu koto nado (1911, in *SZ* 12). *Recollections.* Translated by Maria Flutsch. London: Sōseki Museum in London, 1997.

Rondon Shōsoku (1901, in *SZ* 12). *Letters from London.* In *Tower,* pp. 3–31.

Rondon tō (1905, in *SZ* 2). *The Tower of London.* In *The Tower of London: Tales of Victorian London,* pp. 91–116. Translated by Damian Flanagan. London; Chester Springs, Penn.: Peter Owen, 2005.

Sanshirō (1909, in *SZ* 5). Translated by Jay Rubin. Seattle and London: University of Washington Press, 1977.

Sorekara (1910, in *SZ* 6). *And Then.* Translated by Norma Moore Field. Baton Rouge and London: Lousiana State University Press, 1978.

Sōseki zenshū. 29 vols. Iwanami, 1993–1997.

Wagahai wa neko de aru (1906, in *SZ* 1). *I Am a Cat.* Translated by Katsue Shibata and Motonari Kai. London: Peter Owen, 1971.

"Watakushi no kojinshugi" (1914, in *SZ* 16). "My Individualism." Translated by Jay Rubin. In Kokoro *and Selected Essays.* Lanham, Md.: Madison Books, 1992.

Yume jūya (1908, in *SZ* 12). *Ten Nights of Dream.* Translated by Aiko Itō and Graeme Wilson. In *Ten Nights of Dream, Hearing Things, The Heredity of Taste.* Rutland, Vt.; Tokyo: Charles E. Tuttle Company, 1974.

Sōseki Biography—A Bibliographical Note

Narrative Biographies in English
(1) Jay Rubin's essay, "Sōseki," in *Modern Japanese Writers,* pp. 349–384; (2) Donald Keene's chapter on Sōseki in *Dawn to the West,* pp. 305–355; (3) Van Gessel's account in *Three Modern Novelists,* pp. 11–67; (4) Edwin McClellan's account in *Two Japanese Novelists,* pp. 3–69 (especially 3–15).

Chronologies in Japanese
Of the innumerable available sources, the Sōseki chronology *(nenpu)* in *SZ* 27 (pp. 599–699) is most useful. The ne plus ultra of Sōseki chronologies, though, is Ara Masahito's *Sōseki kenkyū nenpyō,* whose nearly one thousand pages detail virtually every day in the author's life.

Index

About the Author

MARVIN MARCUS has been on the faculty of Washington University in St. Louis since 1985. His teaching has spanned Japanese language and literature, comparative literature, and East-Asian cultural studies. His research, which broadly relates to writers of the Meiji-Taishō periods (1868–1926), has come to focus on the literature of reminiscence and personal reflection. His book, *Paragons of the Ordinary: The Biographical Literature of Mori Ōgai,* was published by University of Hawai'i Press in 1993.

A published poet and avid photographer, Marcus equally relishes the challenge of scholarly research and the pleasure of creative expression. His wife, Ginger, is head of the Japanese language section at Washington University, and their sons, Danny and Steve, indulge their parents' strange obsession with the exotic island civilization off the coast of East Asia.